[Crown Copyright Reserved].

REGULATIONS

FOR THE

CLOTHING OF THE ARMY.

Part I.—REGULAR FORCES.

(EXCLUDING THE SPECIAL RESERVE.)

WAR OFFICE, 1914.

LONDON:
PRINTED UNDER THE AUTHORITY OF HIS MAJESTY'S STATIONERY OFFICE
By HARRISON AND SONS, 45–47, ST. MARTIN'S LANE, W.C.,
PRINTERS IN ORDINARY TO HIS MAJESTY.

To be purchased, either directly or through any Bookseller, from
WYMAN AND SONS, LTD., 29, BREAMS BUILDINGS, FETTER LANE, E.C., and
54, ST. MARY STREET, CARDIFF; or
H.M. STATIONERY OFFICE (SCOTTISH BRANCH), 23, FORTH STREET, EDINBURGH; or
E. PONSONBY, LTD., 116, GRAFTON STREET, DUBLIN;
or from the Agencies in the British Colonies and Dependencies,
the United States of America, the Continent of Europe and Abroad of
T. FISHER UNWIN, LONDON, W.C.

CLOTHING REGULATIONS.

Part I.—REGULAR FORCES.

CONTENTS.

GENERAL REGULATIONS.

(B 10544) Wt. 8343-778 11,500 6/14 H & S P. 13/116

3

CONTENTS—*continued.*

DETAILS OF CLOTHING AND NECESSARIES.

Clothing, &c.

Necessaries.

(C.R. 10544) A 2

4

APPENDICES.

DEFINITIONS.

The following terms used in these Regulations will have the significations shown below :—

UNIT.   As defined in the " King's Regulations."

COMMANDING   The Commanding Officer of a " unit."
OFFICER.

COMPANY.   As defined in the " King's Regulations."

RECRUIT.   A man or boy who has been finally passed by a
                                     Medical Officer empowered to carry out the final
                                     medical examination of recruits, and who has
                                     also been finally approved by an officer authorized
                                     to carry out the final approval of recruits for
                                     the Regular Army.

GEORGE R.I.

A.C.D.
Clo. Reg.
1079

WHEREAS Our Army Council have submitted to Us revised Regulations for the provision of Clothing and Necessaries for Our Army, Part I (Regular Forces, excluding the Special Reserve); and whereas We have been pleased to approve the same:—

OUR WILL AND PLEASURE is, that the Regulations (Part I) established by the Royal Warrant of His late Majesty of the 8th June, 1909, be cancelled, except so far as they refer to the Conditions of the Supply of personal Clothing and Necessaries to Services for which a Consolidated Clothing and Kit Allowance has not been approved, and that, with this exception, these REGULATIONS be the sole and standing authority on the matters herein treated of, excepting all matters relating to the provision of Clothing and Necessaries of such part of Our Army as may be stationed in Our Indian Empire; provided always that Our said Army Council shall, until Our further pleasure be made known, have full power to make any modifications in the details of these Regulations which may be necessary in the interests of Our Service, and also to fix and amend all rates for the upkeep of personal Clothing and Necessaries, the performance of any work that may be executed in Regiments or Corps, or for the local purchase of any article of Clothing or Necessaries. The administration and interpretation of these Regulations shall likewise rest with Our said Army Council.

Given at Our Court at St. James's, this 23rd day of May, 1914, in the 5th year of Our Reign.

By His Majesty's Command,

H. H. ASQUITH.

[As some typographical errors may have occurred in publication, it is requested that, should any be discovered, they may be at once pointed out, in writing, to the Secretary of the War Office.]
The portions of these Regulations which are new are denoted by a black line in the margin.

REGULATIONS FOR THE CLOTHING OF THE ARMY, 1914.

PART I.—REGULAR FORCES.
(Excluding the Special Reserve.)

GENERAL REGULATIONS.

1. All claims to Clothing, Necessaries or other emoluments granted by these Regulations which have not been preferred within a period of twelve months after they accrue, will be deemed to be forfeited, unless under such exceptional circumstances as may be approved by the Army Council, or by an Officer duly authorized by them.

SECTION I.—DUTIES OF OFFICERS AND CONDUCT OF CORRESPONDENCE.

General Officers.

2. General officers commanding will be responsible that the units in their respective commands are complete in clothing and necessaries, and will see that indents are complied with within a reasonable time, also that the clothing records and books are properly posted up. Any delay in supply will be reported to the War Office. They will also be responsible for the efficient custody and turnover of the clothing and necessaries stored for reservists.

A.O. 83
1910

3. Local purchases up to a limit of £5 may be sanctioned by general officers commanding of articles of authorized scale and pattern required for the troops but not available in store, *e.g.*, boots or shoes of abnormal sizes, plain clothes, &c. The prices paid should ordinarily not exceed those laid down in the current Priced Vocabulary of Clothing and Necessaries, and the articles will be examined and brought to account as laid down in paragraph 310.

4. At stations abroad, in cases of urgent necessity, general officers will provide for the requirements of the public service and immediately report their action to the chief ordnance officer, Royal Army Clothing Department.

5. Where a shortage exists in one unit in a district and other units can supply the deficiency out of excess articles in their

possession, the general officer commanding will direct the requisite transfer to be made by voucher.

Commanding Officers.

6. A commanding officer is responsible that the clothing and necessaries of the soldiers under his command are complete and in good order, and that all clothing and boots are carefully fitted in the presence of the officer commanding the company. It is of the utmost importance to ensure that each soldier is at all times in possession of clothing, boots and necessaries in sufficiently good condition to stand three months' wear under service conditions.

A.O.D.
Olo. Reg.
1079

He will also be responsible that a sufficient stock of clothing and necessaries is maintained in store, that this stock is properly cared for, and that articles unlikely to be required are not retained (*see* paragraph 9, Appendix VI.). He will be accountable for any deficiencies and for any loss arising from neglect of these regulations.

7. Officers on assuming command will cause the clothing and necessaries on charge to be verified as directed in paragraph 294, and will satisfy themselves that the articles in store and in wear agree in quantity and condition with those charged in the ledger. Surpluses and deficiencies will be dealt with as directed in paragraph 299.

8. Where a difference of opinion exists between commanding officers, on a change of command or on the occasion of any transfer of clothing or necessaries, as to the condition, quantity or description of the articles to be transferred, application will be made to the general officer commanding, by either of the officers between whom the difference exists, for the assembly of a board to consider and report upon the matter.

9. Commanding officers will bring to the notice of the general officer commanding any inconvenient delay in the supply of clothing or necessaries.

A.O. 48
1914

10. Complaints as to the quality, cut, or workmanship of clothing will be submitted to the general officer commanding, who, if he considers a complaint well founded, will, after consulting other units wearing similar articles, refer the matter to the War Office.

A.O. 216
1912

11. Instructions relative to the storage, inspection and turnover of mobilization clothing and necessaries stored for reservists and for men to be specially enlisted on mobilization will be found in Appendix XIII.

12. On units moving from one home station to another, commanding officers will carry out the instructions contained in Appendix XIV.

Quartermasters.

13. Quartermasters will be responsible to the commanding officers for the care and custody of all unissued articles. Commanding officers will control and supervise the duties with which quartermasters are charged, and will not, under any circumstances, permit them to have direct dealings with soldiers respecting clothing or necessaries.

14. Clothing and necessaries will be issued by quartermasters of units to officers commanding companies and not to the soldiers.

15. Officers commanding companies will indent for all articles of clothing and necessaries required from the quartermaster's store on the prescribed Army Forms (*see* Appendix III).

Conduct of Correspondence.

16. Correspondence relating to indents and vouchers for clothing and necessaries will be addressed to the issuing officer.

All other correspondence relating to clothing or necessaries, except as provided for in the King's Regulations, will be addressed to the assistant director of ordnance stores or chief ordnance officer of the command, who will, if necessary, refer the matter to the chief ordnance officer, Royal Army Clothing Department, Grosvenor Road, London, S.W.

SECTION II.—SUPPLY AND DISPOSAL OF CLOTHING, AND GRANT OF CONSOLIDATED CLOTHING AND KIT ALLOWANCE.

I.—ISSUES AND ALLOWANCES, AND DISPOSAL OF CLOTHING.

17. Soldiers will be entitled to wear clothing according to the classification in Appendix I.

18. The articles of clothing supplied to the soldier (which will be complete with distinguishing badges and chevrons as shown in Table IX), are detailed in Tables I to IV and VI to VIII under the following headings:—

(*a*) *Personal Clothing.*—Articles which after issue are struck off charge in the clothing ledgers.

(*b*) *Public Clothing.*—Articles which after issue are retained on charge in the clothing ledgers.

19. Obsolete articles in store or received from the Royal Army Clothing Department, or other Clothing Depôt, will be used up before any new patterns are taken into wear.

Personal Clothing and Allowance.

20. Soldiers, other than the non-commissioned officers of the West African Regiment referred to on page 110, will receive clothing as detailed in Tables I, II, IV, VI, VII, and VIII under the following conditions:—

A.O. 157
1912

21. The first year's outfit for a recruit will, except in the case of cloth and tweed trousers extra after six months' service for which a money allowance will be granted, be free in kind as detailed in Tables I and II, but in subsequent years the clothing will be maintained by the soldier out of a quarterly clothing allowance, to be credited (except as otherwise provided in these regulations) in the pay list in advance, on each of the following four "clothing quarter-days," viz., 1st January, 1st April, 1st July, and 1st

A.O. 259
1911

A.O. 266
1910

October, and in this allowance will (except for native soldiers of
local forces and boys on the roll as such, other than those placed on
the recognized establishment of the band, trumpeters, drummers,
buglers or pipers) be included a sum of 15s. 3d. per quarter for the
upkeep of the free kit. In the case of soldiers returning home from
stations abroad where service dress is not worn, the purchase of
the second suit of service dress may be deferred until the credit of
clothing allowance permits.

22. The rates for the combined quarterly allowance will be
published in Army Orders from time to time.

23. The first quarterly allowance to a recruit will, except as
provided for in Part III, Clothing Regulations, be credited upon
the fourth "clothing quarter-day" following his enlistment, and
the subsequent allowances will be credited quarterly thereafter,
except on the quarter-day preceding the date on which it is
probable that the discharge or transfer to the Army Reserve may
occur. Should the discharge or transfer to the Army Reserve not
take place by the end of the quarter the allowance so withheld will
then be credited.

24. Soldiers rejoining from the Army Reserve will be treated as
recruits.

25. Transfers from the Royal Marines will receive the first
clothing and kit allowance on the quarter-day following date of
transfer.

26. In the case of soldiers who enlist on the first day of a
quarter and are discharged or transferred to the Reserve on the
last day of a quarter, the allowance for their final quarter will be
credited on the quarter-day preceding discharge or transfer.
When discharge or transfer is delayed until the following quarter
the allowance for the last completed quarter will be credited,
unless the whole of that quarter is spent in hospital.

27. Soldiers who enlist, re-enlist, or rejoin from the Army
Reserve will receive the first allowance on the first day of the quarter
in which the anniversary of the enlistment day occurs, and thence-
forward quarterly, except on the first day of any incomplete quarter
within which it is probable that they will finish their service with
the colours. Should the discharge or transfer to the Army Reserve
not take place by the end of the quarter the allowance so withheld
will then be credited. In the case of promotion to commissioned
rank the allowance becoming due will be credited, unless the date
of the notification of such promotion in the "London Gazette"
coincides with a clothing quarter-day.

28. Soldiers, except native soldiers of local forces, will be credited
on the fourth clothing quarter-day following their enlistment or
re-enlistment with a sum of 30s. 6d. in addition to the first issue
of the combined clothing and kit allowance.

29. Recruits from Special Reserve units will, if enlisted under
the age of 18, be dealt with as in paragraph 28.

30. The clothing allowance of native soldiers of local forces, of
boys on the roll as such, other than those placed on the recognized
establishment of the band, trumpeters, drummers, buglers or pipers,

---

Margin references (left column):

A.C.D.
A.P.C.
10
A.C.D.
Clo. Reg.
1099

A.O. 194
1909

A.O. 75
1911

A.O. 275
1912

A.O. 75
1911

A.O. 157
1912

A.O. 275
1912

A.C.D.
A.P.C.
10

and of men clothed as soldiers, but no longer serving on an army engagement, will not include the 15s. 3d. per quarter for the upkeep of free kit mentioned in paragraph 21.

31. Boys with over 12 months' service who are struck off the boys' roll or who are placed on the recognized establishment of the band, trumpeters, drummers, buglers or pipers, will be credited with the full quarterly rate of clothing and kit allowance from the quarter-day next succeeding the date of removal from the boys' roll or appointment to the establishment of the band, &c. In similar circumstances, boys with less than 12 months' service will receive the full quarterly allowance on the first quarter-day after completing a year's service.

In both cases there will be added to the first full allowance an amount equal to a kit allowance at 2d. per day, from the date of removal from the boys' roll or of appointment to the band, &c., or from the commencement of the seventh month of service, whichever may be the later.

32. The clothing and kit allowance will be expended, at the discretion of the company commander, in the provision and upkeep of such regulation clothing and necessaries as the soldier may, in his opinion, require during the current quarter, and any portion of the allowance that he may cause to be retained to meet probable requirements, for promotion, transfer, &c., will remain in the pay account to the soldier's credit. Any balance not required for clothing or necessaries, or for authorized charges in connection therewith, will (except as provided for by paragraph 33) be included in the current cash payments to the soldier. When the allowance has been expended, any further purchase of clothing or necessaries will be met from the soldier's pay.

33. In the case of a soldier under orders to return home or to embark for a station abroad, the company commander should arrange, as far as possible, for a sufficient balance of clothing allowance being kept to the man's credit to cover the purchase of the additional clothing required at the new station.

34. A soldier on promotion or reduction will be dealt with as follows :—

(*a*) He will receive the higher or lower rate appertaining to his new position from the first clothing quarter-day following the date on which the promotion or reduction was announced in orders, except when the promotion or reduction is announced on the first day of the quarter, with effect from that or earlier date, in which case the allowance at the higher or lower rate will be drawn from the date of announcement.

(*b*) The alterations necessary in his uniform will be effected at the public expense, provided that the cost at authorized rates, including any necessary chevrons, badges or aiguillettes, does not exceed in any case half the value of a new garment. If the cost is estimated to exceed this, half value of a new garment will be credited to the soldier.

(*c*) Should the soldier choose to purchase a new garment in place of the one in possession being converted, the amount for

A.O. 266	
1910	
A.C.D.	
A.P.C.	
10	
A.O. 259	
1911	
A.C.D.	
Clo. Reg.	
1101	
54	
Infantry	
[619	

which the latter could have been converted at the rates shown in the Priced Vocabulary of Clothing and Necessaries, but not exceeding one half of the value of the new garment, may be credited to him.

(*d*) A new garment will not be necessary when the difference is one of material only.

(*e*) Half the value of any other new personal clothing which is necessarily required, owing to difference of pattern or scale, will also be credited, unless the difference is due merely to change of station.

(*f*) At the discretion of the officer commanding the unit, the whole or portion of the next quarterly allowance may be credited in anticipation of the next clothing quarter-day.

35. If, before new articles purchased by a soldier have been worn, any alteration takes place in his rank or position, or he is ordered to another station which involves a change of uniform, the unworn articles (even if they have been fitted and marked) may be returned to regimental store for re-issue, and the value refunded to the soldier, the charge being supported by a reference to the voucher by which the articles are again brought on ledger charge. Specially made garments, or articles trimmed with gold lace, should be dealt with as directed in paragraph 273 at once.

36. Clothing allowance will be withheld from a soldier who is in hospital on the first day of a quarter. The allowance for the quarter in which he leaves hospital will be credited to him on his discharge therefrom, provided it is not then contemplated to carry out his transfer to the Army Reserve or his discharge from the army, within that quarter. Clothing allowance will not be credited to the non-effective account of a deceased soldier whose allowance has been withheld as above.

If, owing to uncertainty as to date of discharge, clothing allowance is withheld from a soldier sent home from abroad (except India) for discharge on account of medical unfitness, it will, if admissible, be issued by the home paymaster into whose payment he is transferred, the charge being supported by the transfer statement of account, which should show the date to which the allowance was last issued.

37. The allowance will not be issued to troops engaged on active service (*see* Clothing Regulations, Part III). From the date of mobilization and during the period of hostilities full dress clothing will be withheld from recruits of all services, unless otherwise ordered.

38. Clothing and kit allowances will be a direct credit in the Pay List.

39. Gold and worsted badges, including aiguillettes and chevrons required on promotion, reduction, transfer, &c., will, when no other alterations in pattern are necessary, be issued free. Garments purchased at the rates shown in Part II of the Priced Vocabulary of Clothing will be issued complete with gold and worsted badges and chevrons, and with flashes for the Royal Welsh Fusiliers. Any such badges and chevrons obtained separately, except as shown above, will be charged for at vocabulary rates.

Good conduct badges and badges denoting special qualifications (*e.g.*, skill-at-arms and signalling badges) will be issued free to men who become entitled to wear such badges. | A.O. 307 1909

Skill-at-arms badges in wear will be transferred from home to colonial pattern garments when a unit proceeds abroad, and from colonial to home pattern garments when a unit returns home. | A.O. 216 1912

Chevrons and badges will not be supplied with drab shirts, and khaki drill frocks or blouses issued free, and one set only will be issued free on promotion, reduction, &c. | A.C.D. Wilts. 680

40. The issue of clothing from store on payment must not be other than that authorized for the rank or appointment held by the soldier who requires the articles. | A.O. 67 1913

41. Metal badges for wear with service dress and khaki drill clothing, and metal band badges for full-dress garments, will be supplied free on appointment or promotion only, any renewals being at the soldier's expense.

42. On re-enlistment, when the service is practically continuous, the soldier will be credited with the allowance for the quarter in which his discharge takes place, and will afterwards continue to receive the normal quarterly allowance ; but where there is a distinct break in his service, and he has left his unit, he will be treated as a recruit.

43. Boys who have outgrown their garments before receiving an allowance will receive new garments free. In other cases of outgrown garments, when general officers are satisfied that a new issue has become necessary from this cause, and that due attention was paid, when fitting, to the instructions in Appendix V, the unexpired value of the garments requiring replacement will be assessed by the officer commanding the unit, and will be credited to the soldier, the new article required being issued on payment. The garments outgrown will be sold for the benefit of the public.

44. Men in detention or prison are dealt with in Section VII.

45. Any portion of the clothing allowance which is credited under these regulations or under special authority in anticipation of the next clothing quarter-day will be deducted from the next allowance due, and if in the meantime the soldier is transferred or attached for pay to another unit, the advance will be notified to the unit and to the regimental paymaster concerned. If the soldier becomes non-effective before the next allowance falls due, the advance will be debited to his non-effective account.

46. The company commander will furnish the regimental paymaster, in advance, with a list of soldiers due or probably due for discharge or transfer to the Army Reserve during the ensuing quarter, showing the dates or probable dates of termination of their colour service.

Public Clothing.

(a.) *General Instructions.*

47. Under ordinary circumstances public clothing will last for the periods laid down in the scales of issue, provided proper care is taken of it, and the necessary minor repairs are executed from time to time as required. When, however, articles become prematurely unserviceable, they will be examined by a board of survey, and if their condition is attributable to their having been subjected to extra wear on the public service under exceptional circumstances, or to fair wear under ordinary circumstances, and not to neglect or wilfulness, the general officer commanding may authorize their replacement.

48. Articles in possession of the soldier will be kept in repair at his expense. Commanding officers will see that all repairs are carried out without delay. The cost of repairing the public clothing of a non-effective will, if the damage has been caused wilfully or by neglect, be recovered from the man's estate if possible. In other cases the cost will be borne by the public.

49. Articles, except bearskin caps, which have been worn the prescribed period will not necessarily be replaced. They will be examined by a board of survey ; repairable articles will be repaired at the public expense, and those unserviceable will be replaced and disposed of as directed in paragraph 89. The report of the board of survey will be annexed as a voucher to the account in which the unserviceable articles are struck off charge, and a copy will in each case be furnished to the local ordnance officer who will record them by units. Should it appear that excessive or undue premature condemnation has taken place the local ordnance officer will forward the proceedings of the board to the chief ordnance officer or assistant director of ordnance stores for the information of the general officer commanding.

50. Bearskin caps which have lasted the prescribed period and are considered fit for further wear will be re-inspected on application to the Royal Army Clothing Department, when a further definite period will be assessed to each. For this purpose such caps will be returned to the Royal Army Clothing Department at convenient times. All bearskin caps which are not considered fit for further wear will be examined by a board of survey, and, if condemned, dealt with as laid down in Appendix XI. Charges for caps re-issued for extended period of wear and lost or damaged will be assessed under paragraph 229, the monthly rates as laid down in the Priced Vocabulary of Clothing and Necessaries for the unexpired portion of the extended period being taken.

51. When boards of survey cannot be held owing to officers not being available, a certificate showing that the articles are unserviceable and why a board cannot be held, will be furnished by the commanding officer.

52. The period of wear will count from the date of issue to the men. Clothing given up by non-effectives will be returned to regimental store for re-issue to other men for whom it may be suitable.

53. Articles out-grown by the wearers may be exchanged for others of suitable sizes.

54. New articles of public clothing will not be issued if part-worn articles of suitable sizes are available.

54
Gen. No.
1199.

A.O. 259
1911

(b.) *Head-Dresses* (*Full Dress*), *and Jack Spurs.*

55. New busby bags and lines will be supplied for time-expired busbies fit to last a longer period. Similarly new leathers and rowels will, when necessary, be supplied for time-expired jack-spurs. A.O. 83
1910

56. The full dress head-dresses and jack spurs of men after completion of training sent from the depôt to the service unit will be retained at the depôt. Transfers will take those in possession provided they are suitable for the new unit. A.O. 138
1913

57. Metal helmets, feather bonnets, and sealskin or bearskin caps will not be allowed in excess of the establishment of a unit.

58. Plumes and hackles- for bandsmen and trumpeters of Dragoon Guards and Dragoons will be provided regimentally.

59. Feather bonnets will be provided regimentally at rates given in the Priced Vocabulary of Clothing and Necessaries. An annual allowance will be granted for repairs and for the renewal of hackles and cases and bonnet covers for the bonnets in wear. When bonnets are transferred from one battalion to another wearing a hackle and border of a different pattern, an estimate of the cost of providing the proper pattern will be forwarded to the chief ordnance officer, Royal Army Clothing Department, whose sanction is necessary before any expenditure on this account can be incurred. The hackles taken from the bonnets in such cases will be returned to the depôt of the battalion from which the bonnets were transferred.

(c.) *Cloaks, Great-coats, Leggings, Pea Jackets and Purses and Belts.*

60. A supply of great-coats that have been condemned as unfit for further general wear under paragraph 49, will be allowed for each general recruiting station for recruits proceeding to other stations. Condemned great-coats received with recruits will, if suitable, be retained for issue to recruits enlisted for other corps, or forwarded for further use to the nearest recruiting officer requiring them. If unfit for further use by recruits they will be disposed of as directed in paragraph 89. In the event of no condemned coats being available, part-worn coats on the verge of condemnation will be supplied.

61. Great-coats and purses and belts taken by drafts of men after completion of training from depôts, will be brought back by the conducting party, unless the service unit requires them, when they may be retained. Any expense for their conveyance will be charged as directed in paragraph 314. Transfers will take the articles in their possession and retain them in wear until exchanged in the usual manner.

62. Worn great-coats will be supplied for insane soldiers at Netley, whenever the assistant adjutant-general, Royal Victoria Hospital, considers them necessary.

63. Leggings will not be taken by drafts of men after completion of training from depôts unless wanted for the journey ;

when taken they will be brought back by the conducting party.
Pea jackets will not be taken from R.E. depôts.

Recruits.

64. Officers commanding companies will indent on the quartermaster for the clothing and necessaries detailed in Tables I, II, III,
VI, VII, VIII, and XVI for recruits after final approval.

65. Recruits finally approved at stations other than those at
which they commence duty will, pending re-examination and final
acceptance, receive only such articles as are absolutely necessary.

66. All personal clothing will be new.

67. In the case of recruits who enlist into the regular forces
from the special reserve and are in possession of two pairs of part-
worn ankle boots or highland shoes, one of the pairs may, if
necessary, be repaired at the public expense.

A.O. 75
―――――
1911

68. Tunics may be supplied on enlistment, except to recruits of
cavalry regiments stationed in or under orders to proceed to South
Africa, who will receive the full dress serge frock in lieu. Knee
boots and cloth pantaloons will not be supplied to recruits of
mounted services with less than six months' service, except in the
case of the Household Cavalry, nor should they be issued until the
men join a service unit ; but the withholding of these articles will
not apply to boys serving at a depôt after twelve months' service
who are likely to remain a further period. The issue of full
dress headdress and gauntlets to recruits of the cavalry will be
withheld at the depôt. Such other articles of the authorized issues
of personal and public clothing as the commanding officer may
consider necessary for drill, parades, duties, and for walking out,
will be issued to recruits during the first three months of their
service, and the remainder on completion of three months' service.

A.O. 75
―――――
1911

69. Recruits who, on enlistment, elect to join cavalry regiments
in India will be clothed in the uniform of the affiliated units to
which, under the Recruiting Regulations, they are posted while
serving at home. Recruits enlisted for cavalry regiments in or
under orders to proceed to Egypt or South Africa will wear the
uniform of these regiments while attached to the affiliated unit at
home (*see* also paragraph 367).

A.O. 112
―――――
1911

70. Recruits posted to India before completing 6 months' service
will be supplied, before embarkation, with the articles of personal
clothing (if any) due on completion of 6 months' service.

71. Boys enlisted to fill vacancies in battalions serving
abroad, except in the case of those under training at the
School of Music, will not be supplied with any home pattern
full dress personal clothing, and only such other articles of home
pattern as are necessary while at home will be issued. The
foreign service full dress frock, which may be lined in the case of
boys remaining at home during the winter months, and trousers
may be issued in lieu of the tunic and home pattern trousers,
and the boys will be credited with the value of any other
articles of home pattern personal clothing withheld. On

A.C.D.
R.S.
―――――
430

embarkation they will be dealt with under paragraph 366, receiving an advance of their clothing allowance, if necessary, to enable them to purchase the personal clothing required. Other boys proceeding to Colonial stations before they have become entitled to their first quarterly clothing allowance, will receive a free issue of such articles as are included in the difference between the home scale and that of their new station.

A.O. 266
1910

72. Boys enlisting in the Royal Field Artillery to be trained as artificers at Woolwich, will be clothed under the scale for Royal Garrison Artillery while under training.

73. For the first two or three months the only head-dresses which will be worn by a recruit will be the caps.

Part-worn and Worn-out Clothing.

74. When any articles of personal clothing in possession of the troops are no longer required for wear, or for the purposes stated in paragraph 78, they may be sold with the written consent and under the direction of the officer commanding the company to other soldiers in the unit for their personal use, the proceeds being credited to the owner's pay account. All such transactions, whether by auction or otherwise, will be entered in Army Book 339, and initialed by officers commanding companies as approving of the sale or purchase. Each entry will give the name of the buyer and seller, and the price paid. Cash payments will be allowed between soldiers not paid on a company pay list, and entries in Army Book 339 will not be necessary.

75. Any articles not so sold will be handed over to the quartermaster by the officer commanding the company (who will obtain a receipt for them) for sale to the authorized contractor for the purchase of worn-out clothing. Badges and buttons may be previously removed and retained by the wearers. All clothing, when taken into store, will be thoroughly examined and the pockets emptied.

76. Clothing will not be sold to any civilian other than the recognized contractor, and it must be distinctly explained to the men that the contractor will pay only the worn-out value. A list of the prices to be paid for worn-out clothing extracted from the Priced Vocabulary of Clothing and Necessaries is to be hung up in one barrack room in each company.

A.O. 275
1912

77. At the time the clothing is handed in by the soldier for sale to the contractor the officer commanding the company will pay to the soldier its worn-out value, for which purpose he may use public money in his possession. Until the value of the clothing is received from the contractor the money advanced for this purpose may be shown in the Cash Reconciliation Statement of the Pay and Mess Book as "Cash due from clothing contractor for worn-out clothing."

78. Soldiers will retain such articles of worn clothing for fatigues, repairs, &c., as the officer commanding the company may deem necessary, and no soldier will be permitted to dispose of any article without the written consent of that officer.

(c.r. 10544)   B

79. Part-worn personal clothing of non-effective soldiers will be sold, either in the unit at not less than contract rates or to the contractor, and the proceeds disposed of as directed in paragraphs 113, 114, or 216.

A.O. 275
1912

80. At home stations the officer commanding a unit will, at intervals not exceeding three months, notify to the authorized contractor that clothing is ready for removal, giving in detail the articles to be removed.

81. As a rule the contractor will personally, or by his agent, remove the clothing within three weeks of the commanding officer's notification, but should a case arise where neither the contractor nor his agent can attend, the clothing may be forwarded to him at his risk, provided payment has been made as directed in paragraph 82.

82. The value of all clothing will be paid by the contractor to the commanding officer before removal, and will be distributed to officers commanding companies under regimental arrangements.

83. Officers commanding companies will keep an account of the receipt and disposal of the sums received for worn-out clothing.

84. Except as directed above, officers, non-commissioned officers and men are forbidden to have any transactions with the contractor, neither will any soldier be permitted to act as his agent or representative.

85. Abroad, if there is no contract at the station, the commanding officer will make his own arrangements for the disposal of worn-out personal clothing, but he will make it one of the conditions of sale that the purchaser shall not, either directly or indirectly, dispose of any tunics, frocks, jackets, or head-dresses, as garments, except to volunteers, unless they have first been so altered that they cannot be recognized as having been used as a uniform of the regular army. Where there is a contract the clothing will be dealt with as directed in paragraph 80.

86. Part-worn public clothing of non-effective soldiers will be taken into the regimental store, and examined by a board of survey (see paragraph 48).

87. To prevent excessive wear of new cloaks, great-coats, and capes, commanding officers will retain such numbers of those condemned as they may consider necessary, and the numbers so retained will be shown on the proceedings of the board of survey which condemns them, and be entered separately in the ledger.

88. Metal ornaments of full dress head-dresses condemned as unserviceable may be retained for reissue, but care will be taken that the head-dresses are not damaged by the removal of the ornaments.

A.O. 112
1911

89. Worn-out public clothing for which there is a contract will be given over to the contractor under the conditions specified in Appendix XI. At Sierra Leone all articles of condemned public clothing will be given in to the Army Ordnance Department, and the ordnance officer will return them to the Royal Army Clothing Department if their value, at the worn out rates shown under home stations in the Priced Vocabulary of Clothing and Necessaries, appreciably exceeds the cost of conveyance, otherwise they will be destroyed.

Regimental Transport and Soldiers Training as Mounted Infantry, &c.

90. Soldiers under training or employed as drivers of regimental transport, non-commissioned officers in charge of the transport, soldiers under training for mounted infantry or mounted duties, and the permanent staff and men under instruction at the camel corps school will require the articles detailed on page 88, in addition to the ordinary supply of clothing, unless otherwise specified. In the case of permanent staff of mounted infantry and the camel corps school, the cord pantaloons, or khaki drill trousers, and puttees will be provided out of the quarterly clothing allowance, but these articles will be issued as public clothing to other dismounted men engaged on, or trained in, mounted duties, under instruction at the camel corps school, or engaged on cyclist duties. Drawers and ankle boots will be provided from the normal allowance, and kilted highlanders will receive one pair of ankle boots free.

A.O. 83 1910

91. At the conclusion of the training or duties the articles (except the boots and those provided out of the clothing allowance) will be returned to store and examined by a board of survey. Repairable articles will, where necessary, be washed at the authorized rates and made serviceable at the public expense ; those unserviceable will be struck off charge, and disposed of to the contractor for worn-out clothing. Condemned spurs will be dealt with as directed in Appendix XI. Articles deficient or damaged by neglect or wilfulness will be charged for as directed in paragraph 229.

Leather Pantaloons and Jack Boots, Household Cavalry.

92. Leather pantaloons and jack boots will be supplied to the Household Cavalry as detailed in Table III. In February and September they will be inspected by officers commanding squadrons, and any requiring repair or renewal will be brought before a regimental board of survey. Application will be made for the attendance of an inspector from the Royal Army Clothing Department, who will assist the board as an expert. The report of the board will be forwarded to the Royal Army Clothing Department with a statement of the probable cost of repair, and with an indent for the replacement of articles condemned as unserviceable. Those condemned will, after replacement, be disposed of as directed in paragraph 89, except that a stock of twenty pairs may be kept in hand for the use of recruits, and repaired at the public expense.

A.C.D. Cav. 1054

93. Small intermediate repairs will be done at the discretion of the commanding officer, and the charge will be included in the pay list supported by the tradesman's receipted bill and the commanding officer's certificate that the repairs have been duly executed.

94. Contractors for the supply of jack boots and leather pantaloons will be placed in communication with the regiment requiring the articles.

95. Supply will be made to the regiment direct, and will be inspected by a board of survey assisted by an inspector from the Royal Army Clothing Department.

96. Articles approved will be stamped by the inspector with the W ⋀ D mark, and the date of issue. The name of the regiment and a consecutive number will also be stamped on them.

97. A separate account will be kept of the leather pantaloons and jack boots as per form, Appendix X. The account will show the date and cost of all repairs. This account will be subsidiary to the clothing ledger (which will show the articles in bulk only), and will be inspected by the board of survey inquiring into repairs or renewals.

Staves and Belts for Serjeant-Drummers.

98. A staff and belt for the serjeant-drummer will be supplied to each battalion of the Foot Guards and infantry, except light infantry and rifle battalions, and will be required to last twelve years ; at the expiration of that period the staff, if serviceable, may be re-gilt, when it will be required to last a further period of eight years.

99. Staves and belts will not be replaced until condemned as unserviceable by a board of survey ; the unserviceable articles may be retained and struck off ledger charge on replacement, otherwise they will be returned to the Royal Army Clothing Department. They must not be disposed of outside the unit.

A.O. 216
1912

State Clothing, Household Cavalry and Foot Guards.

100. State clothing for the trumpeters and band of the Household Cavalry, and for the household drummers of the Foot Guards, will be supplied as detailed in Table XIV.

101. Small intermediate repairs will be arranged for by the commanding officer, but in September all State clothing will be inspected by a representative from the Royal Army Clothing Department, and any further repairs will then be carried out, the cost of these, as well as the intermediate repairs, being charged against the public, if not due to wilful damage.

102. Unserviceable kettledrum and trumpet banners may be retained ; other articles when no longer required will be disposed of under instructions from the chief ordnance officer, Royal Army Clothing Department.

Colours, Standards, and Guidons.

103. Colours, standards, guidons, &c., will be supplied as detailed in Table XIII. The material, colour, and dimensions of standards and colours are shown in Appendix XII.

104. Colours, standards, guidons, &c., which have been in use the prescribed period will not necessarily be replaced, except in the case of Foot Guards, when they will be replaced every fifteen years (all battalions of a regiment at the same time). In the case of all other units they will be examined by a board of survey, and if repairable the repairs will be effected in accordance with paragraph 107. If unserviceable, indents for new ones, accompanied by a copy of the proceedings of the board, will be forwarded to the Royal Army Clothing Department. If colours have not lasted the prescribed period a report will be made of the circumstances in which they became prematurely unserviceable.

105. Commanding officers will arrange for new colours, standards or guidons to be taken into use within three months after receipt ; the provisions of paragraph 287 do not apply to these articles.

106. Drawings for the colours, standards and guidons, will be furnished by the inspector of regimental colours, who will be the sole authority on all details appertaining to these articles.

107. Repairs will be carried out regimentally and charged to the public, but when the cost exceeds £5, authority should be obtained from the Royal Army Clothing Department before the expenditure is incurred.

108. When standards, guidons, or colours are replaced, they remain the property of the State, and should be deposited in some church or other public building. Officers commanding will forward proposals for their disposal to the general officer commanding for submission to the War Office. No one is entitled to sell old standards, guidons, or colours, or to deal in them in any way. In no circumstances may colours or guidons be allowed to pass into the possession of any individual.

A.O. 75
1911
20
Foot Gds.
121

Shoemakers' Tools.

109. One large and four small chests containing tools, &c., as detailed in Table XI, will be allowed for each battalion of Foot Guards and infantry having a serjeant shoemaker, and the sum of five shillings per unit will be allowed annually for the upkeep of the quantities laid down. Credit for the materials used in repairs will be given as directed in paragraph 153. The allowance will be paid by the command paymaster.

A.O. 138
1913

II.—DISCHARGES.

(*See* also paragraphs 23, 26, 27, and 36 for allowances.)

110. Soldiers passing into the army reserve will be treated in regard to clothing as if discharged.

111. Soldiers on discharge may take away the necessaries in their possession, except as provided in paragraphs 146 and 213.

112. Soldiers discharged for any reason (except as provided in paragraphs 113 (1), (2)), will be entitled to take away with them any of the following articles of personal clothing in their possession, viz., boots or shoes, drawers, fezzes, turbans, gloves, service dress and khaki drill trousers, and cardigan waistcoats; also full dress trousers, provided the stripes are removed before the men leave. No other articles of uniform clothing will be retained by the soldier.

113. The personal clothing of soldiers discharged will be dealt with as follows :—

(1) The personal clothing (except drawers and one pair of ankle boots or highland shoes, which may be retained) in possession of a recruit who is discharged within three months of enlistment will, if unworn, be returned to store for re-issue, but, if worn, will be sold, and the proceeds, as shown on Army Form O 1622, credited to the public under the clothing vote, except in the case of a recruit discharged as unlikely on medical grounds to become an efficient soldier who will be treated under paragraph 113 (3).

(2) The personal clothing (except one pair of ankle boots or highland shoes) of soldiers relegated to the army reserve in respect of an offence on enlistment, or discharged—

(a) For fraudulent enlistment or false answer on attestation, or for a mis-statement as to age on enlistment when the discharge takes place after less than twelve months' service,

(b) On sentence of penal servitude,

(c) With ignominy,

(d) For misconduct,

(e) On conviction by the civil power of an offence committed before or after enlistment,

(f) On being claimed by the parish authorities for wife desertion,

will be sold, and the proceeds, as shown on Army Form O 1622, credited to the public under the clothing vote. If, however, the articles are fit for re-issue as new, they will be retaken on charge and utilized.

(3) All other soldiers discharged will be entitled to the proceeds of the sale of the personal clothing in their possession.

114. When a soldier dies, his non-effective account will be credited with the proceeds of the sale of any personal clothing in his possession. In the case of a recruit dying, the value of any clothing and necessaries due, but not issued, will be credited in his non-effective account.

115. A soldier who becomes non-effective before becoming entitled to the issue of his first clothing and kit allowance, will not receive any portion of the 30s. 6d. issuable with that allowance.

116. The following allowances will be granted towards the provision of plain clothes on discharge :—

	s.	d.
Native officers of local forces, warrant officers, and non-commissioned officers entitled to 1st class quality of clothing	15	0
Serjeants	7	6
Rank and file	5	0

A recruit discharged within three months of the date of his enlistment, who is not in possession of sufficient funds to purchase plain clothes, will be supplied with a suit at the public expense, and the allowance will be withheld. Neither plain clothes nor any allowance for their provision will be granted to men who are discharged under Section 81 of the Army Act.

117. Prison warders and barrack wardens are entitled, on resignation, to the allowance granted by paragraph 116 towards the provision of plain clothes.

118. Soldiers discharged and immediately re-attested will not receive a free issue of plain clothes or any allowance in lieu. Soldiers given up as apprentices, and boys discharged for having enlisted without their parents' consent will be similarly treated, except when not in possession of a suit of plain clothes or of sufficient funds to purchase the same.

119. European soldiers discharged between 1st October and 31st March as "no longer physically fit for war service" (*see* King's Regulations) will receive a free issue of a civilian great-coat. Soldiers no longer physically fit for war service, who are discharged between 1st April and 30th September, and soldiers discharged at any time for other causes may purchase such coats at Vocabulary rates. The coats will be indented and accounted for by the unit to which the men belong, or to which they are attached at the time of their discharge.

A.C.D.
A'shot.
2,735

120. Soldiers not entitled to a free issue of plain clothes on discharge may be supplied with a suit on repayment at the rates published in the Priced Vocabulary.

121. Soldiers on discharge or relegation to the Army Reserve whose personal clothing is disposed of under paragraph 113 (2) will, except when sentenced to penal servitude, be supplied with plain clothes as detailed in Table X, unless they are in possession of plain clothes of their own. (*See* paragraph 225 (*a*) as regards the recovery of the value of the plain clothes issued to men relegated to the Army Reserve.)

A.C.D.
Clo. Reg.
982

122. Men released from detention barracks or military prisons who do not return to duty will be supplied with plain clothes by the detention barrack or military prison authorities. If discharged direct from units, they will receive plain clothes from their commanding officers.

123. A suit of plain clothes will be provided by the commanding officer of the man's unit, or of the unit to which he may be attached at the time of imprisonment, for each soldier taken to a civil prison (unless taken to a convict prison to undergo penal servitude) and will be handed over by the escort to the prison authorities, a receipt being obtained for it. Should the man return to duty, the escort which conducts him back to his unit will also bring back the plain clothes, which will be retained for future issue.

124. The plain clothes will be obtained from the clothing depôt supplying the district, or provided locally, by detention barrack or military prison authorities, or by commanding officers, but no money allowance will be paid to the man. The indents will show the articles required and the date of discharge and will be accompanied by size rolls.

125. If provided locally, the cost of the suits, at the rate given in the Priced Vocabulary, will be charged in the pay list, the charge being supported by a certificate on the receipted bill that the articles have been taken on charge. The certificate should state the period of the account in which the articles will be found taken on charge, and the number of the voucher.

III.—SOLDIERS ATTACHED FOR DUTY OR INSTRUCTION TO OTHER CORPS, UNITS, OR INSTITUTIONS.

126. Clothing for soldiers detached from their own units, except those undergoing courses of instruction at the Royal Army Clothing Department and at the School of Instruction for Mounted Infantry, will be indented and accounted for by the unit to which they are attached for pay. The indents for clothing for these men should show clearly the unit to which they belong. The clothing for men at the School of Instruction for Mounted Infantry will be supplied under local arrangements. Non-commissioned officers appointed temporary assistant warders in detention barracks abroad will be clothed by the commandant of the detention barrack.

A.O. 259
1911

127. Soldiers going to the Royal Military School of Music will take their clothing with them, and the quarterly clothing allowances will be drawn at the school. Any renewal of clothing will be obtained by the commandant. The exchange of outgrown public clothing will, when possible, be effected direct with the unit to which the wearers belong. When the unit cannot supply the articles, they will be indented for from the clothing depôt supplying the district, and the part-worn public clothing outgrown will be returned to the unit. Personal clothing of boys outgrown will be dealt with as directed in paragraph 43. Cloth pantaloons will not be worn, and knee boots and jack spurs will be withdrawn before men leave their unit.

128. A blue cloth frock will be supplied for students training for bandmaster and will be transferred from one student to another. The frock will be treated as public clothing.

A.O. 266
1910

129. Clothing of home pattern may be purchased by men of the Royal Artillery sent from abroad to undergo courses of instruction. In the case of men on the Indian Establishment, quarterly allowances will be credited at home rates, and any articles of public clothing which are absolutely necessary will be issued, all such credits and issues being recorded on their transfer clothing statements, and also on Army Form H 1107, rendered in accordance with paragraph 348.

130. Men attached to home depôts, &c, on the expiration of their Indian furlough, pending the return of their unit to the Imperial Establishment, will receive clothing allowances, at home rates, from Imperial funds, and the amounts so credited should be notified to the Assistant Financial Secretary, War Office, when the men rejoin their units.

131. Men and boys of the West India Regiment attending courses of instruction in the United Kingdom will, on arrival, be credited with the value of one service dress suit (including cap), two pairs of woollen drawers, and one cardigan waistcoat.

No addition to the rates of quarterly clothing allowance will be made.

132. Other soldiers sent from abroad to undergo a course of instruction may purchase a service dress suit (including cap), a cardigan waistcoat, and two pairs of woollen drawers, if the articles are not already in their possession (*see* also paragraph 364).

133. In the case of soldiers proceeding to Hythe, the officers commanding the men's units will, before embarkation, forward indents and size rolls to the Royal Army Clothing Department for any articles required, with a request that they may be forwarded to the commandant, School of Musketry, or if the men are to be temporarily attached to another unit, to the officer commanding the latter.

134. Armourers at all stations will be clothed under the scale laid down for the Army Ordnance Corps at the station in question. The unit with which they are serving will indent for the clothing.

135. Non-commissioned officers and men of Royal Engineers, undergoing courses of engine driving on civil railways, will be in possession of the following articles which will be worn in lieu of service dress, canvas clothing, and puttees.

(I) Long course—2 blue serge suits, 1 pea jacket, 1 cap (railway companies') and 2 suits of dungaree.

(II) Short course—1 blue serge suit, 1 pea jacket, 1 cap (railway companies') and 1 suit of dungaree.

One serge suit, one dungaree suit, and the cap will be issued free in each case, and the pea jacket will be held on inventory as public clothing and will be returned to store at the termination of the course. One of the blue serge, and one of the dungaree, suits referred to in (I) will be provided by the soldier out of his quarterly clothing allowance.

SECTION III.—NECESSARIES.

Free Kits.

136. The free kit given to each recruit after final acceptance is detailed in Table XVI. It will be kept up at the expense of the soldier, except in the case of men in military prisons, who will be supplied with necessaries actually required at the public expense. No departure from the articles detailed in the lists will be permitted, nor will the expense of any article not specified in the lists be charged against soldiers except by special authority.

137. The identity disc included in Table XVI will be issued on mobilization only. It will be stored ready marked by the officer commanding the unit in which the soldier is serving, and will be transferred with him on his proceeding to another station either at

Margin notes:
A.C.D.
S. Music.
1420

A.O. 83
1910

A.O. 75
1911

home, in the Colonies, or in India. On transfer to the Army
Reserve the soldier's disc will be passed by the officer commanding
the unit to the officer commanding the depôt in the case of
infantry, and, for other reservists, to the officer in charge of
records who will, in the case of those men who rejoin at depôts,
forward it to the officer commanding the depôt concerned. On
mobilization, identity discs held at record offices will be transmitted to the units to which reservists are allotted. Discs will not
be brought on charge in the regimental clothing ledgers, and those
of non-effectives will be destroyed.

A.O. 75
1911
138. A personal issue of an identity disc fitted with a cord will
be made to each officer.

139. A recruit who purchases his discharge before receiving a
free kit will not be entitled to the kit or to any allowance in lieu.

140. The kits of soldiers who re-engage will not be renewed or
completed at the public expense.

141. A soldier who re-enlists will receive a free kit on the same
conditions as a recruit. This issue will not be made to a soldier
who re-enlists without a break in the continuity of his service.

142. Necessaries will be issued to soldiers in the presence of an
officer ; any objections to articles must be made before they are
taken away from the place of issue.

143. In indenting for necessaries peculiar to Highland regiments
commanding officers will state whether they can be purchased
locally, and at what rate.

144. Necessaries required by small detachments at home or
abroad, will, whenever possible, be obtained on payment from a
unit at the same station.

145. The following articles will be supplied for the use of recruits
waiting at the headquarters of a regimental district or recruits'
barracks :—blacking, combs, forks, knives, spoons, towels ; brushes,
blacking, and polishing. The articles will be issued by the officer
in charge of barracks, who will obtain them from the clothing
depôt supplying the district.

146. The necessaries of soldiers discharged on conviction of
felony will be sold, and the proceeds will be dealt with in accordance with the regulations made under the Regimental Debts
Act.

147. Necessaries which have been used with horses suffering from
contagious disorders will, when authorized to be destroyed, be replaced at the public expense.

A.O. 138
1913
148. A clothes bag for use on board ship will be supplied free
to each soldier whenever he proceeds abroad, and will be retained
in his possession for use on returning home, or on proceeding from
one Colonial station to another or to India.

A.C.D.
Clo. Reg.
1085
149. Soldiers proceeding abroad will, with the following excep-
tions, be supplied with three sets of buttons and rings, and four
waist-hooks, for wear with khaki drill clothing :—

    (*a*) When proceeding to Sierra Leone, except for Royal Army
        Medical Corps, only two sets of buttons and rings will be
        issued.

(*b*) Soldiers of the Royal Army Medical Corps will be supplied with only one set of buttons and rings, but with none if proceeding to Sierra Leone.   No waist-hooks will be issued.

(*c*) Soldiers of the Royal Garrison Artillery proceeding to Ceylon, Mauritius, and the Straits Settlements will be supplied with only two sets of buttons and rings.

No further free issues will be allowed of these articles.

SECTION IV.—ISSUES ON PAYMENT.

Materials and Garniture.

150. All materials for repairs will be indented for from the clothing depôt supplying the district.   The tools, leather, and grindery which can be supplied are detailed in Table XII.   Sewings may be provided locally or indented for from the clothing depôt at the discretion of the commanding officer.

151. Issues of materials or garniture will not include parts or fractions less than as detailed below :—

(*a*) Cloth, serge, and other materials, including twists, laces, cords, braids, &c., measured by the yard—not less than a quarter of a yard.   An issue of twenty yards, or more, may contain from one to three yards more than indented for, to prevent cutting off useless remnants.

(*b*) Buttons, hooks and eyes, and other articles counted by the gross or dozen—not less than one dozen.

(*c*) Articles disposed of by weight—not less than a quarter of a pound.

(*d*) Threads and sewing silks —not less than a skein.

(*e*) Leather will be indented for in hides, not in pounds.

152. Materials will not be indented for for the purpose of enabling serjeant tailors or others to make up clothing or boots for sale to soldiers or other persons (except as laid down in paragraphs 154 and 156).   Materials in small quantities may be issued for the purpose of repairing clothing and necessaries of the authorized scales ; such issues will be on payment.

A.C.D.
Clo. Reg
——
1092
54
——
Gen. No.
1373

153. The articles will be brought on charge in the clothing ledger.   Credit for the articles sold will be given monthly in the accounts of the command paymaster on Army Form P 1925 and the total value of the issues received by the unit on each voucher should, as a rule, be credited within three months of the date of receipt.   Care will be taken to avoid the maintenance of excessive stocks.

154. Neither officers' quality of material nor articles of officers' pattern can be supplied, but materials and articles of clothing and necessaries of army pattern can be issued on payment to officers, provided the quantities asked for are not excessive.   Such issues

A.O. 307
——
1909

A.O. 307
1909
will, as a rule, be obtained through a unit ; when obtained direct from the clothing depôt supplying the area, prepayment will be required.

54
Gen. No.
1373
155. Materials required for the use of families, either of officers of soldiers, or of civilian subordinates, will only be supplied to stations where such or similar materials suitable for use cannot otherwise be obtained, and provided that the quantities asked for are not excessive, and are required for family use only. They will only be issued to home stations in exceptional circumstances which will be explained on the indent ; at stations abroad, 10 per cent. will be added to the rate given in the priced vocabulary of clothing and necessaries. It will be explained on the indents why they are put forward, and the number of families for whom required. Issues under this paragraph are subject to stock permitting.

A.C.D.
Clo. Reg.
1092
156. Soldiers when cycling for recreation may be permitted to wear an undress suit of special pattern as an alternative to service dress, to be provided at their own expense. The provision of this suit is optional. It comprises jacket and knickerbockers of blue serge with blue stockings or blue putties at the option of the wearer. For rifle regiments the suit will be of black tartan and the stockings or putties dark green or black. For Highland and Scottish regiments the knickerbockers will be of regimental tartan. Chevrons, except for Foot Guards, badges of rank and metal titles, as authorized for wear on the tunic, will be supplied on payment for wear on the undress cycling jacket.

Undress cycling clothing will be provided under regimental arrangements, but sample suits with stockings, materials for making up suits, and blue putties may be obtained on payment from the clothing depôt. The charge by the serjeant tailor for making up suits will be adjusted on the basis of the price of the sample suit.

54
Gen. No.
1373
157. Materials required by Colonial Governments will only be issued locally subject to the conditions of paragraphs 166 and 167, as regards the 10 per cent. additional charge.

Clothing and Necessaries.

158. No soldier will be allowed to provide himself with personal clothing by purchase from tradesmen. Soldiers will not be required to purchase necessaries or clothing which are not sanctioned by these regulations.

159. When a new article of personal clothing is issued on payment, it will be charged for at the rate in force at the time of issue (*see* paragraph 40).

160. Public clothing will not be issued on payment.

161. Personal clothing and necessaries for issue on payment will be supplied from the public stores; their provision regimentally is forbidden except under special authority.

162. Soldiers allowed to wear plain clothes may obtain discharged soldiers' suits on payment at the discretion of the officer commanding. Officers' servants and mess waiters may also be supplied with these suits on payment.

163. Necessaries may be sold in regimental institutes, but all such necessaries must be obtained from the quartermaster's stores (*see* paragraph 5, Appendix III), and be sold at government rates to soldiers only. Such sales will be cash transactions. Regimental arrangements must be made for marking. Public charges and credits under this paragraph will be dealt with by the command paymaster.

A.O. 275
1912

A.O. 138
1913

164. A Priced Vocabulary of Clothing and Necessaries, including a table of the clothing and kit allowances, will be published periodically. A detail of the allowances for the provision of certain articles of clothing, &c., will be included in this vocabulary.

165. Clothing and necessaries in store at an Army Ordnance Department station abroad, may be supplied on repayment to civilian subordinates permanently employed.

166. Clothing, or necessaries, required by Colonial Governments, will not be issued locally except in cases of emergency. Such issues will be on repayment.

167. In the case of issues of clothing and necessaries on payment from store at stations abroad, except to officers and soldiers for their own personal use, and of clothing authorized for civilian subordinates in receipt of a clothing allowance, an addition of 10 per cent. will be made to the rate given in the priced vocabulary of clothing and necessaries.

54
Gen. No.
1373

SECTION V.—MISCELLANEOUS SUPPLIES.

Hospital Clothing.
Prison Clothing and Necessaries.
Watch Coats.
Waterproof Clothing.   } as detailed in Table XV.
Working Clothing.
Magazine Clothing.

168. All articles in this section will be dealt with as public clothing.

169. The articles detailed in Table XV except field dressings will be indented and accounted for as follows :—

(*a*) By officers in charge of barracks for articles issued to the troops "on inventory."

(*b*) By ordnance officers for articles supplied to the Army Ordnance Department, and issued "as articles in use."

(*c*) By the officer in charge of the armament district for magazine and other clothing held on armament charge.

A.O. 275
1912

A.O. 259
1911

170. Field dressings for instructional purposes as prescribed in the King's Regulations will be obtained by units for which they are stored with mobilization equipments from the numbers set aside for exchange by the medical officer at his annual inspection. Such units may retain for instruction dressings set aside for exchange up to a maximum number not exceeding 10 per cent. of

A.C.D.
Clo. Reg.
1094

the peace establishment, any balance being returned to the Royal Army Clothing Department.

Other regular units at home may demand from the Royal Army Clothing Department, field dressings for instruction up to a maximum not exceeding 10 per cent. annually of peace establishment.

In the Channel Islands and at stations abroad, other than India, units will obtain field dressings for instruction from the Army Ordnance Department at the station ; supply will be made from the 20 per cent. turned over annually.

These dressings need not be brought on charge.

171. When articles of clothing held under any of the headings named in paragraph 169, become worn out, they will be examined by the officer whose duty it is to account for them. If considered by him to be unserviceable, they will be exchanged, but will subsequently be produced before an inspecting officer or board of survey referred to in the :—

Regulations for Supply, Transport, and Barrack Services. } In the case of articles held under sub-paragraph (*a*).

Regulations for Army Ordnance Services. } In the case of articles held under sub-paragraph (*b*) or (*c*).

172. After approval by the general officer commanding, the recommendations of the board of survey as to the disposal of the condemned articles will be carried out without further authority. The proceedings will be annexed as a voucher to the store account.

173. Articles issued " on inventory," or as "articles in use," will be washed and kept in repair by the officer in charge of barracks (except repairs to clothing and necessaries of soldiers in prison which will be carried out as laid down in paragraph 215), or by the Army Ordnance Department, and materials for repair will be supplied on application to the clothing depôt supplying the district. Old garments returned to store will be utilized for repairs as far as possible, and the certificate of the accounting officer that the garments have been expended in repairs will be attached as a voucher to the account in which the articles are struck off charge. When the washing and repairing are performed under a contract, no materials for repair will be issued.

174. When an article issued "on inventory," or as an "article in use," is lost, made away with, or damaged, the rules for assessing charges laid down in paragraph 229 will be followed. Charges for clothing (other than magazine clothing) held on armament charge, (for which *see* paragraph 175) will be assessed in a similar manner.

175. Magazine clothing held on armament charge will be dealt with—

So far as concerns disposal after condemnation   ... { By the accounting officer under the instructions contained in Appendix XI.

So far as concerns replacement, loss, or damage (wilful or by neglect) ...	In accordance with the rules laid down in the Equipment Regulations, so far as they are applicable.

176. Civilian subordinates will only be supplied with working clothing in very exceptional circumstances. When authorized it will be indented for from the clothing depôt supplying the district, and will be accounted for under the regulations relating to the service concerned. The price at which each article can be procured locally will be shown in the indent.

SECTION VI.—TRANSFERS.

177. Transfers to units in which the uniform is of the same pattern (or can, by changing facings, stripes of trousers, &c., be made of the same pattern) will take all their personal and public clothing with them.

178. Other transfers will take such articles of their public and personal clothing as can be worn in their new unit, with any other articles required for the journey (men going from R.F.A. or R.G.A. to R.H.A. will also take a tunic). If such soldiers are not re-transferred to their corps within three months, the personal articles not required will be disposed of, and the proceeds credited to the man ; any public clothing not required will be returned to their late unit or to the depôt thereof.

179. In the case of a transfer for public reasons between different arms of the service, between the R.H.A., R.F.A., and R.G.A., from dismounted to mounted duties within the unit, from one regiment to another, or from one section of R.E. to another, the entire cost of altering the articles of personal clothing or providing new ones necessitated by difference in pattern or scale will be borne by the public, the man being credited with the value of the new articles required. This will not apply to differences due merely to change of station.   A.O. 266   1910

180. In the case of a transfer at the soldier's request, the man will receive a credit of half the value of new articles of personal clothing required owing to difference in pattern or scale unless the difference is due merely to change of station. Articles in possession, which can be converted, will be altered at the public expense, if the cost of alteration including any necessary chevrons, badges or aiguillettes does not exceed half the value of the new garment ; if the cost is estimated to exceed this, half value of a new garment will be credited to the soldier.

181. Transfers from the Royal Marines will be dealt with for clothing and necessaries under the conditions of paragraphs 179, 180 and 183. (*See* also paragraph 25.)   A.O. 275   1912

A.O. 67
1913

182. Clerks, except those employed in regimental offices, will, on coming to, or being made clerks whilst serving in the London district, be credited with half the cost of the blue tartan frock and the pair of rank and file pattern tweed trousers.

183. Transfers, including those between mounted and dismounted duties within the unit, will be credited with the value of such necessaries as are requisite owing to difference in pattern or scale of issues, except in the case of soldiers re-transferred for misconduct.

184. Men transferred from mounted to dismounted services need not obtain woollen drawers until the cotton drawers in their possession are worn out, and cloth pantaloons and knee boots should be withheld for three months from transfers from dismounted to mounted units.

54
Gen. No.
1338

185. Probationers for the Royal Flying Corps, Army Service Corps, the Royal Army Medical Corps and the Military Provost Staff Corps, also soldiers on probation under paragraph 333 (IV) King's Regulations, will be dealt with as transfers. Any personal and public clothing brought from their former unit will be retained in their new unit until the final disposal of the men is decided upon. The personal clothing of men finally transferred will be disposed of as directed in paragraph 178. Serviceable public clothing not required will be returned to the men's former unit, or to the depôt thereof ; unserviceable articles will be dealt with as directed in paragraph 49. If the men are sent back to their unit the clothing they brought will be returned with them and will be again taken into wear ; the personal clothing they obtained as probationers will be dealt with as directed in paragraphs 74 and 75, and the public clothing will be returned to regimental store.

A.O. 67
1913

186. Probationers for the Army Ordnance Corps, Army Pay Corps, and Gymnastic Staff will bring with them all the clothing in their possession, and will continue to wear it until finally transferred, when they will obtain the articles required to complete their uniform under the conditions for other transfers (*see* paragraph 178). The public clothing not of proper pattern will be dealt with as directed in paragraph 178, and the personal clothing as in paragraphs 74 and 75.

187. Condemned or worn-out cloaks or great-coats will, if possible, be sent with soldiers transferred on probation.

A.O. 216
1912

188. When a soldier is transferred from one unit to another a transfer clothing statement on Army Form H 1157, will be forwarded to the officer commanding the unit to which he is transferred showing the public clothing in wear with the date of issue, and in the case of men who have not been completed with their first outfit of clothing, the articles of personal clothing in wear. This statement will be signed in cavalry or infantry units by the squadron or company commander, and in other cases by the officer commanding the unit.

The form may also be used in cases of inter-company or inter-squadron transfers within a unit, if the commanding officer desires.

189. An abstract of the public clothing, prepared in duplicate on Army Form H 1150 from the transfer clothing statements, will also be sent to the commanding officer of the unit to which the men are transferred.

190. Transfer statements completed as in paragraph 188, will be carefully compared with the articles in possession of the soldier before he leaves the unit. After the statement has been signed by the soldier, he will be responsible for the articles shown to be in his possession. On arrival at the new unit the articles in possession of the man will immediately be compared with the statement.

191. The public clothing will be at once entered in the clothing ledger from the abstract, one copy of which will be signed and returned to the man's former unit.

192. A similar course will be followed when a man is attached temporarily for duty to another unit, unless he remains in the payment of his own unit, when no abstract will be required, and the clothing will not be brought on charge in the clothing ledger. If the man is again moved the statement will be corrected up to date, and signed and transmitted in the usual manner.

193. In the case of men sent from colonial stations to the Discharge Depôt, Gosport, for discharge or for transfer to the Army Reserve, the abstract of public clothing referred to in paragraph 189 will not be required, but transfer statements (showing the articles of public clothing only) will be prepared in duplicate by the unit from which the men are sent and transmitted to the commandant of the Discharge Depôt, who will take on charge the public clothing of such men as are discharged or trans-ferred to the Army Reserve by him, signing and returning to each man's former unit one copy of the transfer statement. The transfer statements of men sent on to the other units for final disposal will be transmitted by the commandant of the Discharge Depôt, as received, to the commanding officer of the unit receiving the men and be similarly dealt with.

194. The abstract of public clothing referred to in paragraph 189 will not be required for men sent from colonial stations to the Royal Victoria Hospital, Netley. Transfer clothing statements (showing the articles of public clothing only) prepared in duplicate by the unit from which the men are sent, will be forwarded to the officer in charge who will, when the question of the men's fitness for further service has been decided by the medical authorities, take on charge the public clothing of those found unfit, signing and returning to each man's former unit one copy of the clothing statement, the other copy being retained as a voucher to the clothing ledger of the hospital. A.O. 307
1909

The public clothing of men fit for further service, and of those to be sent to other hospitals, will not be taken on charge at the Royal Victoria Hospital; and the transfer clothing statements, as received, will be forwarded to the unit or hospital to which the men are transferred, and be dealt with as stated above.

195. The officers in charge at Netley and Millbank, and the Assistant Director of Medical Services at Woolwich, will satisfy

themselves that all men from abroad on leaving hospital are in
possession of at least one cardigan waistcoat, one flannel shirt, one
pair of woollen or cotton drawers, and one pair of worsted socks.
A.O. 259 | Articles required to replace any of the above found deficient will
——— | be issued by them from a stock kept for this purpose (*see* Table
1911 | XV). The issue will be on payment (except as provided below),
credit being given in the pay list of the officer in charge
at Netley, or in that of the R.A.M.C. unit at Millbank or
Woolwich to which the man is attached. In the case of men
coming from a station abroad at which drawers are not worn, and
who have not already received an issue under paragraph 380, the
issue of these articles will be free. The issues will be supported by
a manuscript voucher, which, in the case of men found unfit for
further service, will be attached to Army Form H 1157, as a
voucher to the clothing ledger.

196. Public clothing brought with men from the Special Reserve
will be taken on charge, and the original dates of issue should
appear in the transfer clothing statement, Army Form H 1157.
The men will be clothed as recruits, except as provided for in foot-
notes to Tables I, II, and XVI). Any personal clothing in their
possession will be dealt with under paragraphs 74 and 75.

SECTION VII.—SOLDIERS IN PRISON OR DETENTION.

*Soldiers awaiting trial or undergoing imprisonment by the Civil
Authorities, or sentenced to be discharged with ignominy for
military offences.*

A.O. 259 | **197.** The quarterly clothing and kit allowance will not be
——— | credited to a soldier awaiting trial or undergoing imprisonment by
1911 | the civil authorities, or committed to a military prison. Should he
return to duty, he will, subject to the conditions of paragraphs 23
and 27, be credited with the allowance as from the first day of the
quarter in which he rejoins, unless he has already received the
allowance for that quarter.

198. Soldiers sentenced to be discharged with ignominy will
not wear their uniform clothing (except ankle boots or highland
shoes, canvas clothing, and drawers) in military prisons, but the
articles will be brought back by the escort and disposed of as
follows :—The public clothing will be returned to store, and the
personal clothing (except ankle boots or highland shoes, canvas
clothing, and drawers) dealt with under paragraph 113 (2). Ankle
boots or highland shoes, canvas clothing, drawers, and all necessaries
in possession will be taken to prison. The articles as detailed in
Table XV(*b*) will be used in prison, and such necessaries as are not
required for use in prison will be stored at the prison for re-issue
to the men on release.

199. Soldiers sentenced to be discharged with ignominy, who
are sent home from abroad to military prisons, will embark in
possession of their necessaries, ankle boots or highland shoes,

canvas clothing, drawers, and such other articles of clothing as are considered by the commanding officer to be required for use on the voyage, any necessary articles not in possession being supplied free to prisoners who are without funds. Part-worn articles in good condition should be purchased for this purpose if available. Clothing and necessaries required by men while in detention pending embarkation will be similarly supplied. The articles in possession will be shown in detail in the transfer clothing statements forwarded to the general officer commanding at the port at which the men land. Any articles not taken home by the men will be disposed of as laid down in paragraph 198. Clothes bags (if required) will be supplied at the public expense, if the men are without funds. A.O. 112
1911

200. On arrival at the military prison the clothing in possession (except ankle boots or highland shoes, canvas clothing, and drawers) will be brought back by the escort taking the man to prison at home. The public clothing will be taken on charge by the unit furnishing the escort, and the personal clothing disposed of as laid down in paragraph 198.

201. Clothing and necessaries as detailed in Table XV(*b*) for use in prison will be held on inventory, but the necessaries, boots, canvas clothing, and drawers, brought by the men, will be used until worn out before being replaced by similar articles.

202. On discharge from prison, soldiers sentenced to be discharged with ignominy will be provided by the prison authorities with a suit of plain clothes, and will retain a serviceable pair of ankle boots or highland shoes, drawers, the necessaries in use, and those stored for them. Their canvas clothing will be retained at the prison for further use.

Soldiers in detention.

203. The quarterly clothing and kit allowance will be credited to soldiers undergoing detention, except when it is probable that the discharge from the service or transfer to the Army Reserve will take place within the quarter. Should the discharge or transfer to the Army Reserve not take place by the end of the quarter, the allowance so withheld will then be credited. A.O. 112
1911

The allowance will be credited by the units to which the soldiers belong, and will be utilized for the upkeep of uniform, clothing and necessaries.

204. Soldiers sentenced to confinement in detention barracks will take with them clothing and necessaries completed to scale, except the full dress head-dress at home, and, in mounted services, pantaloons, knee boots and jack spurs. Articles required to complete the scales will be issued on payment, the cost being debited to the man's account. A.O. 157
1912

Men who are to be discharged on the termination of their detention, or whose discharge is to be, or has been, applied for, or about whose discharge there is any uncertainty, will not take full dress, unless already in possession of it. The issue of clothing and

A.O. 157
1912

necessaries to these men will be limited to such articles as are absolutely essential for use during detention, part-worn articles if available being purchased for this purpose. Commanding Officers will be held responsible for unwarranted or unreasonable issues.

During detention replacements will be made by units at the cost of the men.

An inventory in duplicate on Army Form B 253 will accompany each soldier under sentence, and after being duly checked and signed, one copy will be brought back by the escort. A similar inventory will accompany soldiers returning to duty, or will be forwarded with kits returned to special reserve units.

205. A soldier released from detention to proceed abroad will be supplied, as directed in paragraph 366, with the requisite clothing and necessaries by the commanding officer of the unit on the strength of which he is borne, who will also recover from the commandant or superintendent of the detention barrack any articles deposited with him.

206. Except when sentenced to penal servitude, a soldier who is to be discharged on the termination of his detention will take away on release a pair of serviceable boots or highland shoes, and the necessaries and drawers in his possession; plain clothes will be supplied as provided for in paragraphs 121, 122, and 123, and uniform clothing will be returned to the man's unit or depôt, the personal articles being disposed of as directed in paragraph 113 (2).

207. A soldier to be discharged without funds may be supplied with a free issue of a pair of serviceable boots or shoes, a shirt, a pair of socks, and a pair of braces, if not in possession of these articles.

208. The public clothing of a soldier discharged direct from a unit will be taken into store. Personal clothing will be disposed of as directed in paragraph 113 (2). One pair of serviceable boots or shoes, and any necessaries in his possession, may be kept by him.

209. Soldiers under sentence and men of bad character sent home from abroad (including India) for discharge or detention will embark in possession of uniform clothing and necessaries, which will be shown in detail in the transfer clothing statement forwarded to the general officer commanding at the port at which the men land. Any necessaries required by such men will, if they are without funds, be provided before embarkation at the public expense, as laid down in paragraph 204.

210. Clothes bags (if required) will be supplied at the public expense, if the men are without funds.

211. The officer commanding the troops on board will be responsible that the clothing and kits are placed in proper custody, and that only such articles as are required for use are left in the men's possession.

212. The clothing of a soldier discharged on disembarkation will be exchanged for plain clothes by the disembarking staff officer. The necessaries will be retained by the man.

213. The clothing and necessaries of a man sentenced to penal servitude and sent home from abroad will be brought back by the escort taking him to prison at home, and will then be sold, except the public clothing, which will be brought on charge. The proceeds of the personal clothing will be credited to the public, and the proceeds of the necessaries will be dealt with as directed in paragraph 146.

214. The commanding officer of a unit to which a soldier under sentence belongs, or of the unit that furnishes the escort for taking him to a detention barrack, will be responsible that he is in possession of clothing and necessaries as authorized in paragraph 204, or if sent to a civil prison, that a suit of plain clothes, a serviceable pair of boots or highland shoes, a shirt, pair of socks and pair of braces, with any other necessaries or drawers he may have, are left at the prison for issue to him on release, except as provided in paragraph 213. The commanding officer will also be responsible for the recovery from the prison of any clothing which the man is not allowed to take away with him. An additional shirt, pair of socks and pair of drawers, may be issued to soldiers discharged from prison in South Africa and given free passage to England. *(A.O. 112 1911)* *(A.O. 275 1912)*

215. Repairs to prison clothing will, if possible, be carried out in the prison. If the repairs cannot be effected in the prison they will be executed in the nearest military shop, or, if this is not possible, by local tradesmen ; in the latter case the charges should be supported by a certificate from the governor, that the rates are fair and reasonable, and that the work has been satisfactorily performed.

SECTION VIII.—DESERTERS AND FRAUDULENTLY ENLISTED MEN.

Deserters.

216. The deficient public clothing of a deserter will be struck off charge, but will not be included in the monthly return of clothing lost, Army Form P 1954, until he is placed under stoppages on rejoining (*see* King's Regulations). His personal clothing and necessaries will be retained in store for six months for re-issue in the event of his rejoining. After six months the articles will be available · for issue to any rejoined deserter under the terms of paragraph 218, the value of the necessaries so issued being credited to the non-effective account of the original owner. Should there, for any reason, be no such outlet for the part-worn articles of personal clothing, the commanding officer must use his discretion as to the advisability of disposing of them. When disposed of, the proceeds, as shown on Army Form O 1622, will be credited to the public. *(A.C.D Clo. Regns. 1086)*

217. A duplicate (signed by the commanding officer) of the declaration of the court of inquiry recording the circumstances connected with the soldier's absence, and any deficiency in his clothing and necessaries, will accompany the account in which any articles are struck off charge under paragraph 216.

218. A rejoined deserter will be treated as follows :—

A.O. 112
1911

   (*a*) On rejoining he will be supplied with a service dress suit (or khaki, if worn at the station), cap, putties, one pair of boots or highland shoes, and, if necessary, during the winter months, drawers and cardigan waistcoat, and at stations abroad a helmet. Part-worn articles will be issued if in store, or readily obtainable from another unit at the station, or from any soldier who has permission to sell them. In the last case the value of the articles, as assessed by the commanding officer, will be paid, and the amount charged against the public, vouched by the receipt. Such necessaries as may be absolutely essential will also be issued.

If retained in the service he will be further dealt with as follows :—

   (*b*) If a clothing allowance has been drawn before desertion he will be credited with a fresh allowance as from the first day of the quarter in which he recommences his service, unless he has already received the allowance for that quarter. He will pay for any articles required to complete his outfit of clothing and necessaries [including any articles issued under (*a*)]. Should the allowance be insufficient, he will be placed under stoppages of pay for the balance.

A.O. 307
1909

   (*c*) If he rejoins before any clothing allowance has been drawn, his personal clothing will be completed to the authorized scale. Any articles issued under (*a*) will be reckoned as part of the outfit. His kit of necessaries will be completed at his own expense. The first quarterly allowance, to which will (except for native soldiers of local forces) be added a sum of 30*s*. 6*d*., will be credited on the fourth clothing quarter day following the date of re-commencement of service.

A.O. 157
1912

No issues of clothing and necessaries beyond those mentioned in (*a*) will be made to a rejoined deserter until after his case is disposed of, when, if sentenced to detention, the issues will be governed by paragraph 204 subject to (*b*) and (*c*) above.

219. A deserter rejoining will, by sentence of a court-martial, or award of competent military authority dispensing with his trial, be liable to make good any deficiency or damage of public clothing consequent on his desertion; but he will not be charged for any article fit for wear which is in his possession when he rejoins.

220. If he is sentenced to detention and for ultimate discharge, or if any doubt exists as to the ultimate disposal of the man, only such articles (part-worn if available) in addition to those mentioned in paragraph 218, as are absolutely necessary for use while in detention will be supplied, and his account will be debited with the value of all clothing and necessaries supplied since rejoining.

221. A recruit who deserts before receiving his necessaries, if retained in the service on rejoining, will receive a kit at the public expense.

222. A deserter rejoining in plain clothes and discharged at once, will not be supplied with any plain clothes at the public expense, and if he is sentenced to detention before discharge, the clothes in which he rejoined will be sent with him and given to him on his release.

Soldiers Convicted of Fraudulent or Improper Enlistment.

223. A soldier who quits his unit and fraudulently re-enlists will, by sentence of court-martial, or award of competent military authority dispensing with his trial, be liable to make good the value of the unexpired wear of any public clothing deficient on each occasion of his quitting his unit, and also the full value (at the rates published in Army Orders) of each free kit of necessaries obtained by him on each occasion of fraudulent enlistment. If he is not already in receipt of the allowance in his present unit, his first quarterly clothing and kit allowance will be credited on the fourth clothing quarter-day following the date of fraudulent enlistment. If already drawing the allowance, he will continue to draw it quarterly without further adjustment. If he is sent back to the unit he has quitted, he will pay for any personal clothing and necessaries he may require for service in that unit, less those not issued before quitting it. Personal clothing and necessaries which will be of use to him in the unit to which he is relegated, will be sent with him ; the remainder will be sold and the proceeds credited in his account. *(A.O. 75 1911)*

224. A recruit who, before receiving a kit of necessaries, fraudulently re-enlists into, and is retained to serve in another unit, will not pay for the kit so obtained. If sent back to the unit he left, he will take with him the articles which are regulation for that unit, and will have his kit completed to the proper scale at the public expense.

225. Men of the army reserve who rejoin the colours and are convicted of fraudulent or improper enlistment, and re-transferred to the reserve, will be treated under the rules laid down for discharged men in paragraphs 113 (2) and 208.

They will be required to pay—

(a) The value of the suit of plain clothes issued to them on re-transfer to the reserve.

(b) The assessed value of the pair of boots or shoes retained by them.

(c) The value of the free kit of necessaries obtained by them if so sentenced by court-martial within three months of the date of improper enlistment, or if relegated to the Army Reserve without trial within three months of the date of improper enlistment. *(A.O. 138 1913)* (*d*) Any other sums due to the public on account of clothing and necessaries.

226. Sums recovered under paragraph 225 (*b*), (*c*), (*d*) will be entered on Army Form P 1954, for the month in which the man is convicted or relegated to the Army Reserve. The value of the plain clothes referred to in paragraph 225 (*a*) will also be entered on Army Form P 1954 if supplied by the unit.

227. When a man is relegated to the reserve on the expiration of his detention, the commandant or superintendent will include in the report of the advances of subsistence money, the value of any plain clothes bought locally, quoting the authority for the purchase. While awaiting trial, such men will be supplied with one suit (frock or jacket, trousers, cap, and boots) of worn clothing ; and will be allowed the use of a part-worn cloak or great-coat, and such necessaries as may be needful for cleanliness, which will be obtained from the nearest unit.

SECTION IX.—LOSSES AND DAMAGES.

228. Clothing and necessaries lost or damaged, when not in charge of individual soldiers, will be dealt with as laid down in the King's Regulations.

229. Articles of public clothing issued to soldiers, which are lost or wilfully made away with by them, or prematurely worn out through carelessness or neglect, will be replaced from store by new or part-worn articles, and the soldier will be placed under stoppages to make good the unexpired wear value of the lost or worn out garment. In cases where the article is lost or made away with, and it has not lasted its full period, the unexpired wear value will be arrived at by multiplying the monthly rate given in the Priced Vocabulary of Clothing and Necessaries by the number of months which the article has been worn (the month of issue being counted as a full month and the month in which the loss occurred being disregarded), and deducting the result from the new value of the article. When it has lasted its full period, the soldier will be charged the worn-out value of the article only, and when the article, though not lost, has been prematurely rendered unserviceable, the worn-out value will be deducted from the charge arrived at as shown above. Where the date of the issue of the article is not known, or in the case of an article which has no regulation period of wear, the soldier will be charged such amount as may be assessed regimentally from the best evidence available as to the condition of the article at the time of loss ; but the amount of this assessment must not be less than one fourth of the new value of the article, unless it is established by evidence that the actual value (which will then be charged) is less. In no case, however, will less than the worn-out value be charged. For any article of public clothing the maximum charge in any one case will not

A.O. 138
1913.

exceed £2 unless the commanding officer is of opinion that the
missing article has been sold or given away by the soldier, in
which case the unexpired wear value or the assessed value will
be charged. A.O. 138
1913

230. Personal clothing in possession of the soldier will be
taken care of and kept in repair by him. When an article of
clothing has become prematurely unserviceable owing, in the
opinion of the commanding officer, to inferior material or workmanship, the matter will be submitted to the general officer
commanding, who, if he concurs in this opinion, may order replacement at the public expense, at the same time reporting the
circumstances, and forwarding the damaged article to the chief
ordnance officer, Royal Army Clothing Department, for the
information of the Army Council.

A.O. 138
1913

231. The procedure laid down in the King's Regulations to be
followed when clothing and supplies, &c., belonging to the public
are lost or damaged will also apply to clothing and necessaries in
the possession of individual soldiers.

A.O 266
1910

232. When a commanding officer is satisfied that the loss or
damage is due to circumstances beyond a soldier's control, and not
to theft or to wear and tear consequent on inclement weather,
attendance at manœuvres and camps, or other contingencies that
come within the duty of a soldier, he may, subject to paragraph 234, authorize a credit or repairs to the extent of 3s. 6d. per
article, but not exceeding £2 for the unit on any one occasion. If
the cost exceeds this sum the matter will be submitted to the
general officer commanding.

233. When it is decided that the value shall be charged against
the public the soldier will be credited with the full value of the lost
necessaries and with the actual value of the lost personal clothing,
such value being assessed regimentally.

234. Loss by theft of, or malicious damage to, clothing and
necessaries in the possession of the soldier will not be admitted as
a charge against the public, unless some person is convicted of the
offence.

235. Should any deficient article for which a charge has been
made be subsequently recovered, a refund of the amount paid may
be made, if authorized by the general officer commanding. The
refund should be supported by a reference to the cash credit, and to
the voucher and account by which the returned article has been
brought on store charge.

A.O. 67
1913

SECTION X.—PATTERNS.

236. Standard patterns are deposited at the Royal Army Clothing Department, and sealed patterns sent to units agree in all
essential particulars with these. No variation from the standard
pattern is permitted.

237. Sealed patterns of made-up rank and file clothing, complete with badges and shoulder straps, and of articles of free kit will be supplied to units. These sealed patterns will be renewed on receipt of indent whenever officers commanding may deem it necessary, and will not usually be kept more than three years without being replaced. Whenever a change of pattern takes place another sealed pattern will be sent with the first consignment of the altered article from the Royal Army Clothing Department. The latest sealed pattern of each article will be carefully kept for comparison with supplies.

238. Sealed patterns of garments, issued in materials for staff-serjeants and band, will also be supplied, if applied for. The patterns will be part of the supply, and, after serving as a guide for the making up of the materials, and examination of the garments, they will be issued to the soldiers for whom they were indented.

239. Sealed patterns which have been superseded will have the seals removed, and will be issued as articles of supply. If they have deteriorated they will be issued for a shorter period of wear, or sold at reduced rates, as approved by the commanding officer in writing.

SECTION XI.—SERJEANT-TAILORS AND MAKING UP AND FITTING CLOTHING.

240. Clothing will be supplied made up, except the full-dress garments for warrant officers, staff-serjeants and band, which will be issued in material to units that have serjeant-tailors.

241. An allowance will be granted for making up garments from materials and for sewing on free issues of chevrons, badges, &c. A rate per garment will be allowed for fitting made up clothing supplied from the clothing depôt. The rates allowed will be published in the Priced Vocabulary of Clothing and Necessaries. Except in special circumstances, military labour rates only will be allowed in units having a serjeant tailor, and in depôts where the services of a qualified soldier are available. In cavalry regiments where it may not be possible to spare soldiers from regimental duty to assist in the tailor's shop, the general officer commanding may authorize the payment of civilian rates, subject to a certificate from the officer commanding the regiment that military labour is not available. In other cases, with the exception of small units to which no military tailor is appointed, when for special reasons it may be considered necessary to employ temporary civilian assistance, War Office authority will be obtained for charging civilian rates. In all cases civilian rates will be paid only for work performed by civilian tailors. In North and South China, the Straits Settlements and Ceylon, the rates to be paid for tailoring will be those laid down for military labour, irrespective of whether the work is performed by soldiers or by native tailors, local or Indian.

A.O. 83
1910

A.C.D.
S. Settls.
228

242. When the yearly amount for fitting, calculated at a rate per garment, does not equal the minimum fixed annual allowance drawn by a serjeant-tailor appointed before the 1st January, 1894, the difference between that sum and the total amount received for the year will be paid to him.

243. Under special circumstances the general officer commanding, on the recommendation of the commanding officer, may authorize an advance to a newly appointed serjeant-tailor.

244. A serjeant-tailor will receive a gratuity of £2 for each boy trained as a sewing tailor under his superintendence, upon the boy fulfilling the conditions laid down in the King's Regulations.

245. All surplus materials will be delivered to the quartermaster or other accounting officer, who will bring them on charge in the same manner as other receipts.

246. The charges for making up garments will be claimed on Army Form P 1918 as soon as the work has been done. Charges for fitting, except in the case of drafts proceeding abroad (*see* paragraph 369), will be made monthly on Army Forms H 1178 and H 1180 for mounted services, and Army Forms H 1179 and H 1181 for dismounted services. Charges for completing with chevrons, badges, titles, &c., will be claimed as follows :— $\dfrac{\text{A.O. 301}}{\text{1912}}$

(*a*) For drafts proceeding abroad other than India. On Army Form P 1918 by the new unit, except for the khaki drill frocks issued for the voyage.

(*b*) All other clothing. On the voucher on which the articles are struck off charge.

247. Instructions for measurement and fitting are given in Appendix V.

248. Commanding officers are responsible that the men are measured by the serjeant-tailor once in every six months during the first two years of service, and once a year afterwards, and that the entries are accurately made in a measurement roll. This roll will be carefully preserved for use when fitting the men. $\dfrac{\text{A.C.D.}}{\text{Aldershot} \atop 2672}$

249. Officers commanding companies will personally see that the boots are carefully fitted in accordance with the instructions in Appendix V.

250. Ornaments and chains will be fitted to full dress headdresses by the armourer-serjeant or under regimental arrangement, but no allowance for the work will be granted; ornaments for caps will be attached by the men themselves. Swan-neck spurs will be fitted to boots by the armourer-serjeant or corps artificer, without extra pay.

SECTION XII.—MARKING CLOTHING AND NECESSARIES.

Public Clothing.

251. Public clothing issued to individuals will be marked with the initials of the regiment or corps, the soldier's number, and the month and year of issue. When an article is re-issued to another soldier a line will be drawn through the old regimental number and the new one inserted thus:—

	First marking.	Second marking.
Corps	R.I.R.	R.I.R.
Reg. No. ...	1418	~~1418~~ 1520
Month and year of issue	4/02	4/02
Or for cavalry—		
Regiment ...	7 D.G.	7 D.G.
Corps No. ...	3	~~3~~ 27
Month and year of issue.	1/06	1/06

252. If the article is transferred to another regiment a line will be drawn through the initials of the old corps, and the initials of the new one substituted.

253. Articles issued for trial, unless forming part of the annual supply, and those supplied for general use at the School of Military Engineering, and at the School of Gunnery, will not be marked.

254. The personal and public clothing of barrack wardens, pensioner barrack serjeants, or barrack labourers, will be marked with the date of issue and with the name of the man.

255. Clothing issued " on inventory," or as "articles in use," for which there is a fixed period of wear, will be marked with the year and month of issue. For this service one set of ½-inch copper inlaid stamps (figures 0 to 8) for each station, and paint or marking-ink, will, if necessary, be supplied on indent from the Army Ordnance Department, but no charge for the work will be allowed.

256. Clothing and necessaries issued "on inventory," or as "articles in use" for which there is no fixed period of wear, will not be specially marked, the War Department mark being already on such articles.

Personal Clothing and Necessaries.

257. Personal clothing will be marked with the initials of the regiment or corps, the soldier's number, and the month and year of issue. If the article is disposed of to another soldier the marking will be corrected thus:—

	First owner.	Second owner.
Corps	R.I.R.	R.I.R.
Reg. No.	4167	~~4167~~ 4269
Month and year of issue	4/02	~~4/02~~ 6/02
Or for cavalry—		
Regiment	7 D.G.	7 D.G.
Corps No.	3	~~3~~ 27
Month and year of issue	1/06	~~1/06~~ 3/06

258. Soldiers' necessaries will be marked with the initials of the man's regiment or corps, and his regimental or corps number.

259. The personal clothing and necessaries of soldiers transferred to another regiment or corps will be re-marked, but those of transfers between units of the same regiment or corps will retain the original marking.

General Instructions.

260 Re-marking will be done in paint of a different colour from that of the original marking.

261. The marks to be placed upon articles of public and personal clothing and necessaries, and upon condemned clothing delivered to the contractor, are detailed in Appendix VIII.

262. Tools and stamps as detailed in Appendix IX will be provided by the public, on indent from the Army Ordnance Department, but the paint, ink, and pads will be provided by the marker; marking-ink can be obtained from the Army Ordnance Department on payment.

263. An allowance, as laid down in Army Orders, will be granted for marking or re-marking free kits, and personal and public clothing, except spurs, which will be marked, without charge, by the armourer-serjeant, or, in units having no armourer-serjeant, by an artificer.

264. The charge for marking free kits and personal clothing will be made monthly on Army Forms H 1178 and H 1180 for mounted services, and Army Forms H 1179 and H 1181 for dismounted services, and for public clothing on Army Form H 1152 for all services, as soon as the work has been done. The officer commanding the company will certify on the vouchers that it has been performed to his satisfaction.

265. As the price of clothing, &c., includes the cost of marking, the only marking chargeable to the soldier will be for condemned personal clothing handed to the contractor.

SECTION XIII.—INDENTS.

General Instructions.

266. Indents and size rolls will be made out on the Army Forms prescribed for the several services and care will be taken to complete the documents in all their details.

267. Supplementary indents will be clearly described as such at the head of the form. A separate memorandum explaining the necessity for its transmission will accompany it.

268. Commanding officers of units abroad will ascertain from the ordnance officer at the station whether there are any articles in his charge which can be issued in diminution of the requirements, and the ordnance officer will notify on the indent whether such is the case or not, articles that require to be replaced being shown in red ink. If materials for garments are indented for, and there are similar made-up garments in store, or *vice versâ*, the ordnance officer will inform the commanding officer, and ascertain if they can be utilized; if so, he will issue them at the proper time. (*See* also Appendix XV.)

269. Indents on the usual printed forms need not be accompanied by covering letters. Any explanations or special remarks will form the subject of a separate covering letter, and will not be written on the indent.

Regimental Indents.

270. Indents will be transmitted at such times as may be necessary to keep up a sufficient supply at home (*see* also Appendix XIV), and at Mediterranean stations (except Egypt), for three months' requirements, and at other stations for six months' requirements.

271. Care will be taken that at the time the indent is forwarded there shall be a stock in hand to meet the wants of the unit for a period of at least eight weeks at home, and at Mediterranean stations (except Egypt), and three months at other stations.

272. One consolidated indent will be forwarded for the clothing required for the survey companies, Royal Engineers.

273. Commanding officers of units will be careful to indent for only such quantities of clothing and necessaries as will be sufficient for the requirements of the soldiers under their command, and will avoid accumulating unnecessary stock. (*See* paragraph 5.) A stock of garments trimmed with gold lace, &c., or of special dimensions, will not be maintained, and such garments will only be indented for in time to admit of the issue when due. If they cannot, from any casualty or other circumstances, be taken into wear, a report will be made to the chief ordnance officer of the district (see paragraph 9, Appendix VI), who will ascertain whether the garments can be utilized by other units in the district, by alteration or otherwise, and report the result, with particulars, and estimated cost of alterations when proposed, to the Royal Army Clothing Department.

A.O. 49
1912

274. Indents for clothing for drafts proceeding abroad will be prepared immediately after orders are received for the preparation of the drafts. Indents for public clothing will be forwarded whenever it is foreseen that such articles will be required to replace others condemned as unserviceable, or on increase of establishment.

Officers in charge of Barracks and Army Ordnance Department.

275. Indents will be made out annually on Army Form G. 963.

276. Indents will be made out by the officer in charge of barracks at each sub-station of a district, and forwarded to the officer administering barrack services in the district, who will, after examining and arranging to transfer surplus stores as may be necessary from one sub-district to another, and after amending the indents to agree with the transfers ordered, countersign and forward them to the chief ordnance officer. The latter will state what articles can be supplied from the Army Ordnance Department, and return the indents to the officer in charge of barracks. That officer will then forward two copies of each of the indents direct to the clothing depôt supplying the district.

277. Articles for home stations supplied from the clothing depôt will be issued to the stations named on the indents, and the vouchers will be sent to the officer in charge of barracks in the sub-district. Those for stations abroad will be consigned to the Army Ordnance Department in transit, and will be distributed by that Department to the officers who indented for the articles.

278. The articles in charge of the Army Ordnance Department which can be supplied as part of the indent will be issued by the ordnance officer.

279. Indents for clothing or necessaries required by the Army Ordnance Department will be forwarded direct to the clothing depôt.

280. Indents will be despatched in such time as will ensure their receipt by the clothing depôt on or before the following dates :—

Home Stations ...⎫
Mediterranean ...⎬ 1st October⎫ For the service of the year
Hong Kong ...⎫ ⎬ commencing on the suc-
Straits Settlements...⎬ 1st April⎫ ceeding 1st April.
Other stations ... 1st June⎭

281. In framing indents care will be taken to avoid accumulation of unnecessary stocks and that surplus articles not likely to be required at one station are made available for the wants of any other station in the same district before additional articles are indented for.

SECTION XIV.—RECEIPT OF STORES AND BOARDS OF SURVEY.

Receipts—Inspection.

232. Packages on delivery will be carefully weighed and counted before receipt is given to the carrier. If there are no means of weighing, application will be made to the officer in charge of barracks, or other local officer, for the use of a machine. In the event of the weight of a package being less than that marked on it, or should any package show signs of having been tampered with or damaged in transit, the carrier's attention will be drawn to the fact, and the package will be opened in the presence of a witness (and if possible the person who delivered the stores) and the contents compared with the external marks, or with the packing notes or other documents received. | A.O. 48 1911

A.O. 48
1914

283. Should any discrepancy be discovered, or any article be found damaged, the carrier's note or the bill of lading will be endorsed accordingly, the condition of the package on receipt being described, and in the absence of such endorsement the responsibility for loss or damage will rest with the officer receiving the stores.

284. Except as above, packages will be opened as soon as possible after receipt and the contents examined in the presence of two officers.

285. A commanding officer will at once report any discrepancies or damages to the Ordnance Officer of the clothing or ordnance depôt by whom the issue was made. He will also take steps to investigate any loss or damage as laid down in King's Regulations. The quantities received will be brought to account and the vouchers amended.

286. When reporting a discrepancy full information including the cost of repairing any damage will be given ; all numbers and weights together with any marks on the packages affording evidence of their having been tampered with will be carefully recorded. The packages with all wrappers and packing material will be retained until the enquiry closes. Any undue delay in reporting and investigating loss or damage will render the consignee responsible for the full quantities of stores invoiced.

287. When in special cases it is considered that supplies are liable to deteriorate after unpacking, the commanding officer or other responsible officer will cause the packages to be sealed, and will use his discretion as to when they shall be opened. He will sign and return the receipt voucher for the articles sent, noting thereon that the packages have not been opened and the reasons for the same.

288. When the contents are ultimately required the packages will be opened in the presence of two officers. Any discrepancies then discovered will be adjusted in the ledger by a certificate receipt or issue voucher. The discrepancy will be reported and any deficiency or damage investigated as directed in paragraphs 285 and 286.

289. At stations abroad, reports of discrepancies will, if necessary, be forwarded by the Chief Ordnance Officer at the station with his remarks to the Chief Ordnance Officer, Royal Army Clothing Department, at the same time stating whether any deficiency or damage was noted on the bill of lading at the time of receipt. These reports will not, however, delay local investigation into the cause of loss or damage.

290. Articles damaged in transit may be repaired or replaced under the same conditions as articles in possession of the soldier (paragraph 231).

Stock-taking Board.

291. Accounting officers will be held responsible that the clothing and necessaries in their charge are kept and accounted for in accordance with the instructions contained in these regulations. They will satisfy themselves, by frequent inspection of the whole of the articles in possession of the unit, that they are in condition and quantity as described in the clothing ledger.

292. A regimental board of survey will (except for the regular establishment of the Special Reserve) be held on the 30th September in each year to verify the "remain" of clothing and necessaries in store, as shown in the ledgers (*see* paragraph 305), and to report upon the numbers of the articles. Unopened packages will be carefully examined by the board to ascertain whether they have been tampered with. In the case of the regular establishment of the Special Reserve, the ledger remain of clothing and necessaries will be verified at the same time, and by the same board, as that of the Special Reserve unit (*see* Clothing Regulations, Part II).

A.O. 49 1912

A.O. 49 1912

293. The commanding officer may order a stock-taking board to be held on the clothing and necessaries whenever he may consider it desirable to verify his charge. The report of these intermediate boards will be duly recorded in Army Book 106, but will not be sent to the local auditor of the command or the Assistant Financial Secretary, War Office, unless the commanding officer desires to draw attention to any particular point.

294. On a change of command a stock-taking board may be dispensed with when not considered necessary by the incoming officer, and an account need not be rendered ; but the officer taking over charge will be held responsible for the correctness of the clothing, &c., taken over by him, as shown by the balance on the date of the previous account, subject to the variation caused by subsequent duly vouched transactions. Should a board be assembled, however, both the incoming and outgoing officers, or their representatives, should be present and sign the proceedings, which will be recorded in Army Book 106.

295. On a change of quartermaster a stock-taking board may be dispensed with by the commanding officer, but a certificate should be obtained from the incoming quartermaster that the stock was in agreement with the ledger balance. (*See* paragraph 305.)

296. The whole board will, with the exception of the kit bags and parcels of cutlery of Army Reservists, which will be verified as stated below, count all articles in store, and will compare the result with the "remain" in the ledgers, and report any surplus or deficiency. In the case of the kit bags and parcels of cutlery, the board will take at random 15 per cent. of the bags and parcels in store, and count the contents in full and check that they are complete. A further percentage will be verified if the circumstances in any way suggest the necessity for so doing.

A.C.D. Clo. Reg. 1091

297. It is necessary that the whole board should count all the articles, so that each member, if called upon to give evidence on oath, may be able to confirm, from his own knowledge, the statements contained in the proceedings of the board of survey.

298. In small units, if there is a difficulty in assembling a board of survey, the instructions contained in paragraphs 291 to 297 and

299 will be carried out by the commanding officer, whose certificate, on Army Form H 1164, will be sufficient.

299. Surplus articles will be at once brought on charge, and should there be any damage or deficiency, a separate report will be made by the president to the convening officer, who will inform the general officer commanding in order that he may take steps under the King's Regulations to decide upon whom the value of the loss or damage shall fall. The decision of the general officer commanding will be annexed to Army Form H 1164, when forwarded with the account to the local auditor or to the Assistant Financial Secretary, War Office. The absence of such report will not, however, relieve the commanding officer and the quartermaster from responsibility.

300. The stock-taking boards or certificates in lieu will accompany the regimental clothing ledger when forwarded for examination to the local auditor of the command, or to the Assistant Financial Secretary, War Office.

SECTION XV.—ACCOUNTS.

301. The following are direct accounting officers :—

The commanding officers of units. (The clothing of detachments of Royal Artillery which are without officers will be accounted for by the officer commanding the company of Royal Garrison Artillery at the station.)

The officer commanding a wing or detachment, at home or abroad, separated from headquarters for lengthened periods, and by considerable distances.

The officer commanding riding establishment, Royal Artillery.

The commandant {
School of Mounted Infantry.
School of Musketry.
Royal Military School of Music.
Staff College.
Royal Military College.
Royal Military Academy.
Duke of York's Royal Military School.
Royal Hibernian Military School.
Queen Victoria School.
}

The officer in charge, Royal Victoria Hospital, Netley.

The commanding Royal Engineer of a district or sub-district, or the division officer, Royal Engineers, for the supernumerary staff, Royal Engineers.

The inspector of gymnasia, for uniform clothing received at Aldershot.

The officer in charge of barracks for barrack wardens, barrack labourers, and other Army Service Corps subordinates.

The commandant, School of Military Engineering, for depôt companies, Royal Engineers, Chatham.

The superintendent, Fire Brigade, Aldershot, for uniform clothing received at Aldershot.

The senior Army Pay Department officer at the station for clothing of Army Pay Corps.

An officer (appointed by the general officer commanding) for the clothing of the garrison staff, military police (except Aldershot), instructors in established gymnasia, schoolmasters, librarians, &c., in the command. Clothing of instructors in modified gymnasia will be accounted for by the commanding officer of the unit to which they are attached.

Accounts of civilian subordinates' clothing may be rendered by the unit to which the men are attached, if preferred.

The commandant, governor, or superintendent of each detention barrack or military prison for the clothing supplied to the civilian subordinates, warrant officers and non-commissioned officers of the Military Provost Staff Corps, and for plain clothes supplied for discharged prisoners.

The Provost Marshal for Military Police at Aldershot.

302. The following books will be kept as records of the receipt and disposal of clothing and necessaries :—

    (a) Ledger for clothing and necessaries. Army Book 284 for units of more than one company and of depôts, and Army Book 285 for units of one company and detachments.

    (b) Ledger for public clothing in possession of companies (Army Book 340) used only by units which have quartermasters.

303. Instructions for keeping the clothing ledgers will be found in Appendix IV.

304. The company indents (Army Forms H 1178 and H 1180 for mounted services, H 1179 and H 1181 for dismounted services, and H 1152 for all services) will be prepared and forwarded to the quartermaster as directed in Appendix III.

305. The ledgers will (except for the regular establishment of the Special Reserve) be balanced for comparison with the stock remaining in store on the 30th September, on change of command, on change of quartermaster, and whenever the commanding officer considers it desirable to have the stock verified by a board of survey. (*See* paragraph 293.) In the case of the regular establishment of the Special Reserve, the ledger will be balanced on the same date as that of the Special Reserve unit.

306. If avoidable, no issues will be made on the days on which the ledgers are balanced and the stock counted.

807. The clothing ledger ('Army Book 284 or 285) will (except for the regular establishment of the Special Reserve) be closed on 30th September in each year, and will be forwarded by parcel post, with all the necessary vouchers, to the local auditor of the command or to the War Office, not later than 15th October. (*See* paragraph 294 as regards accounts on change of command.) For the regular establishment of the Special Reserve the ledger will be closed on the same date as that of the Special Reserve unit, and will be forwarded for audit within two months after the completion of the training of the Special Reserve unit.

308. When a unit proceeds to India, the clothing ledger will be closed on the date of embarkation, and forwarded for audit as directed in paragraph 307.

309. Charges sanctioned by regulation may be paid on the authority of the commanding officer without pre-audit. Charges for repairs authorized under paragraphs 232 and 290 will be supported by the report of the board of survey, and the authority for the execution of the repairs.

A.O. 48
1914
310. Bills for articles provided locally under special authority will be accompanied by a copy of the authority and the commanding officer's certificate that the articles are of correct pattern, of good quality and fit for the service. The period of the account in which they are brought on charge and the number of the voucher will also be stated.

311. A return by companies will be prepared on Army Form P 1954, showing the names of soldiers placed under stoppages for public clothing during the month, and the amounts recoverable. Nil returns will not be required. The amount shown to be due from each man will at once be charged against him and credited to the public. In the cavalry and infantry the amount due from each company will be published in regimental orders.

312. The value of public clothing found on a soldier's death to be deficient or damaged, either wilfully or through carelessness, will not be charged on Army Form P 1954, unless the deficiency or damage was discovered on his admission into hospital, and there has been no settlement of accounts between his admission and his death. If the death did not take place in hospital, no charge will be admitted unless the deficiency or damage was discovered immediately after death. Any entry in Army Form P 1954, on account of deficient or damaged clothing, will be supported by a certificate to the above effect, signed by the officer commanding the company.

313. Periodical inspections of the clothing store and ledgers of units will be made by officers deputed for the purpose by the Assistant Financial Secretary, and commanding officers will afford every facility in their power for the performance of this duty.

SECTION XVI.—CARRIAGE OF SUPPLIES AND EMPTIES.

314. Packages will be sent by parcel post, goods train, or water carriage, as may be most economical. Military transport will be used, as far as practicable, both by land and water. Where there is no military transport, and a railway or steamship company cannot effect delivery, the consignee will arrange to clear the stores from the railway or steamship, the charges being dealt with as laid down in the Allowance Regulations. When conveyance by passenger train is absolutely necessary, an explanation will be inserted in the carrier's note.

315. Consignments to the Royal Army Clothing Department will be addressed to the ordnance officer and separate vouchers or bills of lading will be furnished. They will be carefully and strongly packed, packing materials received by units with stores being utilised for the purpose, and the labels will show the units from which they are sent. Nails for fastening packages will, if necessary, be provided, and the cost charged against the public. Instructions as to the mode of conveyance will be obtained from the local transport officer. The weights will be distinctly marked on all packages before transmission.

A.O. 266
1910

316. When stores are returned to the Royal Army Clothing Department the name of the railway or steamship company carrying the stores will be written at the top of the carrier's note, which will then be handed over with the stores to the agent of the railway or steamship company collecting them. Officers commanding and other consignees will return carrier's notes, duly receipted, with as little delay as possible, to the delivering railway company, a record being kept of the number of the carrier's note, and of the date on which it was returned to the official of the railway company.

317. Articles which have been exposed to infection will not be sent to the Clothing Depôt without thorough disinfection, and special authority of the officer in charge. The consignor will in such cases certify on the vouchers that the articles have been disinfected as prescribed by regulation.

318. The date and number of the authority for the return of stores will be inserted in the headings of vouchers and bills of lading, and will be conspicuously marked on the outside of each package. Packages will be numbered, and the numbers quoted in the vouchers and bills of lading. An inventory of the contents, signed by the packer, and, if practicable, by the person who witnessed and checked the packing, will be placed in each package.

319. All carrier's notes, both inward and outward, will be made payable at the Royal Army Clothing Department, except those from Weedon, Enfield (Inspection Department), and Birmingham (Inspection Department), to Pimlico, which will be made payable

A.O. 67
1913

by the Transport Officer, Weedon, and those from Kensington to Pimlico,, which will be made payable by the Transport Officer, Kensington, and in all cases the correct weight and the name of the railway or other company will be filled in by the consignor.

320. When packages for which the vouchers have been received have not been delivered within reasonable time, the failure to deliver by the railway or other company concerned will be at once notified to the company; should any further delay take place, the matter will be reported to the issuing officer.

321. At stations in Great Britain, empty packing cases and canvas wrappers received from the Clothing Depôt will be disposed of as follows :—

> (a) Cases not considered worth the cost of return will be broken up and used as kindling wood under instructions from the nearest officer in charge of barracks, whose receipt on Army Form G 1033 will be annexed to the clothing account, in which they are struck off charge.

> (b) Cases and wrappers in a serviceable condition will, if their gross weight is not less than 1 cwt., be returned to the Royal Army Clothing Department, either direct or through the nearest ordnance officer, as may be desirable, on the ground of the cost of carriage, under instructions from the local transport officer. When transferred to the Army Ordnance Department they will be taken on charge by the ordnance officer. Return labels are enclosed in all packages sent out. Wrappers and small cases will be enclosed in larger cases, but all paper and string will be removed.

> (c) When the gross weight is less than 1 cwt., empty packages and wrappers will be handed over to, and taken on charge by, the local ordnance officer for disposal, the usual vouchers being passed.

322. Abroad, in Ireland, in the Channel Islands, and by detachments in Great Britain where there is insufficient storage accommodation, empty packages will be handed over as often as convenient to the Army Ordnance Department, or to the officer in charge of barracks at other than Army Ordnance stations, for disposal.

323. A sufficient stock of empty packing cases will be retained by units for requirements on change of station.

324. Garrison needlework associations may be supplied with empty packing cases or wrappers required for the transmission of shirts to the Clothing Depôt. The entry striking such cases or packing material off charge will be supported by the receipt of the honorary secretary of the association.

A.C.D.
Clo. Reg.
1069

325. The cases or packing materials for articles which have been manufactured at detention barracks will be shown on the Inspection Note, and be struck off charge on receipt of the duplicate reporting the result of the inspection of the goods. Army Form G 1033 will not be required.

SECTION XVII.—PRESERVATION OF CLOTHING, AND DESTRUCTION OF INFECTED CLOTHING.

326. Instructions for the care and preservation of clothing, for removing stains from scarlet tunics or frocks, for the preservation and cleaning of gold embroidery and garniture, and for the treatment of clothing infested with vermin, will be found in Appendix VI.

327. Naphthaline for the preservation of clothing and necessaries in store will be supplied on indent by the Army Ordnance Department, as follows :—

For each unit holding { 20 lbs. annually, for regiments, bat-
stocks of clothing and {   talions, or regimental depôts, and—
necessaries.   { 5 lbs. annually, for other units.

An additional allowance, as laid down in Appendix XIII, is authorized for the preservation of reservists' clothing.

328. Boots, shoes, and leggings should be kept well greased, and not dried before a fire. (*See* also Clothing Regulations, Part II.)

329. Clothing or necessaries that may have been exposed to infection will be dealt with as directed in the Regulations for the Army Medical Service. If the articles are destroyed the authority of the general officer commanding, or of the medical officer, as the case may be, will be forwarded in support of the credit to the soldier of the full value of the necessaries and the actual value as assessed regimentally of the personal clothing destroyed (*see* paragraphs 232 and 233), and the striking off charge of public clothing replaced. A.O. 75 1911

330. Clothing and necessaries worn or used by a soldier attending upon horses infected with glanders or farcy, will not be destroyed without the special sanction in writing of the officer commanding.

331. Field dressings will be carefully inspected annually by a medical officer, and the officer in whose charge they may be will be responsible for seeing that this is carried out. (*See* Regulations for the Army Medical Service.)

SECTION XVIII.—SERVICE ABROAD—RELIEFS.

I.—India.
II.—Other Stations abroad.

I.—INDIA.

General Instructions.

332. Units and drafts proceeding to India are placed on the Indian establishment from the date of embarkation for India. Those proceeding from India to a station at home or abroad (except invalids and time-expired soldiers) are placed on the Imperial establishment from the date of arrival of the ship in port at home, or of disembarkation at a station abroad.

333. Indo-Colonial reliefs at Imperial expense will be placed on the Indian or Imperial establishment respectively, from the date of landing in, or departure from India.

334. No credit will be given from Imperial funds in respect of a clothing allowance falling due on a quarter-day which occurs while the soldier is on Indian establishment, except when he is attached to a home depôt or unit for instruction, or pending the return of his unit (*see* paragraphs 129 and 130).

Clothing allowances which fall due to reliefs while on the sea will be paid by the Indian Government.

Any adjustment which may be necessary with the India Office with regard to these allowances will be effected by the War Office.

A.O. 266
1910

335. Invalids and time-expired soldiers sent home remain on the Indian establishment until discharged or sent to a unit for duty.

Outwards.

336. A special survey on the public clothing, &c., on charge of units will be held before embarkation in the same manner as on the equipment as laid down in the Equipment Regulations, Part I. Any articles found unserviceable will be replaced on receipt of indents signed by the surveying officers and counter-signed by the commanding officer. After the survey has been completed the unit will draw up, on Army Form H 1155, a list of the articles condemned, explaining thereon why articles have become prematurely unserviceable and what charges have been made for those prematurely worn out through unfair usage. Should there be any further number prematurely condemned for reasons as in paragraph 47, and for which it is not proposed to charge the men, the report on Army Form H 1155 will be submitted for the decision of the general officer commanding. The Army Form will finally be forwarded to the Royal Army Clothing Department.

A.C.D.
Inn. F.
509

337. A statement, signed by the commanding officer, will be handed to the surveying officers, showing the condition and dates of issue of all clothing, &c., in possession of absent soldiers.

338. In the case of troops proceeding from home stations, Wolseley pattern helmets will be provided and placed on board the transport in which they proceed, and issued to them prior to landing in India. A khaki drill suit for each soldier will also | A.O. 216
be provided and placed on board the transport and issued to him | 1912
for wear on the voyage when necessary. This suit will be continued in wear after disembarkation, and will be one of the free issues of khaki suits made to all men from home after arrival in India. They will be placed in charge of the quartermaster-serjeant by whom all issues will be made. Officers commanding will, as soon | A.C.D.
as possible after receipt of embarkation orders, forward indents | India
for the numbers of helmets and khaki drill suits, including the | 3422
necessary chevrons and badges required, accompanied by the usual | 3438
size rolls (both in duplicate) to the Superintendent, India Store Depôt, Belvedere Road, Lambeth, London, from whom the forms of indents will be obtained and by whom the articles will be placed on board. Any variation in numbers or sizes between the submission of the indents and embarkation should be promptly notified to the Superintendent.

In the case of units or drafts proceeding to India from Colonial stations, helmets in possession will be taken for wear in India, and will be used on the voyage.

339. Commanding officers of units under orders for India will | A.C.D.
receive, direct from that country, instructions regarding the arrange- | India
ments to be made for the clothing of their units after landing. | 3465
In the case of drafts, other than Royal Engineers, size rolls for clothing required on arrival in India will be forwarded as early as possible direct to the officer commanding the unit they will join.

340. Soldiers proceeding to India from home stations will be in possession, for use on the voyage, of a service dress or blue tartan suit (rervice dress jacket and trews for kilted Highlanders). Soldiers proceeding to India from Colonial stations will be in possession of khaki drill clothing.

341. Each regiment of cavalry and each battalion of infantry will take with it stocks of metal cap and collar badges, and titles for shoulder straps.

The badges in possession of the men will be completed to the | A.O. 216
Indian scale of issue, viz. :—two sets of collar badges, three sets | 1912
of titles, one cap badge in units wearing glengarry caps and one cap badge of Indian pattern in other units. In addition there will be taken a regimental stock of sets of collar badges, sets of metal titles, and cap badges (which should be of Indian pattern in units not wearing glengarry caps) at the rate of 50 per cent. of the strength according to the Indian Establishment of the units.

Army Form H 1107 will be rendered to the Assistant Financial Secretary, War Office, showing :

    (a) The number of badges and metal titles issued to the men under this paragraph.

(b)   The number of badges and metal titles taken as regimental
stock, including any which have been received from
public store, to complete numbers required for Indian
establishment.

342. Credit for repayment issues of the articles referred to in
paragraph 341 will be given in the Indian pay lists.

A.O. 216
1912

343. When a unit proceeds to India a statement, on Army
Form H 1107, showing the strength of the unit and the numbers
and years of issue of the articles of public clothing, will be
forwarded to the Assistant Financial Secretary, War Office, as soon

A.O. 275
1912

as possible after embarkation. A duplicate and a triplicate copy
of Army Form H 1107 will be in possession of the officer commanding a unit on arrival in India, the duplicate for immediate

A.C.D.
India.
3573

transmission to the Controller of Military Supply Accounts,
Calcutta, and the triplicate for the retention of the officer commanding as a supporting voucher to the opening entries made
therefrom in the first Indian clothing ledger.

A.O. 247
1913

344. Soldiers will not, unless absolutely necessary to enable
them to preform their duties before embarkation, or to meet the
requirements of paragraph 340, be required to purchase articles
included in the undermentioned lists (A) and (B) after the unit
has appeared in the preliminary programme of reliefs, or, in the
case of drafts, after instructions to prepare the draft have been
received. Those in the possession of the men will be taken to India,
except tunics of services, other than cavalry, and forage caps of all
services, which must be disposed of prior to embarkation.

(A.)—*Articles which are not part of the scale for India.*

All services ...	Bag, helmet, Wolseley pattern ; cap, forage ; cap, service dress ; frock and trousers, canvas ; jacket and trousers, service dress ; drawers, woollen (except kilted Highlanders and pipers of Highland Light Infantry) ; tunics (except cavalry).

A.O. 216
1912

R.A.	Puttees, drab (R.H.A., R.F.A., and mounted men of heavy brigades and batteries, R.G.A.) ; girdles R.F.A.
Infantry ...	Shoes, canvas.
Schoolmasters	Frock coat ; frock, cloth.

(B.)—*Articles not of India pattern, but which may be continued in
wear in lieu of corresponding items in the Indian scale.*

All services ...	Puttees (except as in list A) ; trousers, cloth or tweed ; waistcoats, cardigan.
Cavalry ...	Frock, serge ; pantaloons, cord.
R.A.	Pantaloons, cloth and cord ; trousers, tartan.
R.E.	Frock, serge ; pantaloons, cloth or cord ; trousers, serge or tartan.
Infantry ...	Drawers, woollen (kilted men only) ; frock, serge ; gaiters, drab.
A.O.C. ...	Frock, serge.

Knee boots, leggings and home pattern full dress head-dresses of all services will be returned to store prior to embarkation, and will be disposed of as directed in paragraph 345. Jack spurs will not be taken by drafts.

345. At home, a return of the surplus clothing and necessaries will be forwarded, before embarkation, to the assistant director of ordnance stores, or chief ordnance officer of the command, who, if he cannot arrange for their disposal in the command, will report to the chief ordnance officer, Royal Army Clothing Department. Full dress head-dresses will be dealt with under the conditions laid down in paragraph 376.

A.O. 49
1912

346. Abroad, surplus clothing and necessaries will be given up to the ordnance officer at the station before embarkation for appropriation as directed in paragraph 268. As soon as it is known that a unit is to be relieved, the officer commanding will report to the ordnance officer at the station the probable quantity, in detail and by sizes, of the clothing and necessaries which will be handed in to the army ordnance department and this, together with a detail of the clothing and necessaries already on army ordnance charge will be reported to the chief ordnance officer, Royal Army Clothing Department, at the earliest possible date. A report will also be rendered as to any articles not likely to be utilized within a reasonable period, when instructions as to their disposal will be given.

347. A statement of the articles of public clothing authorized to be taken, showing the month and year of issue, will be prepared on Army Form H 1157 for each man of a draft proceeding to India, for transmission to his new unit, and an abstract of the public clothing, prepared in duplicate on Army Form H 1150 from the transfer clothing statements, will also be forwarded.

348. Immediately after the embarkation of each draft, a return of the clothing in possession will be forwarded to the Assistant Financial Secretary, War Office, on Army Form H 1107, by the commanding officer of the unit, from which the draft is sent.

349. Clothing regulations for British troops serving in India are issued by the Government of India.

Homewards.

350. A special survey on the public clothing, necessaries, &c., of units proceeding from India to home stations or the colonies will be held in the same manner as on the equipment as laid down in the Equipment Regulations, Part 1.

351. Commanding officers will hand to the surveying officers statements on Army Form H 1107 of the necessaries in possession, showing their number and condition, and also of—

(a) Clothing brought from India (Army Form H 1107).
(b) Clothing in possession of all absent soldiers.
(c) Surplus materials or garniture brought from India.
(d) Necessaries sold during the voyage in those cases where the survey is held after disembarkation.

The statements will show what articles are obsolete, or cannot for other reasons be utilized by the unit.

352. Any articles not taken over by the Imperial Government will be disposed of under instructions from the inspector of military equipment, India Office.

353. The clothing, necessaries, materials, &c., taken over from the Indian Government as serviceable, and of the pattern and scale worn at the new station, will be taken on Imperial charge, with the exception of any personal clothing in possession of the men. A list of the articles taken over will be attached as a voucher to the clothing and necessaries ledger.

354. No complaint of unfitness for service of any article passed as serviceable by the joint committee of survey will be entertained.

355. After the survey, indents for replacement of unserviceable articles will be at once forwarded to the chief ordnance officer of the clothing depôt supplying the district.

356. Returns will be sent to the Assistant Financial Secretary on Army Form H 1107 of the personal and public clothing in possession of soldiers who, on return from India, join a unit for duty, specifying its condition and dates of issue. These returns will not include the clothing of soldiers who are immediately discharged or transferred to the Army Reserve.

A.O. 67
1913

357. In the case of details and individuals returning from India, transfer clothing statements will be rendered in duplicate, one copy being receipted and returned to the unit in India, and the other retained as a voucher to the clothing ledger.

358. Soldiers arriving from India for duty at home or colonial stations will complete their personal clothing at their own expense to authorized scales, except that men arriving home who are within six months of discharge, or who are likely to proceed abroad again within six months, will purchase only such articles as are considered necessary. Such men will continue to wear the serge frocks in possession (in lieu of tunics) which they may have lined at their own expense. The purchase of the second suit of service dress may be deferred until the credit of clothing allowance permits.

A.C.D.
Clo. Reg.
1099

359. Clothing brought from India and included in the scale for the new station will be continued in use.

360. Soldiers returning as invalids, or for discharge, will wear the clothing in their possession until they are discharged, or until their fitness for further service has been finally determined upon. If retained in the service, they will be dealt with under paragraph 358 (see also paragraph 195).

361. Soldiers on return from India will be treated as if the clothing in their possession had been issued to them under these regulations.

362. Purses and belts will be brought on charge as public clothing, and the men credited with the worn-out value.

II.—OTHER STATIONS ABROAD.

363. Soldiers proceeding abroad will draw the quarterly allow-ance for the new station from the quarter-day coinciding with, or following embarkation, and those returning home for further service will draw the quarterly allowance for home from the quarter day coinciding with, or following embarkation. Soldiers who rejoin the Imperial Establishment for further service on ter-mination of Colonial employment will draw the quarterly clothing allowance from the quarter day coinciding with or following the date of rejoining. Those who rejoin from employment in tropical Africa will receive in addition a special credit of one quarter's clothing allowance at Home rates and the value of a free kit of necessaries, to be paid by the War Department, and subsequently recovered from the Crown Agents for the Colonies. *A.O. 49 1912*

364. Soldiers returning home for a course of instruction will draw the home rate of clothing allowance from the quarter day coinciding with, or following embarkation, and on again proceeding abroad will draw the colonial rate from the corresponding date. If returning home on furlough they will continue to draw the colonial rate during the furlough period, but if permitted to attend courses of instruction during such furlough, they will receive clothing allowance at home rates on any quarter-days that fall within the period of instruction. *A.O. 266 1910* *A.O. 247 1913*

365. Soldiers who proceed to the Colonies or Egypt (except the Mountain Battery, Royal Garrison Artillery), before becoming entitled to their first quarterly clothing allowance will be credited with an advance of one quarter's allowance to assist them in purchasing the required personal clothing. *A.O. 194 1909*

366. Soldiers proceeding abroad will be completed with clothing as follows :— *A.O. 49 1912*

(*a*) All soldiers, other than those joining the Mountain Battery, Royal Garrison Artillery, in Egypt, and the West African Regi-ment, will, before embarkation, obtain from their allowance any new articles of personal clothing necessary owing to difference of pattern or scale. Two of the khaki drill suits, one only in the case of R.A.M.C., shown in the scales will be supplied free in the first instance, except that, in the case of men for Sierra Leone and Royal Garrison Artillery for Ceylon, Mauritius and the Straits Settle-ments, a free issue of one drab shirt with detachable collar, and the back pad will be substituted for one free suit of khaki drill. *A.C.D. Clo. Reg. 1099* *A.C.D. W. African 158*

(*b*) Soldiers joining the Mountain Battery, Royal Garrison Artillery, in Egypt, will be clothed by the battery on arrival, except that khaki helmets and white covers will be issued on pay-ment prior to embarkation. Their greatcoats will continue to be dealt with as public clothing under these regulations.

(*c*) European non-commissioned officers appointed to the West African Regiment will be supplied before embarkation with a free outfit of articles as in Table VIII, page 110.

A.O. 75
1911

367. Recruits enlisted for cavalry regiments in Egypt or South Africa will, if they proceed abroad before becoming entitled to a clothing allowance, receive a free issue of the third suit of khaki drill clothing, the colonial pattern helmet and two pagris shown in the scale.

A.O. 247
1913

A.C.D.
Clo. Reg.
1095

368. Men proceeding to North China will, before embarkation, provide at their own expense woollen vests and drawers (Table II), and for the lining of their serge frocks and service dress jackets if already in possession of the unlined garments. They will also on arrival at the station receive, as a free issue, fur caps, British warm coats, and leather mitts lined with lambskin (Table III). Indents for these three items will be forwarded to the chief ordnance officer, North China, at the earliest possible date, and, as far as possible, so as to reach him by the 1st of June ; the indents from home stations will be addressed " *via* Siberia."

A.O. 301
1912

369. In the case of drafts proceeding abroad, the fitting marking and completing with chevrons, badges, titles, &c., of the colonial pattern garments [except (a) serge frocks supplied to cavalry recruits on enlistment (*see* paragraph 68 and Appendix V, paragraph 6), and (b) the completing with chevrons, badges, &c., of the khaki drill suit issued for the voyage] will be deferred until the men reach their new unit ; the service dress (or blue tartan) in possession will be retained in wear until the new garments have been fitted and completed. A suit of khaki drill clothing, of a size suitable without being fitted or marked, but completed with chevrons, badges, &c., will be kept in the clothes bag for each man proceeding from home to stations beyond the Mediterranean for use on the voyage when it becomes too hot for the service dress, and whilst the canvas suit is being washed. The colonial pattern

A.O. 138
1913

helmets will be marked prior to embarkation.

The charges made by the unit abroad for fitting, marking and completing with chevrons, &c., will appear on Army Form P 1918.

370. Soldiers (other than those sent home for discharge) embarking from a station abroad, will complete their clothing to the scale at the new station on arrival, except that those coming home who are likely to proceed abroad again within six months will

A.C.D.
Clo. Reg.
1099

not be required to provide themselves with tunics, or the second suit of service dress. Such men may continue to wear the serge frocks in possession, which they may have lined at their own expense. In the case of those returning home from stations where service dress is not worn, the purchase of the second suit of service dress may be deferred until the credit of clothing allowance permits.

371. Men sent home from abroad for discharge should, if their discharge is not carried out at once on arrival, be required to purchase only such articles of the home scale as are considered absolutely necessary.

In the case of men within six months of discharge, tunics need not be provided, but the foreign service full-dress frock (which they may have lined at their own expense) may be continued in wear until date of discharge or transfer to the army reserve.

372. Invalids sent home for discharge will retain in their possession sufficient personal clothing for a complete change of garments in the event of the weather being cold or wet during the voyage, and while awaiting discharge at home.

373. New clothing or necessaries in possession of a unit moving between stations abroad other than India, or returning home, if surplus or not of the pattern worn at the station to which the unit is ordered will be given into store at the station the unit is leaving, and appropriated by the army ordnance department to meet the indents forwarded under paragraph 268. Such articles as may be authorized to be worn at the new station and which are not authorized for other units at the station of departure, will be taken to the new station. As soon as it is known that a unit is to be relieved, the officer commanding will report to the ordnance officer at the station the probable quantity in detail and by sizes of the clothing and necessaries which will be handed in to the army ordnance department, and this, together with a detail of the clothing and necessaries already on army ordnance charge, will be reported to the chief ordnance officer, Royal Army Clothing Department, at the earliest possible date. A report will also be rendered as to any articles not likely to be utilised within a reasonable time, when instructions as to their disposal will be given. A.O. 216 1912

374. Commanding officers of units placed under orders to proceed from one foreign station to another, will, on the earliest possible date, forward indents and size rolls direct to the chief ordnance officer, Royal Army Clothing Department, for such articles of clothing and necessaries as are required on arrival at the new station, and these articles will be sent direct to the new station, less such as are reported to be available under paragraph 371. (For North China *see* also paragraph 368.)

375. When a unit is ordered to a station abroad, surplus articles purchased locally or made up regimentally will be transferred to the depôt. A list of the remaining surplus articles will be forwarded to the assistant director of ordnance stores or chief ordnance officer of the command, who, if he cannot arrange for their disposal in the command, will report to the chief ordnance officer, Royal Army Clothing Department.

376. When units proceed abroad a board of survey will be held on the home pattern full dress head-dresses, and all those found to be unserviceable (except bearskin caps) will be disposed of as directed in para. 89. Cloth helmets which have been worn three years and cannot be made fit for a further two years' wear may be considered unserviceable. The remainder (except bearskin caps) will be dealt with in the manner laid down in para. 375. A.O. 49 1912

All bearskin caps will be sent to the Royal Army Clothing Department.

377. Soldiers returning to the United Kingdom from abroad will bring their helmets with them, if required for use on the voyage, and will on arrival receive home pattern full dress head-dresses.

378. When a unit in possession of leggings is ordered to a station abroad, a board of survey will be held on them before the unit embarks. Those serviceable will be sent to the clothing depôt supplying the district, and those unserviceable will be disposed of as directed in paragraph 89.

379. Leggings in possession of drafts proceeding to stations abroad will not be taken by the men, but will be retained by the unit from which they proceed.

380. Invalids due to arrive home from colonial stations between 1st October and 31st March will be supplied, before embarking, with a free issue of a pair of woollen drawers, if the articles are not in possession ; other soldiers of dismounted services due to arrive home between the above dates from stations at which woollen drawers are not worn will provide themselves with two pairs, but in the case of those for early discharge or transfer to the army reserve, one pair only will be necessary (*see* also paragraph 195).

381. Invalids and time-expired men sent home from colonial stations for discharge or transfer to Army Reserve, &c., whose greatcoats are in good and serviceable condition, should, as far as possible, be supplied before embarkation with a condemned or nearly worn-out greatcoat, the serviceable garment in possession of the man being withdrawn and retained for further wear in the unit.

Officers commanding units should see that a sufficient stock of condemned greatcoats is retained in regimental charge to enable this to be carried out. Knee boots and jack spurs should be withdrawn from such men before embarkation.

DETAILS OF CLOTHING AND NECESSARIES.

CLOTHING, &c.

NECESSARIES.

Table I.—Personal Clothing—Mounted Services.

HOUSEHOLD CAVALRY.

Home Stations.

	Boots, ankle	pairs 2
	„ Wellington	pair 1
A.O. 157	Cap, forage, with chin strap	.. 1
1912	„ service dress	.. 1
	Drawers, cotton	pairs 2
	Frock coat, bandmaster only	.. 1
	„ serge, blue	.. 1
	Gloves, leather	pair 1
	Jacket, undress, except bandmaster	.. 1
A.C.D.	„ service dress	.. 1
Cav.	Pantaloons, cloth	pair 1
1052	„ cord	„ 1
	Puttees, blue	pairs 2
	„ drab	pair 1
...	Trousers, tweed	„ 1
1052	„ service dress	„ 1
	Tunic	.. 1

MOUNTED SERVICES—*continued.*

CAVALRY OF THE LINE.
ROYAL HORSE ARTILLERY.
ROYAL FIELD ARTILLERY. (**W.Os.**, **N.C.Os.,*** and Drivers only), and permanently mounted **W.Os.**, **N.C.Os.** and men of heavy brigades and heavy batteries, **Royal Garrison Artillery.**
ROYAL ENGINEERS. (Except Sappers and Pioneers of Signal Companies.)
ARMY SERVICE CORPS.
ARMY VETERINARY CORPS.

	Home Stations.	Stations Abroad.	
Boots, ankle ... ... pairs	2‡	2‡	
„ Wellington ... ... pair	1	1	
Cap, forage	1	1	
„ service dress	1	1	
Drawers, cotton ... ... pairs	2‡	2‡	
Frock, canvas, rank and file (except lance-serjeants), and artificers of all ranks	1	1	
Frocks, khaki drill	...	3	
Frock, serge (except Cavalry in Egypt and R.H.A.)	...	1	
„ coat, bandmaster (Cavalry only)	1	1	
Gauntlets, pair (Dragoon Guards, Dragoons and Lancers only)††...	1	1	
Girdle ‡‡	1	1	
Gloves, leather ... ... pair	1	1	A O. 307
Helmet, Wolseley pattern, with chin strap, cover, badge and bag	...	1	1909
Jacket, dress (R.H.A. only)	1	1	
„ service dress	2	1‖	
Pantaloons, cloth ... ... pairs†	1	1	
„ cord ... ... „	1	1	
Pagris	...	2	
Puttees, blue ... ... pairs	...	1¶	
„ drab ... ... „	2	2	
Trousers, canvas, pairs, rank and file (except lance-serjeants), and artificers of all ranks	1	1	
Trousers, tweed ... ... pairs**‖	1	1	
„ khaki drill ... ... pairs	...	3	
„ service dress, pairs	1	1‖	
Tunic (except R.H.A.)	1	1§	
Waistcoat, cardigan	1	1	

* Except Wheelers, Fitters and Saddlers, who will be clothed under the scale for Gunners, R.F.A.   A.O. 75 / 1911
  † Recruits not to be supplied until after 6 months' service.
  ‡ Recruits from Special Reserve in possession of 2 pairs of ankle boots or 2 pairs of cotton drawers will receive only 1 pair of each as a first issue.   A.O. 259 / 1911
  § Cavalry in Egypt only.
  ‖ Cloth for 11th Hussars.
  ¶ A.S.C. and A.V.C. in South Africa only.   A.C.D. / Clo. Reg.
  ** A recruit will receive a money allowance at the end of 6 months' service in lieu of an issue of an extra pair of tweed trousers.   1099 / A.C.D.
  †† Not to be supplied to recruits at the Depôt.
  ‡‡ Lancers, R.F.A., and A.S.C. only at home; Lancers (Egypt only) abroad.   Malta / 2281
  ‖ Malta, Gibraltar, Egypt and South Africa only.

MOUNTED SERVICES—*continued.*

ROYAL FIELD ARTILLERY. (Gunners; also Wheelers or Fitters and Saddlers of all Ranks.).

	Home Stations.	Stations Abroad.
Boots, ankle .. .. pairs	2*	2*
„ Wellington .. .. „	1	1
Cap, forage	1	1
„ service dress	1	1
Drawers, cotton .. .. pairs	2*	2*
Frocks, canvas	1	1
„ khaki drill	..	3
„ serge	..	1
Girdle	1	..
Gloves, leather .. .. pair	1	1
Helmet, Wolseley pattern, with chin strap, cover, badge and bag..	..	1
Jacket, service dress	2	1‡
Pantaloons, cord.. .. .. pairs	1	1
Pugris	..	2
Puttees .. .. pairs	2	2
Trousers, canvas.. .. .. „	1	1
„ tweed .. .. „	1†	1†
„ khaki drill .. .. „	..	3
„ service dress .. .. „	1	1‡
Tunic	1	..
Waistcoat, cardigan	1	1

A.O. 307
1909

A.O. 259
1911
A.C.D.
Clo. Reg.
1099
A.C.D.
Malta
2281

* Recruits from Special Reserve in possession of 2 pairs of ankle boots or 2 pairs of cotton drawers will receive only 1 pair of each as a first issue.
† A recruit will receive a money allowance at the end of 6 months' service in lieu of an extra pair of tweed trousers.
‡ Malta, Gibraltar, Egypt and South Africa only,

MOUNTED SERVICES—*continued.*

MILITARY MOUNTED POLICE.

	Home Stations.	Egypt.
Boots, ankle pairs	1	1
,, Wellington ,,	1	1
Caps, forage	2	1
,, service dress	..	1
Drawers, cotton pairs	2	2
Frock, khaki drill	..	3
,, tartan	2	1
Gloves, leather pairs	2	2
Helmet, Wolseley pattern, with chin strap, cover, badge and bag..	..	1
Jacket, service dress	..	1
Pantaloons, cloth pairs	1	1
,, cord .. ,,	1	1
Pagris	..	2
Puttees pairs	2	2
Trousers, tweed ,,	1	1
,, khaki drill ,,	..	3
,, service dress	..	1
Tunic	1	1
Waistcoat, cardigan	1	1

A.C.D.
Mil. P.
2085

A.O. 307
1909

ROYAL ARTILLERY BAND.

Mounted Men.

Boots, ankle..	pair	1
Boots, Wellington ..	,,	1
Cap, forage ..	..	1
Frock coat, bandmaster	..	1
Frock, tartan (except bandmaster)	..	1
Girdle	..	1
Gloves, leather	pair	1
Knot, sword for bandmaster	..	1
Pantaloons, cloth	pair	1
Trousers, tweed	,,	1
Tunic	..	1

MOUNTED SERVICES—*continued.*

**SAPPERS AND PIONEERS OF SIGNAL COMPANIES, R.E.,
OTHER THAN "K" COMPANY.**

	Home Stations.	Stations Abroad.
Boots, ankle .. .. pairs	2	2
„ Wellington .. .. „	1	1
Cap, forage	1	1
„ service dress	1	1
Drawers, cotton .. .. pairs	2	2
Frock, canvas	1	1
„ khaki drill	..	3
„ serge	..	1
Gloves, leather .. .. pair	1	1
Helmet, Wolseley pattern, with chin strap, cover, badge and bag..	..	1
Jacket, service dress	2	1*
Pantaloons, cord.. .. .. pair	1	1
Pagris	..	2
Puttees .. .. pairs	2	2
Trousers, canvas.. .. .. pair	1	1
„ khaki drill .. .. pairs	..	3
„ service dress .. .. pair	1	1*
„ tweed, mounted pattern .. .. „	1	1
Tunic	1	..
Waistcoat, cardigan	1	1

A.O. 307
1909

A.C.D.
Malta
2281

* Malta, Gibraltar, Egypt, and South Africa only.

Table II.—Personal Clothing—Dismounted Services.

ROYAL GARRISON ARTILLERY and boys of R.F.A. under training as Artificers.
ROYAL MALTA ARTILLERY.
ARMY SERVICE CORPS (except drivers of vehicles with internal combustion engines).
ARMY ORDNANCE CORPS.
ARMY PAY CORPS.

	Home Stations.	Stations Abroad.	
Boots, ankle ... ... pairs	2*	2*	
Cap, forage	1	1	
„ „ railway pattern ¶	1	1	
„ service dress	1	1	
Drawers, woollen ... ... pairs	2*	2†	
Dungaree clothing ¶ ... ...suits	2	2	
Frocks, canvas	1‡	1‡	
„ khaki drill	...	3††§	
„ serge	...	1§	
„ tartan blue (clerks employed in London district only)	1	...	A.O. 307
Helmet, Wolseley pattern, with chin strap, cover, badge and bag	...	1	1909
Jacket, service dress	2	1‡‡	
Pagris...	...	2	
Puttees (except A.O.C.) ... ...pairs	2	2	
„ (A.O.C. only) ... ... pair	1	1	A.O. 259
Shoes, canvas (R.G.A. and R.M.A. only, except heavy batteries, siege companies, trumpeters, clerks and boys)... ... pair	1	1	1911
Sleeping suits	...	2‖	
Trousers, canvas ... ... pair	1‡	1‡	
„ khaki, drill ... ...pairs	...	3††§	
„ service dress ... ... „	2	1‡‡	
„ tartan or serge ... ..., pair	...	1§	
„ tweed ... ... „	1	...	A.O. 67
„ „ rank and file pattern, (clerks employed in London district only) ... ... „	1	...	1913
Tunic	1	...	
Waistcoat, cardigan	1	1	

* Recruits from Special Reserve in possession of 2 pairs of ankle boots, or 2 pairs of drawers, will receive only 1 pair of each as a first issue.
† Hong Kong only.
‡ Not for mechanical transport branch, Army Service Corps; otherwise for rank and file (except lance-serjeants) and artificers of all ranks. Men of the Army Ordnance Corps and boys of the Royal Artillery undergoing training as artificers will receive 2 canvas suits on enlistment. Supplied on enlistment only to clerks.
§ At Sierra Leone for all services, and at Ceylon, Mauritius, and the Straits Settlements for Royal Garrison Artillery, arriving after 1st September, 1912, 3 drab shirts with detachable collars, 1 back pad, 1 black tie (provided locally) and 1 sash or kamarband will be supplied. Two of the shirts and the remaining articles will form part of the scale in lieu of the serge frock and full dress trousers. The third shirt will be in lieu of one of the suits of khaki drill.
‖ At Hong Kong, Singapore, Ceylon, Mauritius, Jamaica and Sierra Leone only. (Provided locally.)
¶ Mechanical Transport Branch, Army Service Corps only.
†† In North China 1 suit of service dress (jacket lined) will form part of the scale in addition to the above. The serge frock will be lined, and 2 pairs of woollen drawers and 2 woollen vests will be kept up by all soldiers.
‡‡ Malta, Gibraltar, Egypt, and South Africa only.

A.O. 266
1910
A.O. 216
1912
A.C.D.
Reserves
3152
A.C.D.
Malta
2281

DISMOUNTED SERVICES—*continued.*

DRIVERS OF VEHICLES WITH INTERNAL COMBUSTION ENGINES, ARMY SERVICE CORPS.

	Home Stations.	Malta.
Boots, ankle ... ... pairs	2	2
Breeches, cloth, blue ... ... pair	1	1
Cap, forage, railway pattern	1	1
„ „	1	1
„ service dress	1	1
Covers, cap, white	2	2
Drawers, woollen ... ... pairs	2	...
Dungaree clothing ... ... suits	2	2
Frock, khaki drill	...	3
„ serge, blue working	1	1
„ „ dress	...	1
Gloves, leather, brown ... ... pair	1	1
Helmet, Wolseley pattern, with chin strap, cover, badge and bag	...	1
Jacket, service dress	2	1
Leggings, leather, working ... ... pair	1	1
Pagris	...	2
Puttees ... ... pairs	2	2
Trousers, khaki drill ... ... „	...	3
„ service dress ... ... „	2	1
„ tartan ... ... pair	...	1
„ tweed ... ... „	1	...
Tunic	1	...
Waistcoat, cardigan	1	1

A.C.D.
Reserves
3152

DISMOUNTED SERVICES—*continued.*

ROYAL ARTILLERY BANDS. (Dismounted Men.)

	Woolwich.	Ports mouth, and Ply-mouth.	Gibraltar and Malta.
Boots, ankle .. .. pairs	2	2	2
„ Wellington .. .. pair	1	..	..
Cap, forage	1	1	1
„ service dress	..	1	1
Drawers, woollen .. .. pairs	..	2	..
Frock, canvas	..	1‡	..
„ cloth (except bandmaster)	1	..	..
„ coat, bandmaster	1	1	1
„ khaki drill	..	..	3
„ serge	..	..	1
Girdle	..	1	..
Helmet, Wolseley pattern, with chin strap, plume, cover, badge, and bag	..	..	1
Jacket, service dress	..	1	1
Knot, sword, bandmaster	1	..	1
Pagris	..	..	2
Puttees.. .. .. pair	..	1	1
Trousers, canvas .. .. „	..	1‡	..
„ khaki drill.. .. .. pairs	..	..	3
„ serge, bandmaster.. .. .. pair	..	..	1
„ service dress .. .. .. „	..	1	1
„ tartan (serjeants and rank and file) .. „	..	..	1
„ tweed .. .. pairs	2	1	..
Tunic	1	1	..
Waistcoat, cardigan	..	1	1

‡ Except bandmaster and band-serjeants.

54
Gen. No.
1214

A.O. 307
1909

DISMOUNTED SERVICES—*continued.*

ROYAL ENGINEERS [except Band, Soldiers employed on Electric Light duties, dismounted men of the Searchlight Company, Military Mechanists (including Coxswains), and "K" Signal Company].

	Home Stations.	Stations Abroad.
Boots, ankle ... ... pairs	2‖	2‖
Cap, forage	1	1
„ service dress	1	1
Drawers, woollen ... ... pairs	2‖	2†
Frock, canvas	1‡	1‡
„ khaki drill	...	4††*
„ serge*	...	1
„ tartan blue**	1	...
Helmet, Wolseley pattern, with chin strap, cover, badge and bag	...	1
Jacket, service dress	2	1‡‡
Pagris	...	2
Puttees ... ... pairs	2	2
Shoes, canvas ... ... pair§	1	1
Sleeping suits	...	2¶
Trousers, canvas ... ... pair	1‡	1‡
„ khaki drill ... ... pairs	...	4*
„ service dress ... ... „	2	1‡‡
„ tartan... ... ... pair*	...	1
„ tweed...	1	...
„ „ rank and file pattern ... ...pair**	1	...
Tunic	1	...
Waistcoat, cardigan	1	1

A.O. 307 1909

A.O. 67 1913

* At Sierra Leone, 3 drab shirts with detachable collars, 1 back pad, 1 black tie (provided locally), and 1 sash or kamarband will be supplied, 2 of the shirts and the remaining articles will form part of the scale in lieu of the serge frock and full dress trousers. The third shirt will be in lieu of one of the suits of khaki drill.

† Hong Kong only.

‡ Rank and file and artificers of all ranks. Supplied on enlistment only to clerks.

§ For drivers of stationary engines employed on Engineer services.

‖ Recruits from Special Reserve in possession of 2 pairs of ankle boots or 2 pairs of drawers will receive only 1 pair of each as a first issue.

¶ At Hong Kong, Singapore, Ceylon, Mauritius, Jamaica, and Sierra Leone only. (Provided locally).

†† Three only for drivers of engines employed on Engineer services.

** Clerks employed in other than regimental offices, in London District only.

‡‡ Malta, Gibraltar, Egypt, and South Africa only.

A.C.D. Malta 2281

BAND, ROYAL ENGINEERS.

Boots, ankle ... ... pairs	2
Cap, forage	1
Frock, cloth	1
Frock-coat, bandmaster	1
Trousers, tweed ... ... pairs	2
Tunic	1

54 Gen. No. 1214

DISMOUNTED SERVICES—continued.

All MECHANISTS (except Coxswains) SOLDIERS employed on Electric Light duties, and dismounted men of Searchlight Companies.

	Home Stations.	At Bermuda, Malta, Gibraltar, Hong Kong and South Africa.	At Singapore, Ceylon, Mauritius, Jamaica, and Sierra Leone.
Boots, ankle ... ... pairs ††	2	2	2
Cap, forage	1	1	1
„ service dress	1′	1	1
Drawers, woollen ... ... pairs	2††	2†	...
Frock, canvas (for ranks below serjeant) ...	...	...	1
Frocks, khaki drill	...	3	4*
„ serge, blue	2	2	...
„ serge, scarlet	...	1	1*
Helmet, Wolseley pattern, with chin strap, cover, badge, and bag	...	1	1
Jacket, service dress	1	1**	...
Jerseys, blue, rank and file	2	2	2
Pagris	...	2	2
Puttees ... ... pairs	2	2	2
Shoes, canvas ... ... „	...	1‡	2‖
„ „ ... ... pair	1§	1§	...
Sleeping suits	...	2¶	2
Trousers, canvas (for ranks below serjeant) ... ... pair	...	...	1
Trousers, khaki drill ... ... pairs	...	3	4*
„ serge, blue ... ... „	2	2	...
„ service dress... ... ... pair	1	1**	...
„ tartan ... ... „	...	1	1*
„ tweed ... ... „	1	...	...
Tunic	1	...	...
Waistcoat, cardigan (W.Os., staff serjeants, and serjeants)	1	1	1

A.O. 307 / 1909

*. At Sierra Leone, 3 drab shirts with detachable collars, 1 back pad, 1 black tie (provided locally), and 1 sash or kamarband will be supplied. 2 of the shirts and the remaining articles will form part of the scale in lieu of the serge frock and full dress trousers. The third shirt will be in lieu of one of the suits of khaki drill.
† Hong Kong only.
‡ At Hong Kong only. (Royal Army Medical Corps pattern).
§ For engine drivers of Defence Electric Lights at Home Stations, Bermuda and Malta only.
‖ To be provided locally for Singapore, Ceylon and Mauritius.
¶ At Hong Kong only (provided locally).
†† Recruits from Special Reserve in possession of 2 pairs of ankle boots or 2 pairs of drawers will receive only 1 pair of each as a first issue.
** Malta, Gibraltar, and South Africa only.
N.B.—The instructors in the Electrical School, S.M.E. will be clothed under the scale for ordinary dismounted Royal Engineers.

A.O. 266 / 1910

A.C.D. / Malta / 2281

DISMOUNTED SERVICES—*continued.*

ROYAL ENGINEERS ("K" Signal Company).

Home Stations.

Boots, ankle	pairs	2
Cap, forage	..	1
„ service dress	..	1
Drawers, woollen	pairs	2
Frock, canvas	..	1*
„ tartan, blue	..	1
Jacket, service dress	..	1
Puttees	pair	1
Trousers, canvas..	„	1*
„ tartan, blue	„	1
„ service dress	„	1
„ tweed	„	1
Tunic	..	1
Waistcoat, cardigan	..	1

* Rank and file and artificers of all ranks.

MILITARY MECHANISTS (Coxswains).

Home Stations.

Boots, ankle	pairs	2
Caps with peak	..	2
Frock, cloth, blue	..	1
„ serge, blue	..	1
Jersey	..	1
Trousers, serge	pair	1
„ tweed	pairs	2

DISMOUNTED SERVICES—*continued.*

FOOT GUARDS. (Except Band and Pipers.)

—	Home Stations.	Egypt.	
Boots, ankle .. .. pairs	2*	2*	A.C.D.
Cap, forage	1	1	Guards
Cap, service dress	1	1	1215
Drawers, woollen .. .. pairs	2*	..	
Frock, canvas	1†	1†	
Frock, khaki drill	..	3	
Frock, tartan	..	1	
Gloves, leather, warrant officers, staff-serjeants, and serjeants only .. .. pair	1	1	
Helmet, Wolseley pattern, with chin strap, cover, badge and bag..	..	1	A.O. 307 1909
Jacket, service dress	1	1	
Jacket, white, serjeants and rank and file‡ ..	1	..	
Knot, sword, warrant officers and staff-serjeants ..	1	1	
Pagris	..	2	
Puttees .. .. pair	1	1	
Sash, warrant officers, staff-serjeants, and serjeants only	1	1	
Shoes, canvas .. .. pair	1	1	
Tassel for serjeant-drummer	1	1	
Trousers, canvas.. .. .. pair	1†	1†	
„ khaki drill .. .. pairs	..	3	
„ service dress .. .. pair	1	1	
„ tartan.. .. .. „	1	1	
Trousers, tweed .. .. „	1	..	
Tunic, dress	1	..	
Tunic, undress, warrant officers, staff-serjeants, and colour-serjeant-instructor in musketry	1	..	
Waistcoat, cardigan	1	1	

* Recruits from Special Reserve in possession of 2 pairs of ankle boots or 2 pairs of drawers will receive only 1 pair of each as a first issue.

† Rank and file (except lance-serjeants) and artificers of all ranks.

‡ Orderly room serjeants, and the battalion drill serjeant will wear undress tunics in lieu of white jackets. Serjeants employed on recruiting duties, orderlies (other than cyclist orderlies) employed at the Horse Guards and at the regimental headquarters and military police of Foot Guards, will each require an *extra* tunic in lieu of the white jacket.

Extra garment for colour-serjeant-instructors in musketry—
        At home   ...   . 1 jacket, service dress.
        Abroad   ...   . 1 frock, khaki drill.

A.O. 275
1912

DISMOUNTED SERVICES—*continued.*

BANDS, FOOT GUARDS.

Boots, ankle	pairs	2
Cap, forage	..	1
Gloves, leather (bandmaster and band-serjeant)	pair	1
Knot, sword (bandmaster and band-serjeant)	..	1
Sash (bandmaster and band-serjeant)	..	1
Shoes, canvas	pair	1
Trousers, tartan	„	1
Trousers, tweed	„	1
Tunic, dress	..	1
Tunic, undress (bandmaster and band-serjeant)	..	1

PIPERS OF THE SCOTS GUARDS.

		Home Stations.	Egypt.
A.C.D.	Apron, kilt	1	1
Guards	Cap, glengarry	1	1
1215	Drawers, woollen pairs	2	..
	Frock, canvas (except serjeant piper)	1	1
	„ khaki drill	..	3
	„ tartan	..	1
	Gloves, leather, serjeant piper pair	1	1
A.O. 307	Helmet, Wolseley pattern, with chin strap, cover,		
1909	badge and bag	..	1
	Jacket, service dress	1	1
	Jacket, white	1	..
	Kilt	1*	1*
	Pagris	..	2
	Scarf	1	1
	Sash, serjeant piper	1	1
	Shoes, canvas pair	1	1
	Shoes, Highland pairs	2	2
	Trousers, canvas (except serjeant piper) pair	1	1
	„ khaki drill pairs	..	3
	Tunic	1	..
	Waistcoat, cardigan	1	1

* To be made into trews at the public expense when replaced.

DISMOUNTED SERVICES—*continued.*

INFANTRY OF THE LINE (except **KILTED, TREWED,** and **RIFLE REGIMENTS**), including **SCHOOLS OF MUSKETRY** at **HYTHE** and **BLOEMFONTEIN.**

	Home Stations.	Stations Abroad.	
Boots, ankle* .. .. pairs	2	2	
Cap, forage	1	1	
„ service dress..	1	1	
Drawers, woollen* .. .. pairs	2	2§	
Flash (R. Welsh Fus. only)	1	1	
Frock, canvas	1†	1†	54
Frock coat, bandmaster	1	1	Gen. No.
„ khaki drill	..	3‡	1214
„ serge	..	1	
Helmet, Wolseley pattern, with chin strap, cover,			A.O. 307
badge and bag..	..	1	1909
Jacket, service dress	2	1**	
Pagris	..	2	
Puttees .. .. pairs	2	2	
Sash, warrant officers, staff-serjeants, and serjeants ..	1	1	
Shoes, canvas .. .. pair	1	1	
Sleeping suits	..	2¶	
Trousers, canvas .. .. „	1†	1†	
„ khaki drill .. .. pairs	..	3‡	
„ serge .. .. pair	..	1	
„ service dress .. .. pairs	2	1**	
„ tweed .. .. pair	1	..	
Tunic	1	..	
Waistcoat, cardigan	1	1	

Extra garments for colour-serjeant-instructors in musketry, and all warrant officers, staff-serjeants, company-serjeant-major instructors, and serjeant-instructors of the Schools of Musketry at Hythe and Bloemfontein :—

    At home..   .. 1 jacket, service dress.
    Abroad ..   .. 1 frock, khaki drill.

  * Recruits from Special Reserve in possession of 2 pairs of ankle boots or 2 pairs of drawers will receive only 1 pair of each as a first issue.
  † Rank and file (except lance-serjeants) and artificers of all ranks.
  ‡ In North China one suit of service dress (jacket lined) will form part of the scale of clothing, in addition to the above. The serge frock will also be lined, and 2 pairs of woollen drawers and 2 woollen vests will be kept up by all soldiers.
  § Hong Kong only.
  ¶ At Hong Kong, Singapore, Ceylon, Mauritius, Jamaica, and Sierra Leone only. (Provided locally.)
  ** Malta, Gibraltar, Egypt, and South Africa only.

A.C.D.

Malta

2281

Table II.—Personal Clothing—Dismounted Services.

DISMOUNTED SERVICES—*continued.*

RIFLE REGIMENTS. (Including **SCOTTISH RIFLES.**)

	Home Stations.	Stations Abroad.
Boots, ankle* .. .. pairs	2	2
Cap, glengarry (Scottish Rifles)	1	1
„ forage (except Scottish Rifles)	1	1
„ service dress (except Scottish Rifles)	1	1
Drawers, woollen* .. .. pairs	2	2§
Frock, canvas	1†	1†
„ khaki drill	..	3
„ „ extra, for colour-serjeant-instructor in musketry	..	1
„ tartan	..	1
Helmet, Wolseley pattern, with chin strap, cover, badge and bag	..	1
Jacket, service dress	2	1**
„ „ extra, for colour-serjeant-instructor in musketry	1	..
Pagris	..	2
Puttees, ... pairs	2	2
Shoes, canvas .. .. pair	1	1
Sleeping suits	..	2¶
Trousers, canvas .. .. „	1†	1†
„ khaki drill .. .. pairs	..	3‡
„ service dress .. .. pair	2	1**
Trousers or trews, tartan .. .. .. „	1	1
Tunic	1	..
Waistcoat, cardigan	1	1

A.O. 307
1909

* Recruits from Special Reserve in possession of 2 pairs of ankle boots or 2 pairs of drawers will receive only 1 pair of each as a first issue.
† Rank and file (except lance-serjeants) and artificers of all ranks.
‡ In North China, one suit of service dress (jacket lined) will form part of the scale of clothing in addition to the above. The tartan frock will also be lined, and 2 pairs woollen drawers and 2 woollen vests will be kept up by all soldiers.
§ Hong Kong only.
¶ At Hong Kong, Singapore, Ceylon, Mauritius, Jamaica, and Sierra Leone only, (Provided locally.)
** Malta, Gibraltar, Egypt and South Africa only.

A.C.D
Malta
2281

DISMOUNTED SERVICES—*continued.*

HIGHLAND KILTED REGIMENTS AND PIPERS OF HIGHLAND LIGHT INFANTRY.

	Home Stations.	Stations Abroad.	
Apron, kilt...	1	1	
Cap, glengarry	1	1	
Drawers, woollen‖ ... ...pairs	2	2*	
Frock, canvas	1†	1†	
„ khaki drill	...	3‡	
„ „ „ ... extra, for colour-serjeant instructor in musketry	...	1	
„ serge	...	1	
Gaiters, white ... ...pair	1	1	
„ drab ... ... „	1	1	
Helmet, Wolseley pattern, with chin strap, cover, badge and bag	...	1	A.O. 307 1909
Jacket, service dress	1	1**	
„ „ „ ... extra, for colour-serjeant instructor in musketry	1	...	
„ white, all ranks...	1	1	
Kilt	1§	1§	
Plaid, other ranks...	1	1	
Pagris	...	2	
Sash, warrant officers. staff-serjeants, and serjeants ...	1	1	
Scarf, warrant officers, staff-serjeants, band, and pipers ...	1	1	
Shoes, canvas ... ...pair	1	1	
„ Highland‖ ... ...pairs	2	2	
Sleeping suits	...	2¶	
Trews, tartan, pair	1	1	
Trousers, canvas ... ...pair	1†	1†	
„ khaki, drill ... ...pairs	...	3‡	
Tunic	1	...	
Waistcoat, cardigan	1	1	

---

   * Hong Kong only.
   † Rank and file (except lance-serjeants) and artificers of all ranks.
   ‡ In North China 1 Jacket service dress (lined), 2 pairs trousers service dress, 1 pair puttees, and 1 pair boots, ankle, in lieu of 1 pair highland shoes, will form part of the scale of clothing in addition to the above. The serge frock will also be lined, and 2 pairs of woollen drawers and 2 woollen vests will be kept up by all soldiers.
   § To be made into trews at the public expense when replaced.
   ‖ Recruits from Special Reserve in possession of 2 pairs of highland shoes or 2 pairs of drawers will receive only 1 pair of each as a first issue.
   ¶ At Hong Kong, Singapore Ceylon, Mauritius, Jamaica, and Sierra Leone only. (Provided locally.)
   ** Malta, Gibraltar, Egypt and South Africa only.

A.O. 275 1912

A.C.D. Malta 2281

DISMOUNTED SERVICES—*continued.*

SCOTTISH TREWED REGIMENTS. (Except SCOTTISH RIFLES and PIPERS OF HIGHLAND LIGHT INFANTRY.)

—	Home Stations.	Stations Abroad.
Boots, ankle* .. .. pairs	2	2
Cap, glengarry	1	1
Drawers, woollen* .. .. pairs	2	2†
Frock, canvas	1§	1§
„ khaki drill	..	3‡
„ „ extra, for colour-serjeant-instructor in musketry	..	1
„ serge	..	1
Helmet, Wolseley pattern, with chin strap, cover, badge and bag..	..	1
Jacket, service dress	2††	1**
„ „ „ extra, for colour-serjeant-instructor in musketry	1	..
„ white, all ranks (H.L.I. only)..	1	1
Pagris	..	2
Puttees .. .. pairs	2	2
Sash, W.O., staff-serjeants and serjeants	1	1
Scarf, W.O., staff-serjeants, band and pipers (H.L.I. only)	1	1
Shoes, canvas .. .. pair	1	1
Sleeping suits	..	2‖
Trews, tartan .. .. „	1	1
Trousers, canvas .. .. „	1§	1§
„ khaki drill .. .. pairs	..	3‡
„ service dress .. .. „	2	1**
Tunic	1	..
Waistcoat, cardigan	1	1

* Recruits from Special Reserve in possession of 2 pairs of ankle boots or 2 pairs of drawers will receive only 1 pair of each as a first issue.
† Hong Kong only.
‡ In North China, one suit of service dress (jacket lined) will form part of the scale of clothing in addition to the above. The serge frock will also be lined, and 2 pairs of woollen drawers and 2 woollen vests will be kept up by all soldiers.
§ Rank and file (except lance-serjeants) and artificers of all ranks.
‖ At Hong Kong, Singapore, Ceylon, Mauritius, Jamaica, and Sierra Leone only. (Provided locally.)
** Malta, Gibraltar, Egypt, and South Africa only.
†† One jacket only for H.L.I.

DISMOUNTED SERVICES—*continued.*

ROYAL ARMY MEDICAL CORPS, except Non-European
Section of 29th Company.

———	Home Stations.	Stations Abroad.	
Boots, ankle§ .. .. pairs	2	2	
Cap, forage	1	1	
„ service dress	1	1	
Drawers, woollen§ .. .. pairs	2	2†	
Frock, khaki drill	2‡	3***	
„ serge***	..	1§§	
„ tartan blue*	1	..	
Helmet, Wolseley pattern, with chin strap, cover, badge and bag	..	1	A.O. 307 1909
Jacket, service dress	1	1†††	
„ „ „ lined	..	1**	
Pagris	..	2	
Puttees .. .. pair	1	1	
Shoes, canvas .. .. „	1	1††	
Sleeping suits	..	2‡‡	
Trousers, khaki drill .. .. pairs	2‡	3***	
„ service dress .. .. .. pair	1	1‡‡‡	
„ tartan*** .. .. „	..	1	
„ tweed .. .. „	1	..	
„ „ rank and file pattern* .. „	1	..	A.O. 67 1913
Tunic	1	..	
Waistcoat, cardigan	1	1	

N.B.—For extra articles issuable to warrant officers engaged on mounted duties, *see* page 88.
* Clerks employed in other than regimental offices in London District only.
† Hong Kong and North China only. Two woollen vests will also be kept up in North China.
‡ Worn-out or old khaki drill clothing should be retained for use on coal fatigues. Two suits per annum for every 18 N.C.Os. and men on the strength may be purchased at the rates for worn-out khaki drill clothing for the use of soldiers having no worn-out or old garments during their first year of service.
§ Recruits from Special Reserve in possession of 2 pairs of ankle boots or 2 pairs of drawers will receive only 1 pair of each as a first issue.
** North China only.
†† These may be provided locally at warm stations abroad.
‡‡ At Hong Kong, Singapore, Ceylon, Mauritius, Jamaica, and Sierra Leone only (provided locally).
§§ Lined, in North China.
*** At Sierra Leone, 3 drab shirts with detachable collars, 1 back pad, 1 black tie (provided locally), and 1 sash or kamarband will be supplied. 2 of the shirts and the remaining articles will form part of the scale in lieu of the serge frock and tartan trousers. The third shirt will be in lieu of a suit of khaki drill.
††† Malta, Gibraltar, Egypt and South Africa only.
‡‡‡ Malta, Gibraltar, Egypt, South Africa and North China only.

A.O. 266 1910
A.C.D. Malta 2281

DISMOUNTED SERVICES—*continued.*

ROYAL FLYING CORPS.

A.O.D. Royal Flying Corps. 1	—	Home Stations.
Boots, ankle .. .. pairs		2†
Cap, forage		1
„ field		1
Drawers, woollen .. .. pairs		2†
Girdle		1
Jacket, service dress		2
Pantaloons, cord .. .. pair		1
Puttees .. .. pairs		2
Shoes, canvas .. .. pair		1
Trousers, tweed .. .. „		1
„ service dress .. .. „		1
Tunic..		1
Waistcoat, cardigan		1

† Recruits from Special Reserve in possession of 2 pairs of ankle boots or 2 pairs of drawers will receive only 1 pair of each as a first issue.

DISMOUNTED SERVICES—*continued.*

MILITARY FOOT POLICE.

—		Home Stations.	Egypt, Gibraltar, and Malta	
Boots, ankle .. .. pairs		2	2	
Cap, forage		2	1	
„ service dress		..	1	
Drawers, woollen .. .. pairs		2	..	
Frock, khaki drill		..	3	
„ tartan		2	1	
Helmet, Wolseley pattern, with chin strap, cover, badge, and bag		..	1	A.O. 307 / 1909
Jacket, service dress		..	1	
Pagris		..	2	
Puttees.. .. .. pair		. ..	1	
Shoes, canvas .. .. „		1	1	
Trousers, khaki drill .. .. pairs		..	3	
„ service dress		..	1	
„ tartan .. .. pair		..	1	
„ tweed .. .. pairs		2	..	
Tunic		1	..	
Waistcoat, cardigan		1	1	

DRILL STAFF AND BAND OF THE ROYAL MILITARY COLLEGE.

Boots, ankle .. .. pairs	2	
Cap, forage	1	
„ service dress	1	
Drawers, woollen .. .. pairs	2	54
Frock coat, bandmaster	1	Gen. No. / 1214
Jacket, service dress	1	
Puttees .. .. pair	1	
Sash, warrant officers, staff-serjeants, and serjeants	1	
Trousers, service dress .. .. pair	1	
„ tweed .. .. „	1	
Tunic	1	
Waistcoat, cardigan	1	

DISMOUNTED SERVICES—*continued.*

GARRISON STAFF (including Garrison Provost Serjeants, Permanent Staff of the Fire Brigade, of the School of Signalling, Aldershot, and of the Camel Corps School, Egypt).

GYMNASTIC STAFF (including Serjeant-Instructors).

MILITARY STAFF CLERKS.

WARRANT OFFICERS AND NON-COMMISSIONED OFFICERS OF THE DUKE OF YORK'S AND ROYAL HIBERNIAN MILITARY SCHOOLS, AND OF THE STAFF COLLEGE.

VICTORIA AND GARRISON LIBRARIANS.

	Home Stations.	Stations Abroad.
Boots, ankle .. .. pairs	2	2
Cap, forage	1	1
„ service dress	1¶	1
Drawers, woollen.. .. .. pairs	2	2*
Frock coat, bandmaster	1	..
Frock, khaki drill	..	3
„ serge	..	1
„ tartan, blue (clerks' pattern)	1†	..
Helmet, Wolseley pattern, with chin strap, cover, badge and bag..	..	1
Jacket service dress	1¶	1**
Pugris	..	2
Puttees .. .. pair	1¶	1
Sash, warrant officers, staff-serjeants, and serjeants ..	1‡	..
Sleeping suits	..	2§
Trousers, tweed, R. & F. pattern (clerks only).. pair	1†	..
„ khaki drill .. .. pairs	..	3
„ serge .. .. pair	..	1
„ service dress .. .. .. „	1¶	1**
„ tartan, blue (except clerks) .. „	1†	..
„ tweed .. .. „	1	..
Tunic	1	..
Waistcoat, cardigan	1	1

A.O. 307 / 1909

A.O. 67 / 1913

A.C.D. / Malta / 2281

* Hong Kong only.
† Warrant officers and non-commissioned officers of the Duke of York's and Royal Hibernian Military Schools and Military Staff Clerks employed in the London District only. Also the serjeant-major at the School of Music, except that the students' pattern blue cloth frock will be issued in lieu of the tartan frock.
‡ Except Clerks at the School of Gunnery, who wear R.A. pattern clothing.
§ At Hong Kong, Singapore, Ceylon, Mauritius, Jamaica, and Sierra Leone only. (Provided locally.)
¶ Not for warrant officers and non-commissioned officers of the Duke of York's and Royal Hibernian Military Schools and the serjeant-major at the School of Music.
** Malta, Gibraltar, Egypt, and South Africa only.

DISMOUNTED SERVICES—*continued.*

WARRANT OFFICERS AND NON-COMMISSIONED OFFICERS, EXCEPT SERJEANT-PIPER, OF THE QUEEN VICTORIA SCHOOL.

Boots, ankle	pairs 2
Cap, glengarry	1
Drawers, woollen	pairs 2
Frock, blue tartan (clerk's pattern)	1
Sash	1
Trews	pairs 2
Tunic	1
Waistcoat, cardigan	1

SERJEANT-PIPER OF THE QUEEN VICTORIA SCHOOL.

Cap, glengarry	1
Drawers, woollen	pairs 2
Frock, blue tartan (clerk's pattern)	1
Gaiters, white	pair 1
Kilt*	1
Scarf	1
Shoes, highland	pairs 2
Trews	pair 1
Tunic	1
Waistcoat, cardigan	1

* To be made into trews at the public expense when replaced.

Extra Articles (sanctioned by paras, 90 and 91).

MOUNTED INFANTRY, REGIMENTAL TRANSPORT DRIVERS, CAMEL CORPS SCHOOL, and other Dismounted Soldiers engaged on, or under training for, Mounted Duties.

	All Stations.		
	Regimental Transport Drivers and Permanent Staff of Mounted Infantry.	Permanent Staff and Men under Instruction, Camel Corps School, Egypt.	Men engaged on, or under training for, mounted duties.
Drawers, cotton ... ... pairs	2 (e)	2 (e)	2 (e)
Pantaloons, cord ... ... pair	1	... ...	1
Puttees ... ... ,,	1	1 ⎫ Replaced in the case of men under instruction when condemned by a Board of	1 (d) ⎫
Trousers, khaki drill ... ,,	... ...	1 ⎰ Survey.	...
Bag, stable	1 (a)	1 ⎱ Replaced when condemned by a Board of	1 (b)
Knife clasp, with marlin-spike, tin opener and lanyard ...	1 (a)	1 ⎰ Survey.	1 (b)
Spurs, jack ... ... pair	1 every 5 years	... ...	1 (c)
Strap, chin (Scottish Regts. only)	1	1	

Replaced when condemned by a Board of Survey.

Men of Highland (kilted) regiments undergoing training will be supplied free with a pair of ankle boots.

Canvas clothing at the rate of three suits per company will be held at the school of instruction for mounted infantry at Aldershot for the use of lance-serjeants of line battalions, and will be replaced on being condemned as unserviceable by a Board of Survey.

(a) Supplied free on joining, and kept up at the men's expense.

(b) For men under training for mounted infantry a supply equal to one per horse will be held on charge at the school of instruction for use as required.

(c) A stock of spurs will be held at the school of instruction for mounted infantry at Aldershot, and men proceeding for a course of instruction will not be supplied with spurs by their units.

(d) Two pairs for men of Highland battalions.

(e) These may be purchased in lieu of woollen drawers.

For Dismounted Men engaged on Cyclist Duties.

—		Home Stations.	Stations Abroad.
Pantaloons or breeches, cord, pair	⎧ Replaced annually for orderlies, biennially for permanent staff, and, for other men, as condemned by Board of Survey. ⎫ ..	1	1
*Puttees, pair (if not already in possession)	⎩ ⎭ ..	1	1

* An annual allowance for the provision of stockings in lieu of puttees will be granted for the number of authorized cyclists of Highland (kilted) battalions.

An annual allowance for the provision of uniform is granted for the two cyclist orderlies attached to the headquarters of the Eastern Command, and for the fifteen employed in the London District.

Table III.

PUBLIC CLOTHING (for Services Clothed under Tables I and II).

Service.	Home Stations.	Period of wear. — Years.	Stations Abroad.	Period of wear. — Years.
Household Cavalry	1 cloak and cape ..	8		
	1 coat, great, drab, mounted men ...	8		
	1 pair gauntlets ..	8		
	1 helmet, metal, { warrant officers and Q.M. corpl.-major	}20		
	other ranks ..	8		
	1 pair spurs, jack ..	5		
	1 pair pantaloons, leather ..	*		
	1 pair spurs for jack boots	*		
	1 pair boots, jack ..	*		
	1 pair boots, knee ..	8		
Dragoon Guards and Dragoons, except 2nd Dragoons	1 coat, great, mounted men..	5		
	¶1 helmet, metal, with bag	8		
	†1 pair boots, knee ..	8		
	1 pair spurs, jack ..	5		
2nd Dragoons ..	1 coat, great, mounted men..	5		
	¶1 cap, bearskin (without hackle) and bag	9	1 coat, great, mounted men ..	5
	¶1 hackle feather for ditto	3	1 pair boots, knee ..	8
	†1 pair boots, knee ..	8	1 pair spurs, jack ..	5
	1 pair spurs, jack ..	5		
Lancers	1 coat, great, mounted men..	5		
	¶1 cap, lance, without cover or line ..	6		
	¶1 cover and line for ditto	3		
	†1 pair boots, knee ..	8		
	1 pair spurs, jack ..	5		

* Replaced when condemned by a Board of Survey.
† Recruits not to be supplied until after 6 months' service.
¶ Not to be supplied to recruits at the Depôt except the lines for Lancers required for wear with tunic.

A.O.
1911

TABLE III—*continued.*

Service.	Home Stations.	Period of wear. — Years.	Stations Abroad.	Period of wear. — Years.
Hussars and Royal Horse Artillery	1 coat, great, mounted men	5	1 coat, great, mounted men ..	5
	¶1 busby and bag ..	6		
	¶1 set of lines for ditto	3	1 pair boots, knee ..	8
	†1 pair boots, knee ..	8	1 pair spurs, jack ..	5
	1 pair spurs, jack ..	5		
Royal Artillery Mounted Band	1 coat, great, mounted men	5		
	1 busby ..	4		
	1 bag for ditto ..	2		
	1 pair boots, knee ..	4		
	1 pair spurs, jack ..	5		
Other mounted services, including permanently mounted men of heavy brigades and heavy batteries, Royal Garrison Artillery and Sappers and Pioneers of signal companies Royal Engineers, except K Company	1 coat, great, mounted men	5	1 coat, great, mounted men	5
	1 helmet, cloth, with bag	6		
	†‡1 pair boots, knee ..	8	‡1 pair boots, knee ..	8
	1 pair spurs, jack ..	5	1 pair spurs, jack ..	5
All dismounted soldiers, except as detailed below	§1 coat, great, dismounted men ..	*5	§1 coat, great, dismounted men ..	*5
	‖1 helmet, cloth and bag	6		
Master Gunners, Royal Artillery	1 coat, great, dismounted men ..	5		
	1 hat, cocked, with box	6		

C.D.
serves
3152

* 7 years for drivers of vehicles with internal combustion engines, Army Service Corps.
† Recruits not to be supplied until after 6 months' service.
‡ Not supplied to wheelers, saddlers, or gunners of R.F.A., to sappers and pioneers of Signal Cos. R.E., nor to A.S.C. and A.V.C. in South Africa.
§ Including Mounted Infantry and Infantry Regimental Transport.
‖ Not supplied to Military Mechanist Coxswains, R.E., and Royal Flying Corps, military wing.
¶ Not to be supplied) to recruits at the Depôt, except the lines required for wear with tunic or dress jacket.

O. 259
————
1911

TABLE III—*continued*.

Service.	Home Stations.	Period of wear. — Years.	Stations Abroad.	Period of wear. — Years.
Royal Artillery Bands, At Woolwich..	1 coat, great, dismounted men ..	5		
	1 busby	4		
	1 bag for ditto ..	2		
At Dover, Plymouth, and Portsmouth	1 coat, great, dismounted men ..	5		
	1 busby and bag ..	6		
At Gibraltar and Malta	.. ..	..	1 coat, great, dismounted men ..	5
Royal Engineers Band	1 coat, great, dismounted men ..	5		
	1 cap, bearskin, and bag	7		
Foot Guards ..	1 coat, great, and cape	5	1 coat, great, and cape	5
	1 cap, bearskin ..	9		
	2 chains for ditto ..	9	1 purse ⎫ pipers of and belt ⎬ Scots	8
	†2 plumes for ditto (except Scots Guards)	9	1 tassel for ⎭ Guards ditto .. ⎰ only ..	4
	2 bags for ditto ..	9		
	‡1 pair leggings, leather	6		
	1 purse and ⎫ pipers of belt .. ⎬ Scots	8		
	1 tassel for ⎭ Guards ditto .. ⎰ only ..	4		
King's Royal Rifles, Royal Irish Rifles, and Rifle Brigade	1 coat, great, dismounted men ..	5		
	*1 busby and bag ..	6		
Fusiliers	1 coat, great, dismounted men ..	5	1 coat, great, dismounted men ..	5
	1 cap, sealskin, and bag	6		
Highland Light Infantry (except band and pipers), and Scottish Rifles	1 coat, great, dismounted men ..	5		
	*1 chaco	6		

* The chin-strap will be renewed (if necessary) after 3 years' wear.
† For the band of Irish Guards a plume will be supplied annually.
‡ The laces will be renewed (if necessary) after 18 months' wear; they will be provided locally by the Commanding Officer at a rate published in Army Orders.

TABLE III—*continued.*

Service.	Home Stations.	Period of wear. Years.	Stations Abroad.	Period of wear. Years.
Highland kilted regiments and band and pipers of Highland Light Infantry	1 coat, great, dis-mounted men ..	5	1 coat, great, dis-mounted men ..	5
	*1 bonnet, feather, with badge	12		
	†1 purse and belt ..	8	†1 purse and belt ..	8
	†1 set of tassels for ditto	4	†1 set of tassels for ditto	4
Royal Scots and King's Own Scottish Borderers	1 coat, great, dis-mounted men ..	5	1 coat, great, dis-mounted men ..	5
	1 bonnet, Kilmarnock, with badge.. ..	3		
	.1 feather, for ditto ..	1		
	1 bag for ditto ..	6		
Warrant officers and non-commissioned officers, Queen Victoria School	1 coat, great, dis-mounted men ..	5		
	1 purse and Belt .. } serjeant-piper only	8		
	1 set of tas-sels for ditto .. }	4		

* Not supplied to pipers of the Highland Light Infantry. An annual allowance will be granted for keeping the bonnet in repair.
† Not supplied to band of the Highland Light Infantry.

TABLE III—*continued.*

WATERPROOF AND WORKING CLOTHING.

(All Stations.)

ROYAL ENGINEERS.

*Coats, waterproof, with wrappers ..	field units and divisional signal companies	1 per set of saddlery .. 1 per set of double harness	Every 6 years.
Hat, sou'wester, frock and trousers, oilskin, and boots, knee C.P.	military mechanist coxswains, each 1		Every 2 years.
Waders, pairs ..	field companies and bridging trains, each .. 16 field troops, each .. 8		Replaced when condemned by Board of Survey.
†Caps, forage railway companies	railway companies, each company .. .. 10 drivers of engines employed on engineer services 1		Annually.
†Dungaree clothing	railway companies and drivers of engines employed on engineer services, each man 2 suits		Biennially.
Jackets, pea ..	railway companies, each company .. .. 35 platelayers, each man 1 soldiers employed on electric light duties .. } each man, 1		Every 4 years.
	military mechanist coxswains, each man .. .. 1 drivers of engines employed on engineer services 1		Biennially.

INFANTRY.

Capes, waterproof (oil-dressed), transport drivers, each battalion of infantry, 4	Replaced when condemned by Board of Survey.

A.O. 49
1912

A.O. 275
1912

* Oil-dressed capes in lieu of waterproof coats will be supplied for men employed on long rein driving only.
† Drivers employed on electric light duties excepted.

TABLE III—*continued.*

ARMY SERVICE CORPS.

A.O. 49	*Coats, water-proof, india-rubber, or frocks, oilskin	No. 1 depôt Co. 10		Every 2 years for oilskin frocks and trousers.
1912		,, 3 ,, ,, ... 20		
		Other depôt Co.'s, each 34		
		60th M.T. Co. 5		3 years for india-rubber coats.
		Other Service Co.'s, each 19		
		Each remount Co. .. 6		
		Drivers and Assistant drivers of motor ambu-lances and motor lorries, each man 1		
	Trousers, oilskin, pairs	Remount Co., Ireland .. 12		

Caps, bakers, each man 2		Annually.
Jackets and waistcoats, kersey, bakers, each man 1		Biennially.
Trousers, moleskin, pairs, bakers, each man 2		Triennially.
Frocks, butchers' jean, each man 1		Annually.
Jerseys, butchers, each man 1		Annually.
Leggings, leather, pairs, butchers, each man 1		Triennially.
Trousers, canvas, pairs, butchers, each man 2		Annually.

	Coat, great, blue, working ..	Drivers of vehicles with internal combustion engines	1 Biennially.
	Coats, drabbett ..		2 Triennially.
A.O 266 1910	Jacket, pea ..	Men of mechanical trans-port branch (except drivers of vehicles with internal combustion engines), each man 1	Artificers, Triennially. Other men, Biennially.
A.C.D. A.S.C. 5794	Jacket, waterproof Leggings, pair ..	Motor cyclist, each machine on charge 1	Biennially.

ROYAL FLYING CORPS—(Military Wing).

A.C.D. R.F.C. 18	Coats, waterproof, indiarubber for drivers of W.D. motor vehicles	Each aeroplane squadron 24	Every 3 years.
		Airship squadron .. 15	
		Headquarters (military wing) 1	
		Central Flying School .. 16	

* Oil-dressed capes in lieu of waterproof coats will be supplied for men employed on long rein driving only.

TABLE III—*continued.*

ROYAL FLYING CORPS.

Gauntlets, leather, pairs .. 50			
Goggles, pairs 40	Per Aeroplane Squadron ..		
Helmets, Aviation .. 25		Military Wing.	
Coat, leather, per man .. 1	For 50 per cent. of Establishment.		A.C.D. R.F.C. 1
Trousers, leather, pair .. 1			
Jean clothing, combination suits, 2 per man, biennially			
Helmets, Aviation .. 50			
Coats, leather 25			
Trousers, leather, pairs .. 25	Will be supplied for use during course of instruction at Central Flying School.		
Goggles, pairs 50			
Gauntlets, leather, pairs .. 100			

ROYAL ARMY MEDICAL CORPS.

1 Helmet, Wolseley pattern ..	For men on duty in Imperial transports	To last 3 trooping seasons.	A.O. 83 1910 120 India 8401
2 Pugris			

MISCELLANEOUS PUBLIC CLOTHING.

All soldiers serving in South Africa ..	1 bag spare field kit every 4 years.	
All dismounted services not supplied with puttees	1 pair leggings every 3 years.*	
Household Cavalry, pom-pom section ..	2 canvas suits every 3 years.	
Drum carriages and instrument slings for bandsmen of the Foot Guards ..	Annually as required.	
1 hat, pith, without cover, for Royal Garrison Artillery, at Sierra Leone, Mauritius, Straits Settlements and Ceylon, if their work necessitates their exposure to the sun for long periods, also for Armament Artificers at the same stations	Replaced when worn out.	A.O. 247 1913
Soldiers employed on the public works, and working parties in South Africa ..	Felt hats as may be required	Replaced when condemned by a Board of Survey.
Mechanical Transport section A.S.C., smiths R.G.A., R.E. and A.O.C. at Malta	86 pith hats biennially.	A.O. 247 1913
Soldiers in N. China, each man	1 cap, fur .. .. .. 1 coat, warm British .. 1 pair mitts, leather, lined with lambskin	Replaced when condemned by a Board of Survey.

* The laces will be renewed (if necessary) after 18 months' wear; they will be provided locally by the commanding officer at a rate published in Army Orders.

TABLE III—*continued.*

MISCELLANEOUS.

A.O. 112 / 1911	1 cape, waterproof, for each bicycle allowed, under Equipment Regulations. Part I.	Replaced when condemned by Board of Survey.
	1 frock, serge, blue 1 pair trousers, serge .. .. 1 cap .. .. } Clerk measuring baggage at Southampton	} Annually.
	Schools of Gunnery, Shoeburyness and Lydd ..	{ Duck clothing for use of officers undergoing instruction.
A.C.D. / Dep. E. / 3127	School of Gunnery, Shoeburyness.. .. .. School of Military Engineering, Chatham .. .. Inspection Department, Woolwich	Such articles and quantities as may be required for the numbers employed, except that canvas clothing will not be issued to men receiving it in their personal scale.
A.O. 275 / 1912	School of Military Engineering, for wear by non-commissioned officers and men undergoing instructions in the driving of engines and in foundry work	{ Caps, with peak, 15 ... Dungaree clothing suits, 15 ... ... Jackets, pea, 15 ... } For engine drivers. Trousers, moleskin, pairs, 6 ... ... Waistcoats, moleskin, 6 } For moulders. Shoes, wood-soled, pairs, 6
	Other Schools of Gunnery	{ Canvas clothing will be supplied for the use of the instructional staff and of non-commissioned officers undergoing instruction who are not in possession of canvas clothing. Boots, knee, C.P., and jackets, pea, will also be supplied for Assistant Instructors.
	Dowlas clothing*	{ For men employed in cookhouses and bakehouses on Indian transports } { 12 suits for each transport every trooping season.
120 / India / 8401	Helmet, Wolseley pattern*	} R.A.M.C. on Indian transports 1 per man.
	Khaki drill clothing*	{ For the quartermaster-sergeant and four troop deck serjeants on Indian transports } { 2 suits per man each trooping season.
	Helmet, Wolseley pattern*	„ „ „ 1 per man.
A.O. 67 / 1913 / A.C.D. / 4 / 2515	Goggles	{ For drivers of internal combustion engined vehicles (except A.S. Corps.) } 1 pair per vehicle.

* Issued by the Embarkation Commandant, Southampton.

Table IV.

MILITARY PROVOST STAFF CORPS AND WARDERS, TEMPORARY ASSISTANT WARDERS AND SERVANTS OF DETENTION BARRACKS AND MILITARY PRISONS.

	Home Stations.	Stations Abroad.
PERSONAL CLOTHING.		
Boots, ankle .. .. pairs	2	2
Caps, forage..	2	1
Cap, service dress	..	1
Drawers, woollen .. .. pairs	..	2*
Frock, khaki drill	..	3‡
Frock, tartan‡	1	1
Helmet, Wolseley pattern..	..	1
Pagris	..	2
Sleeping suits	..	2†
Trousers, khaki drill .. .. .. pairs	..	3‡
„ tartan‡ .. .. pair	..	1
„ tweed .. .. pairs	2	..
Tunic	1	..
Waistcoat, cardigan	..	1
PUBLIC CLOTHING.		
Coat, great .. .. triennially	1	..
„ „ .. .. .. quadrennially	..	1

A.O. 307
1909

* Malta, Gibraltar. Egypt, South Africa and Hong Kong only.
† At Hong Kong, Singapore, Ceylon, Mauritius, Jamaica, and Sierra Leone only.
‡ At Sierra Leone 3 drab shirts with detachable collars, 1 back pad, 1 black tie (provided locally), and 1 sash or kamarband will be supplied. 2 of the shirts and the remaining articles will form part of the scale in lieu of the tartan frock and full dress trousers. The third shirt will be in lieu of one of the suits of khaki drill.
N.C.Os. appointed temporary assistant warders in detention barracks at stations abroad will not receive a duplicate issue of such articles as caps, boots, khaki drill frocks and trousers, and helmets ; the clothing issued to them will be limited to such articles as will be necessary to complete them to above scale, and will be supplied by the commandant of the detention barracks. Their regimental serge or tartan trousers will not be replaced free, and the drill frocks and greatcoats in possession will be continued in wear and made suitable for their new duty by the addition of any necessary pockets, initials, &c.

(c.r. 10544)   G

TABLE IV—*continued.*

SCHOOLMASTERS.

—	Home Stations.	Stations Abroad.
PERSONAL CLOTHING.		
Boots, ankle .. .. pairs	2	2
Cap, forage	1	1
Drawers, woollen.. .. .. pairs	..	2*
Frock, cloth	1	..
Frock coat	1	..
„ khaki drill	..	3
Frock, serge	..	1
Helmet, Wolseley pattern	..	1
Knots or cords, shoulder‡ .. .. .. pairs	2	2
Pagris	..	2
Sleeping suits	..	2†
Trousers, khaki drill .. .. pairs	..	3
„ serge .. .. pair	1	1
„ tweed .. .. „	1	..
Waistcoat, cardigan	..	1
PUBLIC CLOTHING.		
Coat, great .. .. .. every 10 years	1	1
Leggings, leather, pair .. .. every 3 years	1	..

* In Egypt, South Africa, Malta, Gibraltar and Hong Kong only.
† At Hong Kong, Singapore, Ceylon, Mauritius, Jamaica, and Sierra Leone only. (Provided locally.)
‡ Knots for Warrant Officers, cords for Schoolmasters who are not Warrant Officers.

A.O. 307 / 1909

MILITARY STUDENTS.

PERSONAL CLOTHING.	
Boots, ankle .. .. pairs	2
Cap, forage	1
Cords, shoulder .. .. pairs	2
Frock, cloth	1
„ coat	1
Trousers, tweed .. .. pair	1
„ serge .. .. „	1
PUBLIC CLOTHING.	
Coat, great .. .. every 10 years	1

PERSONAL CLOTHING.

Table V.

	Civilian Students.	Barrack Wardens.	Pensioner Recruiters and Pensioner Conductors.	Barrack, Water, and Gas Labourers, Pump Masters, Conservancy Men and Pioneers at Discharge Depot, Fatiguemen, Ordnance College.	Civilian Boats' Crews.	Military Foster Wardens, Aldershot, Norwich and Colchester, Woodmen and Caretakers, Chattenden, Islingham, Twydall and Darland and Woodman and Assistant Woodman at Aldershot.	Chapel Keeper, Wellington Barracks.	Once Keepers and Men Messengers, Bathmen at Recruiting Stations, Orderlies at Discharge Depot, Library Assistants.*	Custodian and Model Cleaner at the Rotunda Museum, Woolwich, and Pensioner on Embarkation Duties, Southampton.	Lift Attendant, Nursing Sisters Home, Millbank.	Pensioner Librarians.
Boots, ankle, pairs	2	2	1d	1	2	2	1	1	1		1
Boots, wellington, pair	1	1	1	1	1	1	1	1	1	1	1
Cap, forage											
Cap, Navy pattern											
Coat, velveteen	2			1a	1	1					
Cords, shoulder, pairs	1										
Frock ...			1								
Frock coat ...									1c		
Frock, tartan, blue (clerks' pattern)											
Girdle ...											
Hat and band ...		1	1		1	1	1	1		1	1
Hat, straw ...	1										
Hat, ⎰ moleskin											
⎱ serge					1						
Jacket, ⎰ moleskin											
⎱ serge		1	1			1	1	1		1	1
Jerseys, blue ...											
Leggings, leather, pair											
Pantaloons, cord, pair	1	1	1	1	2	1					
Trousers, ⎰ moleskin				2a							
pairs ⎱ serge											
⎱ tweed											
Tunic ...	1	1	1	1	1	1	1	1	1	1	1
Waistcoat, moleskin	1			1							
Waistcoat ...										1	

* The clothing for Library Assistants will be of Royal Military College (servants') pattern.

a. For men sweeping chimneys.

b. Except for Library Assistants, the cap will only be issued when necessitated by the amount of outdoor work

c. Frock coat for custodian.

d. 2 pairs for Pensioner Conductors.

G 2

PERSONAL

TABLE V—cont.	Royal Military Academy and Ordnance College. Servants.*	Royal Military College and Staff College.		Messengers.*	Gate Keepers.	Ex-Soldiers at Royal Victoria Hospital, Netley, employed as Police.	Reservists and Ex-Soldier Grooms, Royal Military College, and the Cavalry School.	Pensioner Labourers (including Coal Carriers and Sweeper) at Royal Victoria Hospital, Netley.
		Mess Butlers.† Mess Waiters.	Servants and Porters.*					
Armlet, worsted, M.P....	...	...	...	...	...	1	...	...
Apron	...	1	1	1	...	...	...	...
Boots, ankle, pairs ...	...	...	...	...	1	1	2	1
Cap	1	...	...	...	1	1	...	1
Coats { dress... ...	1	1	1	2d	...	...	...	...
Coats { frock... ...	...	...	...	...	1	1	...	...
Coats { undress ...	...	1a	...	...	...	...	...	...
Frock { canvas ...	...	...	...	...	...	...	...	...
Frock { tweed ...	...	...	...	...	1	1	...	...
Frock { Dowlas ...	...	...	...	...	...	...	...	...
Hat	1	1c	1c	1	...	...	...	...
„ felt	...	...	...	...	...	...	1	...
Jackets { moleskin	...	...	...	...	...	...	...	1
Jackets { serge ...	...	...	...	...	...	...	...	...
Jackets { undress	...	...	1	...	...	...	2	...
Jackets { working ...	1	...	...	...	...	...	...	...
Pantaloons, cord, pair	...	...	...	...	...	...	1e	...
Puttees, pairs	...	...	...	...	...	...	2e	...
Trousers { canvas, pairs	...	...	...	...	...	...	...	...
Trousers { duck „	...	...	...	...	...	...	...	...
Trousers { dress „	1	1	1	2d	2	2	...	...
Trousers { undress „	...	1	1	...	...	...	1	...
Trousers { moleskin „	...	...	...	...	...	...	...	1
Trousers { working „	1	...	...	...	...	...	...	...
Trousers { tweed „	...	...	...	...	...	...	...	...
Waistcoats { dress ...	1	1	1	2d	...	...	...	...
Waistcoats { undress ...	...	1	1	...	...	...	1	...
Waistcoats { moleskin ...	...	...	...	...	...	...	...	1
Waistcoats { serge ...	...	...	...	...	...	...	...	...

A.O. 83
———
1910

A.O. 266
———
1913

A.O. 259
———
1911

a. Tweed for mess butler, jean for mess waiters.
b. For three cooks only.
c. A felt hat for two years in succession and a silk hat every third year.
d. Messenger at Staff College to wear 1 dress suit (servant's pattern), and 1 undress suit (butler's pattern).

CLOTHING.

(b) Cooks at Discharge Depôt.	Reservists and Ex-Soldiers employed at the School of Musketry and at Kneller Hall, as Storemen at the Discharge Depôt, and as Clerks and Caretakers (except Caretakers, War Department Lands, Ordnance College and Military Cemeteries) employed under authority of War Office letter 7615/312.	Ex-Soldiers at the School of Mounted Infantry.	Range Wardens and Range Policeman.	Central Flying School (f).		
				Messengers and Recreation Room Attendant.	Officers' Servants.	Pioneer.
...	...	...	...	...	...	...
3	...	...	...	...	...	...
...	2	2	2	1	2	2
...	1	1	1	1	1	1
...	...	...	...	...	...	...
...	...	...	...	...	...	...
...	...	...	1	...	...	...
...	...	...	...	...	..	...
3	...	...	...	...	...	...
...	...	...	...	...	..	...
...	...	...	...	...	...	1
...	...	...	...	1	...	...
...	2	2	2	...	2	...
...	...	...	...	...	...	...
...	...	...	...	...	...	...
...	...	...	1	...	...	...
3	...	...	...	...	...	...
...	2	2	2	...	2	...
...	...	...	...	...	...	1
...	...	...	...	1	...	...
...	2	2	1	...	2	...
...	...	...	...	1	...	1
...	...	...	...	1	...	...

e. Except farriers, shoeing smiths, carpenters, cooks, valets, officers' mess waiters, serjeants' mess waiters and storemen at the Cavalry School, who get an additional pair of trousers in lieu.

  (*f*) 42/Flying School/64.

* If entitled to uniform clothing.   † Royal Military College only.

A.O. 138
1913   **PERSONAL**

TABLE V—*continued.*		Duke of York's Royal Military School.		
		Master Cook.	Pioneers.	Night Watchmen.
Boots, ankle ... ... pairs		1	2	1
Cap		...	1	1
Frock, dungaree		...	...	...
Jacket, moleskin		...	1	...
„ serge		1	...	1
Trousers, dungaree ... ... pairs		...	...	...
„ moleskin ... ... „		...	1	...
„ serge ... ... „		1	...	...
„ tweed ... ... „		...	...	1
Waistcoat, moleskin		...	1	...
„ serge		1	...	1

PUBLIC CLOTHING—

TABLE V—*continued.*		Civilian Students.	Barrack Wardens.	Pensioner Recruiters, and Pensioner Conductors.	Barrack, Water, and Gas Labourers, Pump Masters and Conservancy men, Fatiguemen, Ordnance College.	Military Estate Warders, Aldershot, Norwich, and Colchester, Woodman and Caretaker, Chattenden and Islingham, and Woodman and Assistant Woodman at Aldershot.
(1)		(2)	(3)	(4)	(5)	(6)
Coat, great	every 10 years	1	...	...	...	...
	every 6 years	...	...	...	...	1
	every 5 years	...	1	1	1	...
	every 4 years	...	...	...	...	...
Jacket, pea	every 3 years	...	...	...	...	...
Watchcoat	every 6 years	...	...	...	...	...

CLOTHING.

Queen Victoria School.			Royal Hibernian Military School.		
Pioneers.	Engineers and Assistant Engineers.	Assistant Cook, Gate Porter and Night Watchmen.	Laundry Engineer and Night watchmen.	Master Cook and Hospital Orderly.	Pioneers.
2	1	1	1	1	2
1	1	1	1	1	1
...	2	...	2 (a)	...	...
1	...	...	...	...	1
...	1	1	1	1	...
...	2	...	2 (a)	...	...
1	...	...	...	1	1
...	...	1	...	...	...
...	1	1	1	...	...
1	...	...	...	...	1
...	1	1	1	1	...

(a) Laundry Engineer only.

HOME STATIONS.

Chapel Keeper, Wellington Barracks.	Servants, Royal Military Academy, and Ordnance College.	Gate Keepers, Royal Military College, and Staff College.	Civilian Boats' Crews.	Pensioner Librarians.	Master Cook, and Pioneers, Duke of York's Royal Military School.	Nightwatchman Duke of York's Royal Military School.	Pioneers, Assistant Cook, Gate Porter and Nightwatchmen, Queen Victoria School.	Laundry Engineer, Master Cook, Hospital Orderly and Pioneers, Royal Hibernian Military School.	Night Watchman, Royal Hibernian Military School.
(7)	(8)	(9)	(10)	(11)	(12)	(13)	(14)	(15)	(16)
...	...	...	...	...	...	...	...	...	...
...	...	...	...	...	...	...	...	...	...
1	...	1	...	1	1	...	1	1	...
...	1	...	...	...	...	...	...	...	...
...	...	...	1	...	...	...	...	...	...
...	...	...	...	...	...	1	...	...	1

TABLE V—*continued.*

Duke of York's Royal Military School, Royal Hibernian Military School, and Queen Victoria School.

Female servants, and boys at the Duke of York's Royal Military School, Royal Hibernian Military School and Queen Victoria School are supplied with clothing, for the local provision of which a commuted rate is allowed.

STATIONS ABROAD.

An annual allowance is granted for the provision and upkeep of clothing for civilian messengers, native boats' crews, range wardens, transport carters, &c., employed at stations abroad, at rates shown in the Priced Vocabulary of Clothing and Necessaries, promulgated by Army Orders. These amounts are the maximum allowances and should be charged against Army Votes only on the production of evidence of expenditure by the officer concerned.

A O. 266 / 1910

The scale of clothing for Pensioner Librarians is the same as that for Home Stations.

A.O. 75 / 1911

The following will be the scales of Personal Clothing for Barrack Wardens and Barrack Labourers abroad :—

	Barrack wardens at Malta, Gibraltar, and Egypt.	Barrack labourers at		
		Malta and Gibraltar.	South Africa.	Bermuda and Jamaica.
Boots, ankle .. pairs	2	1	1	1
Cap, forage	1	1	1	1
Drawers, woollen.. pair	1	1	..	..
Frock, khaki drill ..	2	2	1	2
Frock, serge blue ..	..	..	1	..
Hat, straw	..	..	..	1
Trousers, khaki drill, pairs	2	2	1	2
Trousers, serge, blue, pairs	..	..	1	..
Waistcoat, cardigan ..	1	1	..	..

Table VI.

ROYAL GARRISON ARTILLERY.

PERSONAL CLOTHING.

	Non-European Officers (all stations).	Hong Kong-Singapore Battalion.	Sierra Leone Company Royal Garrison Artillery.
Blouses, khaki drill	..	..	2
Boots, ankle .. .. .. pairs	2	2	..
Fez	..	..	2
Frocks { serge†	..	1	..
" patrol†	1	..	..
khaki drill	2	3	..
canvas	..	1c	1c
Jacket, blue cloth	1	..	..
Knickerbockers { tartan† .. pairs	2	1	..
khaki drill "	2	3	2
Puttees† .. .. .. "	1	2b	1
Sash or kamarband, Navy blue ..	..	..	1
Shirt, drab	..	..	3
Tassel for fez	..	..	2
Trousers, canvas .. .. pairs	..	1c	1c
Turban { khaki	1a	1a	..
dress	1a	1a	..

British N.C.Os and men and the Royal Malta Artillery are clothed under Tables II. and III.

a. To be provided locally.
b. One pair blue and one pair drab.
c. Rank and file and artificers of all ranks.
† At Mauritius and the Straits Settlements, 3 drab shirts with detachable collars, 1 back pad, 1 black tie (provided locally), and 1 kamarband will be included in the scale for non-European officers in lieu of the frock, serge, patrol, and 1 pair tartan knickerbockers; and 3 drab shirts and 1 kamarband for non-commissioned officers and men Hong Kong-Singapore Battalion in lieu of the serge frock, tartan knickerbockers and blue puttees.

A.O. 216
―――
1912

TABLE VI—*continued.*

PUBLIC CLOTHING.

For each soldier...	1 cape	Sierra Leone Company, Royal Garrison Artillery, (except Europeans)	every 5 years.
	1 coat, great	For all stations except Sierra Leone	every 5 years.
	coats, great, for men on guard only	Sierra Leone 15	...every 5 years.
	1 frock, oilskin		every 3 years.
	1 pair trousers, oilskin		every 2 years.
	1 hat, sou'wester ...		every 3 years
	2 caps, naval pattern ...		annually.
	2 covers for ditto ...	For boatmen of Sierra Leone Co....	annually.
	1 frock, serge, B.C. ...		annually.
	3 shirts, flannel, white...		annually.
	1 pair trousers, serge, B.C.		annually.
	1 pair trousers, serge, B.C.		biennially.

A.O. 157 1912	Sandals (provided locally) will be allowed to the extent of 20 per cent. of the strength for men of the Sierra Leone Company, Royal Garrison Artillery, with sore feet, when certified to be necessary by medical authority.

Table **VII.**

ROYAL ENGINEERS.

NON-EUROPEANS SERVING WITH THE FORTRESS COMPANY AT SIERRA LEONE.

PERSONAL CLOTHING.

A.O. 157
1912

Blouses, khaki, drill	2
Fez	2
Frock, canvas*	1
Knickers, khaki drill .. .. pairs	2
Puttees, drab .. .. „	1
Sash, (or kamarband), Turkey, red	1
Shirt, drab	3
Tassel for fez	2
Trousers, canvas* .. .. pairs	1

* Rank and file and artificers of all ranks.

PUBLIC CLOTHING.

1 cape .. .. Every 5 years.

Sandals (provided locally) will be allowed to the extent of 20 per cent. of the strength for men with sore feet, when certified to be necessary by medical authority.

Table VIII.

A.O. 49
1912 | **WEST INDIA REGIMENT AND NON-EUROPEAN SECTION OF 29th COMPANY R.A.M.C.**

PERSONAL CLOTHING.

Boots, ankle	pairs 2
Breeches, serge, blue	pair 1
Cap, forage (except natives)	1
„ service dress (except natives)	1
Fez and tassel (except Europeans)	1
Frock, canvas*	1
„ khaki drill	2
„ „ „ .. (extra for colour-serjeant instructor in musketry only)	1
„ serge (non-European section R.A.M.C. only)	1
Gaiters	pairs 2
Jacket, Zouave (except non-European section R.A.M.C.)	1
Helmet, complete, except cover	1
„ cover (Europeans and non-European section R.A.M.C. only)	1
Pagris	2
Puttees	pairs 2
Shoes, canvas	pair 1
Sleeping suits, Europeans only (provided locally)	2
Stockings, cotton	pairs 2
Trousers, canvas*	pair 1
„ khaki drill	pairs 2
Turban (except Europeans)	1
Waistcoat, white, dress (except non-European section R.A.M.C.)	1

* Rank and file (except lance-serjeants) and artificers of all ranks.

PUBLIC CLOTHING.

For each soldier, 1 coat, great	every 5 years.

Table VIII.— 109

TABLE VIII—*continued.*

WEST AFRICAN REGIMENT.

(Natives only.)

PERSONAL CLOTHING.

Blouses, khaki drill 2	A.O. 157
Boots, ankle, pairs (Signalling and Telephone Section only) .. 2	1912
Fez 2	
Frock, canvas* 1	
Knickerbockers, khaki drill.. .. .. pairs 2	
Puttees, drab 1	
Sash (or kamarband) Turkey red 1	
„ (Serjeants only) 1	
Shirt, drab 3	
Tassel for fez 2	
Trousers, canvas, pair* 1	

* Rank and file (except lance-serjeants) and artificers of all ranks.

TABLE VIII—*continued.*

PUBLIC CLOTHING (West African Regiment only).

A.O. 157 1912 A.C.D. W. Africa 496	For each soldier (except Europeans), 1 cape .. .. every 5 years. 1 frock, oilskin.. .. .. triennially ⎫ 1 pair trousers, oilskin .. .. .. biennially ⎪ 1 hat, sou'wester .. .. triennially ⎪ 2 caps, naval pattern .. .. annually ⎪ For 2 covers for ditto .. .. „ ⎬ each 1 frock, serge, B.C. .. .. „ ⎪ boatman. 3 shirts, flannel, white.. .. .. .. „ ⎪ 1 pair trousers, serge, B.C. .. .. .. „ ⎪ 1 „ „ „ „ .. .. .. biennially ⎭
A.O. 157 1912	Sandals (provided locally) will be allowed to the extent of 20 per cent. of the strength for men with sore feet, when certified to be necessary by medical authority.

European Non-Commissioned Officers of the West African Regiment.

	Badge for cap	1
	Boots, ankle (for N.C.Os. of kilted regiments) .. .. pair	1
	Frocks, khaki drill	1
	Helmet, complete with cover	1
	Initials for shoulder straps .. .. pairs	3
	Jacket, serge, drab, thin	1
	Pad, back	1
	Pagris	2
	Puttees (for N.C.Os. of kilted regiments) .. .. .. pair	1
A.C.D. Clo. Reg. 1006	Sash (Turkey red)	1
	Shirts, drab, with detachable collars	2
	Sleeping Suits (provided locally)	2
	Tie (provided locally)..	1
	Trousers, khaki drill .. .. pair	1
	„ serge, drab, thin .. .. „	1

These articles are supplied only on appointment. An annual allowance is granted for their upkeep.

Table IX.

BADGES.—ALL STATIONS.

The following badges are supplied under the conditions laid down in the Regulations, instructions, &c., governing the various competitions.

		Regulations for qualifying.	
For Good Swordsmanship in Cavalry Regiments.			
(1) Crown and crossed swords	Best swordsman in regiment		
(2) Crown and crossed swords	Best swordsman in each squadron		
(3) Star and crossed swords	Best swordsman in each troop		
(4) Swords crossed	One to every 20 men competing in addition to (1), (2), and (3). (For this computation preliminary trials to be included.)	Cavalry Training.	

For (1).—All the squadrons of a regiment to have competed
For (2) and (3).—60 men per squadron to have competed
For (4).—When the number competing in each squadron is not an exact multiple of 20 the surplus numbers in the squadrons shall be added together and an additional badge granted for every 20 such competitors. These additional badges to be distributed among those squadrons which have the highest surplus numbers			

For Batteries and Companies, Royal Artillery.			
Crown and crossed guns	For Coast Defence companies of Garrison Artillery and companies of Siege and Movable Armament classified as " special " (including Royal Malta Artillery and local battalions and companies).	Instructions for Practice —Seawards, R.G.A. Coast Defences, R.G.A. Siege and Movable Armament.	A.O. 191

(Indents for badges from units at home to be accompanied by a certificate from the Camp Commandant, or by a certified extract from District Orders. Those for units abroad will be countersigned by the Commandant, School of Gunnery, Shoeburyness.)

TABLE IX—*continued.*

					Regulations for qualifying.

Gunnery Badges.

). 266 910	G. with laurel wreath and crown (1st prize)	Two of each per company for siege artillery one of each for battery of 4 or 6 guns, movable armament (R.G.A.) and one of each per battery or company for other British Artillery, and for Royal Malta Artillery		One of each per company for local battalions and companies.	For British Artillery—Instructions for Practice, Horse, Field, and Heavy Artillery. Garrison Artillery Training, Vol. 1.
). 275 912	G. with laurel wreath and star (2nd prize)			.. ..	For Royal Malta Artillery and local battalions and companies—Pay Warrant.
	G. with laurel wreath (3rd prize)				

Two badges (1st or 2nd prize) allowed in addition to companies of R.G.A. (except heavy batteries) for serjeants.

* *Layers' Badges.*

L. with laurel wreath	Three per company for Royal Malta Artillery, and two per company for local battalions and companies.	}	Pay Warrant.

Badges for Qualified Range Takers and Range and Position Finders.

R. in wreath	Royal Horse Artillery } Royal Field Artillery } Two per battery .. Royal Garrison Artillery. Six per company..	{	Handbooks of Range Finding Instruments. Garrison Artillery Training, Vols. I. and II.

For 1st Class Machine Gunners.

). 21)14	M.G. in wreath { Cavalry. Fourteen per regiment .. { Infantry. Fourteen per battalion ..	}	Musketry Regulations.

Field Works, Royal Engineers.

A badge, Q.I. in wreath, for each Qualified Instructor below the rank of serjeant.	Royal Engineers Corps Memorandum, Part II.

For Skill in Driving.

266)lo	Crown, crossed whips and spur (1st prize)	1st, 2nd, 3rd, and 4th prizes, one of each, for each battery of Royal Horse, Royal Field, and Heavy Artillery.
	Whips crossed and spur (2nd, 3rd, and 4th prizes)	1st, 2nd, and 3rd prizes, one of each, for each field unit and for the field training depôt in the Royal Engineers.

* Layers' badges for British Artillery, are issued as badges of appointment. (See page 115.)

TABLE IX—*continued.*

		Regulations for qualifying.	
For Judging Distance.			
Star	16 per regiment of cavalry 48 „ battalion of infantry 6 „ company of R.E. (Not allowed for Depôt squadrons and companies.)	Musketry Regulations.	A.O.D. E. Yorks. 643
For Good Shooting.			
Crown, crossed rifles and wreath	One per regiment or battalion ..		
Star, crossed rifles and wreath	One per regiment or battalion ..		
Crown and crossed rifles..	One per commander of each section in the best shooting squadron of a regiment of cavalry and best shooting company of a battalion of R.E. or infantry.	Musketry Regulations.	A.C.D. Manch. 671
Star and crossed rifles ..	One per squadron, company or band.		
Rifles crossed	One per marksman in Cavalry, R.A., R E , Infantry, A.S.C., and A.O.C.		A.O. 266 1910

The badges are gold embroidered for full-dress and worsted embroidered for service dress (serge and khaki drill). They will not be supplied for wear on cotton, duck, canvas or working frocks, nor will 1st class machine gunners, judging distance and good shooting badges be worn on the white jackets of the Foot Guards and Highland Regiments.   A.C.D. / Infantry / 3784

The crown and crossed swords for the best swordsman in a cavalry regiment, and the crown and crossed rifles for section commanders of best shooting squadrons, &c., will be worn on the right forearm ; the judging distance " star " on the right forearm above any other badges ; all other badges will be worn on the left arm below the elbow.

DISTINGUISHING BADGES

Ranks.	Chevrons. No. of bars.	Distinguishing Worn on Cloaks and Great Coats.	
Subadar, Jemadar ... ... }	...	No chevrons or badges on arm.	1
Schoolmaster			
Conductor, A O.C. ... ... }	...	Crown and wreath	2
1st Class Staff Serjeant-Major, A.S.C. and A.P.C. ...			
Sub-Conductor, A.O.C.	...	Crown	3
Bandmaster	...	Special†	4
Farrier Corporal-Major, Household Cavalry	...	Crown	5
Other Warrant Officers	...	Crown	6
Master Gunner, 1st and 2nd Class	...	Crown and gun ...	7
„ „ 3rd Class	...	Gun	8
Regimental Quartermaster Corporal-Major, Household Cavalry ...	4	Star	9
„ „ Serjeant	4	Star	10
Non-Commissioned Officers holding the rank of—			
Quartermaster Corporal-Major, Household Cavalry ...	4	... ...	11
„ „ Serjeant	4	... ...	12
Squadron Corporal-Major, and Quartermaster-Corporal, Household Cavalry	4	Crown (crossed rifles in addition for Instructor in Musketry)	13
Farrier Quartermaster-Corporal			
Farrier Staff-Corporal			
Saddler Corporal of Horse			
Corporal of Horse Trumpeter ... ... } Household }	4	... ...	14
Drill Corporal ... ... } Cavalry }			
Hospital Corporal			
Squadron Corporal-Major Instructor in Fencing and Gymnastics			
Serjeant Bugler, Drummer, or Piper	4	Drum or bugle, except Serjeant Pipers	15
„ Trumpeter	4	... ...	16
Company Serjeant-Major, A.S.C. *	4	... ...	17
Armourer Quartermaster-Serjeant...	4	... ...	18
Farrier Corporal of Horse ... ... } Household }	3	... ...	19
Corporal of Horse ... ... } Cavalry }			
Band Corporal...	3	... ...	20
Squadron Serjeant-Major Instructor in Fencing and Gymnastics			
Squadron Serjeant-Major, or Quartermaster-Serjeant ...		{ Crown (crossed rifles in addition for Squadron Serjeant Major Instructor in Musketry)	21
Farrier, Wheeler, Saddler, or Smith Staff-Serjeant ...			
Troop, Battery or Company Serjeant-Major, or } ...	3		
Quartermaster-Serjeant ... ... }			
Serjeant of Mounted Band, and ... ...}			
Staff-Serjeant of Regimental Band, R.A. }			
Havildar Major, and ... ... }			
Company Serjeant-Major Photographer, R.A. }			
Colour-Serjeant	3	Crown	22
Other Non-commissioned Officers holding the rank of Colour-Serjeant		{ Crown (crossed rifles in addition for Colour Serjeant Instructor in Musketry)	23
Armament Staff-Serjeant			
Staff-Serjeant, A.S.C., A.O.C., R.A.M.C., A.P.C., and Royal Military College	3		
Company Serjeant-Major Instructor in Gunnery, R.A., and W. India Regiment			
Battery or Company Serjeant-Major Instructor, School of Musketry			
Armourer Staff-Serjeant			
Band-Serjeant	3	... ...	24
Serjeant Instructor School of Musketry	3	Crossed rifles	25

* If promoted to that rank before November 1, 1898.

AND CHEVRONS.

Badges.		
	Worn on Frocks, Frock coats (except Household Cavalry), Jackets (dress, undress, and service dress) Tunics (except undress Tunics in Foot Guards), and Waistcoats W. India Regiment.	Remarks.

<table>
<tr><td></td><td></td><td style="text-align:center">Household Cavalry.</td></tr>
<tr><td>1</td><td>No chevrons or badges on arm.</td><td>Warrant Officers and Non-commissioned Officers wear aiguillettes instead of chevrons on tunics. Farrier Quartermaster-Corporal, Farrier Staff Corporal, Squadron Corporal-Major Instructor in Fencing and Gymnastics, Squadron Corporal-Major Rough Rider, Corporal of Horse Trumpeter, Farrier Corporal of Horse and Drill Corporal, wear a crown in addition.</td></tr>
<tr><td>2</td><td>Crown and wreath — except on khaki drill frocks.</td><td></td></tr>
<tr><td>3</td><td>Crown ...</td><td></td></tr>
<tr><td>4</td><td>Special.</td><td>All Warrant Officers (except Bandmaster) and Non-commissioned Officers wear crowns on frock and jacket.</td></tr>
<tr><td>5</td><td>Crown and horseshoe.</td><td></td></tr>
<tr><td>6</td><td>Crown.</td><td>Crowns are worn on cloaks by Non-commissioned Officers holding the rank of Squadron Corporal-Major.</td></tr>
<tr><td>7</td><td>Crown and gun.</td><td></td></tr>
<tr><td>8</td><td>Gun.</td><td>Crossed swords are worn by Squadron Corporal-Major Instructor in Fencing and Gymnastics and Drill Corporals.</td></tr>
<tr><td>9</td><td>Crown on frock and jacket.</td><td></td></tr>
<tr><td>10</td><td>Star.</td><td>Trained Squadron Scouts wear a brass fleur-de-lis badge on tunics, serge frocks, and undress jackets; Scout Corporals of Horse and Regimental Scouts wear the same badge, with the addition of a bar below the fleur-de-lis. The badges will be worn on the right arm above the elbow, and in the case of Non-commissioned Officers, above the chevrons.</td></tr>
<tr><td>11</td><td>Crown on frock and jacket.</td><td></td></tr>
<tr><td>12</td><td>... ... ...</td><td></td></tr>
<tr><td>13</td><td>Crown on frock and jacket (crossed rifles in addition for Instructor in Musketry).</td><td></td></tr>
<tr><td></td><td></td><td style="text-align:center">Cavalry of the Line.</td></tr>
<tr><td>14</td><td>Ditto. Crossed trumpets in addition for Corporal of Horse Trumpeter.</td><td>Special badges are worn in certain regiments, see page 121.
Trained Squadron Scouts wear a brass fleur-de-lis badge on tunics or serge dress frocks, and on service dress jackets or khaki drill frocks; Scout Serjeants and Regimental Scouts wear the same badge, with the addition of a bar below the fleur-de-lis. The badges will be worn on the right arm above the elbow, and, in the case of Non-commissioned Officers, above the chevrons.</td></tr>
<tr><td>15</td><td>Drum or bugle (except Serjeant Pipers).</td><td style="text-align:center">Royal Artillery.</td></tr>
<tr><td>16</td><td>Crossed trumpets.</td><td rowspan="3">All Non-commissioned Officers above the rank of Corporal wear a gun on tunic, frock, and jacket. Gun layers wear an " L. and laurel wreath " on the right arm, above the elbow and above chevrons if in possession of any. Similarly observers wear an " O " with laurel leaf. The number of layers authorized to wear badges is :—</td></tr>
<tr><td>17</td><td>... ... ...</td></tr>
<tr><td>18</td><td>Hammer and pincers.</td></tr>
<tr><td>19</td><td>Crown on frock and jacket.</td><td></td></tr>
</table>

20	Crown and crossed swords.	In R.H.A. and R.F.A. batteries, 18.	A.O. 138
		In coast defence companies, R.G.A., 15 per cent. of the peace establishment of each company.	1913
		In heavy batteries, R.G.A., 12.	A.O. 112
21	Crown (crossed rifles in addition for Squadron Serjeant-Major Instructor in Musketry).	In siege companies, R.G.A., 24.	1911
		In movable armaments 3 per sub-section or gun. The number of observers authorized to wear badges is :—In siege companies, R.G.A., 24, and in a Howitzer Battery R.G.A. 8.	A.C.D.
			Malta
			2348

<table>
<tr><td>22</td><td>Colour badge on tunic and full dress khaki drill frock, crown on khaki drill frock, and service dress jacket, but not worn on white jacket in Highland Regiments.</td><td style="text-align:center">Royal Engineers.
All Non-commissioned Officers (except Serjeant Bugler) above the rank of Corporal wear a grenade on tunic, frock, service dress jacket, and great coat.
A special badge is worn by Serjeant Bugler.
A grenade and chevrons, according to rank, are worn on the jersey by soldiers employed on electric light duties.</td></tr>
<tr><td></td><td></td><td style="text-align:center">Foot Guards.</td></tr>
<tr><td>23</td><td>Crown (crossed rifles in addition for Colour-Serjeant Instructor in Musketry, and hammers and pincers for Armourer Staff-Serjeants).</td><td>Serjeant-Majors wear a special badge on dress tunic. No chevrons or badges are worn on undress tunics.
The Serjeant Piper of Scots Guards wears a crown on tunic, undress jacket, and service dress jacket.
The Scout Serjeant and 1st Class Scouts in each battalion wear a brass fleur-de-lis badge with bar below on tunics, white jackets, and service dress jackets and khaki drill frocks. The badges should be on the right arm above the elbow, and, in the case of Non-commissioned Officers, above the chevrons.</td></tr>
<tr><td>24</td><td>Special.</td><td></td></tr>
<tr><td>25</td><td>Crossed rifles.</td><td></td></tr>
</table>

† Except in regiments of Household Cavalry and Foot Guards.

DISTINGUISHING BADGES

Ranks.	Chevrons. No. of bars.	Distinguishing Badges.	
		Worn on Cloaks and Great Coats.	Worn on Frocks. Frock coats, except Household Cavalry), Jackets (dress, undress, and service dress) Tunics (except undress Tunics in Foot Guards), and Waistcoats W. India Regiment.
Serjeant. Havildar. Lance-Serjeant. Kettle Drummer, 3rd Hussars...	3	... ...	... ...
Corporal. Naique....	2	... ...	... ...
2nd Corporal. Lance-Corporal. Bombardier, and Acting Bombardier.	1	... ...	... ...
Bandsman or Musician	...	... ...	Special.
Bugler or Trumpeter	...	... ...	Crossed trumpets, or bugle (on frocks and service dress jackets only in Light Infantry Regiments), not worn in Household Cavalry.
Drummer or Fifer	...	... ...	Drum on frocks and service dress jackets only, not worn in Foot Guards
Gunner	...	... ...	... ...
Pioneer	...	... ...	Crossed hatchets with grenade, bugle, rose or star according to regiment or service. Grenade for Grenadier Guards and Fusilier Regiments; rose for Coldstream Guards; star for Scots and Irish Guards; bugle for Light Infantry and Rifle Regiments. On the service dress jacket of Foot Guards crossed hatchets only will be worn.
Private	...	... ...	... ...

Remarks.

Infantry.
The Scout Serjeant and 1st Class Scouts in each battalion wear a brass fleur-de-lis badge with bar below on tunics or full-dress frocks, on service dress jackets or khaki drill frocks, and on white jackets in Highland battalions (including Highland Light Infantry).
The badges should be on the right arm above the elbow, and, in the case of Non-commissioned Officers, above the chevrons.

Royal Army Medical Corps (including Non-European Section of 29th Company).
All ranks wear a Geneva cross on tunic, frock, service dress jacket, and great coat.
1st Class Orderlies wear two straight bars of braid, and 2nd Class Orderlies one bar, on tunics, frocks, and service dress jackets. Hospital Serjeants and Hospital Orderlies of the Royal Malta Artillery and the West India Regiment also wear a Geneva cross.

School of Musketry.
The Serjeant-Major, Quartermaster-Serjeant Instructor, and Company Serjeant-Major Instructor wear a crown and crossed rifles, and Serjeant Instructor crossed rifles on tunic and frock.
The Serjeant-Major, Quartermaster-Serjeant Instructor, and Company Serjeant-Major Instructor wear a crown and crossed rifles on great coat.

School of Gymnastics and Gymnastic Instructors.
The following will be worn by Warrant and Non-commissioned Officers of the gymnastic staff on tunic, frock, and great-coat:—

Serjeant-Majors	Crown (large) and crossed swords.
Quartermaster-Serjeant	Chevron, four-bar, and crossed swords and crown.
Company Serjeant-Major Instructor	Chevron, three-bar, and crossed swords and crown.
Serjeant Instructor	Chevron, three-bar, and crossed swords.

Warrant and Non-commissioned Officers in possession of army physical training certificates, may wear crossed swords in addition to badges of rank on the tunic, the frock, and the service dress jacket. The badge will be worn on the right arm above the chevrons, except by colour-serjeants, who will wear it open immediately below the chevrons.

A.O. 67
1913

Royal Flying Corps.—(Military Wing).
Warrant and Non-commissioned officers and men of the Royal Flying Corps or of the Central Flying School who are in possession of certain qualifications wear a flying badge on the left breast. All non-commissioned officers above the rank of corporal wear a four-bladed propeller on tunic and service dress jacket.

A.O. 40
1913
20

Miscellaneous.
Range and Laboratory Quartermaster-Serjeants, Assistant and Acting Assistant Instructors in Gunnery wear crown, crossed guns, and grenade on chevron.
Assistant Instructors in Signalling and trained Signallers authorized to wear badges, wear crossed flags.
Rough riders wear a spur.
Warrant Officers, Non-commissioned Officers, and Privates who are employed as artificers wear the following badges, on tunics, frocks, and jackets:—

Saddlers, a bit, except in cavalry regiments.
Farriers and Shoeing-smiths, a horseshoe.
Wheelers* and Carpenters, a wheel.
Armourers, Fitters, Machinery Artificers, Machinery Gunners, and Smiths,* hammer and pincers.
Bandmasters' and Bandsmen's special badges are not worn on white jackets in Highland Regiments.
Cavalry bandsmen wear no badge.
Chevrons and badges of rank are worn on pea jackets.
Large crowns are worn on frocks and tunics by warrant officers of all services, and also by non-missioned officers of the following services entitled to wear crowns:—
Cavalry (except Household Cavalry), Royal Engineers, Army Service Corps, Army Veterinary Corps, Army Ordnance Corps and Military Police. Small crowns are worn by infantry (orderly-room clerk ranking as colour-serjeant, and non-commissioned officers holding rank of colour-serjeant), Royal Army Medical Corps, Army Pay Corps and Military Provost Staff Corps.
Gilding metal crowns for service dress garments are of the same size for all ranks.
Band badges will not be worn on tunics of R.G.A. bandsmen of Sheerness, Portsmouth and Plymouth Bands, or on tunics and frocks of R.A. band, Aldershot.

R.F.C.
25
A.C.D.
Tel. E.
1713
A.O. 259
1911
A.O. 75
1911
A.O. 49
1912

* All men who have qualified at the Ordnance College will receive a badge.

DISTINGUISHING BADGES AND CHEVRONS—*continued.*

1. Chevrons and badges of rank, and Geneva crosses, will be worn on both arms of drab shirts, khaki drill frocks, and service dress jackets and drab great-coats. In the case of other garments the articles named, and also badges of appointment for all garments will be worn on the right arm only.* Badges and chevrons will be worn above the elbow in all cases except the following, when they will be worn below the elbow :—

All badges and chevrons on cloaks and grey great-coats.

All badges for warrant officers and badges and chevrons for staff-serjeants wearing 4-bar chevrons (Foot Guards excepted).

Musicians' badges, Royal Artillery.

2. Four-bar chevrons worn below the elbow will be worn with the point upwards; all others will be worn with the point downwards. Good conduct badges will be worn below the elbow on the left arm, with the point upwards.

3. The braid worn by second class orderlies of the Royal Army Medical Corps will be placed one inch above the knot of the tracing on the right sleeve of tunic and frock. The second bar, worn by first class orderlies, will be half an inch above the first.

4. The chevrons and badges of rank (except those worn on drab shirts, khaki drill, service dress, canvas, or duck frocks) will be for :—

Household Cavalry   ...Gold lace and embroidery for all ranks.

Cavalry, and Military Mounted and Foot Police — Gold lace and embroidery for all ranks, except the spurs for privates employed as rough-riders, crossed trumpets for the trumpeters, and horse shoes for the shoeing-smiths, which will be worsted.

Royal Artillery (including Royal Malta Artillery, Local Battalions and, Companies, Schools of Gunnery, Royal Military Academy), Royal Engineers — Gold lace and embroidery for all ranks, except the crossed trumpets for trumpeters or buglers, and the chevrons and grenades on the jerseys worn by Royal Engineers, which will be worsted.

A.O. 275
1912

* A signaller, if a colour-serjeant, will wear the Signaller's badge on the left arm above the elbow. Non-commissioned officers and men employed as signallers, but who have not the assistant instructor's certificate will, while so employed, wear the signaller's badge on the left arm below the elbow.

DISTINGUISHING BADGES AND CHEVRONS—*continued.*

Foot Guards	Serjeant-piper, Scots Guards—Silver lace and embroidery for both tunic and jacket. Dress tunics—Gold lace and embroidery for all ranks above lance-serjeant and for corporals in the band (silver lace for the corporal piper); worsted lace and embroidery for all other ranks. White jackets—Worsted lace and embroidery for all ranks, except the serjeant-piper and corporal-piper, Scots Guards.
Infantry of the Line† (except Highland and Rifle Regiments), West India Regiment, School of Musketry	Gold lace and embroidery for all ranks above lance-serjeant ; worsted lace and embroidery for all other ranks.
Highland Regiments†	Tunics and frocks—Gold lace and embroidery for all ranks above lance-serjeant ; worsted lace and embroidery for all other ranks. White jackets—Gold lace and embroidery for colour-serjeants and all of equal or superior rank ; worsted lace and embroidery for all other ranks.
Rifle Regiments † ...	Tunics and frocks—Badges for serjeant-bugler (except Rifle Brigade) colour-serjeant instructor in musketry, and pioneer serjeant in gold embroidery ; for the bandmaster and serjeant-bugler Rifle Brigade, in gold and silk. The chevrons for ranks above lance-serjeant in the Rifle Brigade are edged with gold braid. All other chevrons and badges are of worsted lace and silk or worsted embroidery.
Royal Flying Corps ...	Gold lace and embroidery for all ranks.
Army Service Corps, Army Ordnance Corps, Army Pay Corps ...	Gold lace and embroidery, except badges for trumpeters and buglers, and for privates employed as shoeing-smiths, rough-riders, and carriage-smiths, which will be of worsted embroidery.

54
Misc.
212

† Band-serjeants and bandsmen wear metal badges.

DISTINGUISHING BADGES AND CHEVRONS—*continued.*

Royal Army Medical Corps	Gold lace and embroidery, except the Geneva cross worn by corporals and lance-corporals on frocks, and by buglers and privates on both tunics and frocks, and the cherry red braid for first and second-class orderlies of the nursing section, which will be worsted ; but orderlies appointed to Queen Alexandra's Imperial Military Nursing Service will receive bars of gold braid for wear on tunics and full dress frocks.
Army Veterinary Corps	Gold lace and embroidery, except badges for privates, which will be of worsted embroidery.
Gymnastic Staff ... ... Staff and Garrison Districts Royal Military College ... Staff College... ... ... Duke of York's Royal Military School, Royal Hibernian Military School, and Queen Victoria School	Gold lace and embroidery.
Military Provost Staff Corps	Gold lace and embroidery for all ranks.

Chevrons worn on drab shirts, khaki drill and service dress clothing will be made of worsted lace. Badges will be in metal.†

Chevrons only, of worsted lace, will be supplied for canvas or duck clothing, and will be worn on the right arm only.

Chevrons for cloaks, greatcoats, blue working greatcoats and pea jackets for all services will be made of worsted lace, except for the Foot Guards, which will be of cloth. Badges for drab greatcoats will be in metal, and a free issue will be made on appointment or promotion only, any renewals being at the soldier's expense. Badges for pea jackets will be of worsted embroidery.

5. Good conduct badges for tunics, dress jackets and frocks (except khaki drill frocks and service dress jackets) will be made of—

Gold lace for non-commissioned officers in the	Cavalry. Military Mounted and Foot Police. Royal Artillery. Royal Engineers. Royal Flying Corps.. Army Service Corps. Royal Army Medical Corps. Army Ordnance Corps. Army Pay Corps. Army Veterinary Corps.

† For Royal Flying Corps, chevrons and badges for service dress will be of worsted lace and embroidery, except the signaller's badge which will be of gold embroidery.

DISTINGUISHING BADGES AND CHEVRONS—*continued.*

Gold lace for bandsmen of the ... ...
{ Household Cavalry.
Royal Artillery.
Royal Engineers.
Foot Guards (for tunics only).
Royal Military College (for tunics only). }

And of worsted lace for non-commissioned officers and bandsmen in other services and for privates of all services, except Household Cavalry and Royal Flying Corps who receive gold badges.

Good conduct badges for khaki drill frocks and service dress jackets of all services will be made of worsted lace. Good conduct badges will not be worn on canvas frocks.

6. The following special badges will be worn on the tunic above the chevron by the regiments specified, viz. :—

1st Dragoon Gds.	Austrian Eagle ...	
2nd Dragoon Gds.	{ "Bays" within a laurel wreath, surmounted by a crown	
3rd Dragoon Gds.	{ Prince of Wales's Plume	
4th Dragoon Gds.	{ Star of the Order of St. Patrick ...	
7th Dragoon Gds.	Ligonier Crest ...	
1st Dragoons ...	Royal Crest... ...	
2nd Dragoons ...	Eagle	
6th Dragoons ...	Castle of Inniskilling	
3rd Hussars ...	White Horse ...	
5th Lancers ... 8th Hussars ...	} Harp and Crown ...	
9th Lancers ...	{ A.R. Cypher and Crown	
10th Hussars ...	{ Prince of Wales's Plume	
11th Hussars ...	{ Crest and motto of His Royal Highness the late Prince Consort	
12th Lancers ...	{ Prince of Wales's Plume	
14th Hussars ...	Prussian Eagle ...	
15th Hussars ...	Royal Crest... ...	
17th Lancers ...	Death's Head ...	
18th Hussars ...	Q.M.O. in monogram	
19th Hussars ...	Elephant	
21st Lancers ...	{ Imperial Cypher and Crown	

A.O. 266 ——— 1910

The badges will be worn by corporals, lance-serjeants, and serjeants of all grades in the 2nd Dragoon Guards and 14th Hussars, and by serjeants of all grades above the rank of lance-serjeant in other regiments. They will be made of sterling silver (oxidized for 14th Hussars), except those for the 2nd Dragoon Guards and 18th Hussars, which will be made of white metal, the 7th Dragoon Guards, which will be made of gilding metal and those for lance-serjeants and corporals of 14th Hussars, which will be made of oxidized German silver.

A.O. 49 1912

These badges are not worn by Warrant Officers.
They will be required to last 12 years, and if lost during the first

year's wear full value will be charged for them ; in the case of
silver badges one twenty-fourth will be deducted from the full
value for each year's wear if worn more than one year.

7. A silver star, to last eight years, will be supplied for the forage
and service dress caps of each warrant officer and staff-serjeant of
the Coldstream, the Scots and the Irish Guards. Two gilt
grenades will be supplied for the forage and service dress caps of
each warrant officer and staff-serjeant of the Grenadier Guards on
promotion ; these grenades will be kept up at the expense of the
warrant officer and staff-serjeant.

8. In services in which embroidered badges are supplied at the
public expense, a badge will be supplied with each cap.

9. Badges will be supplied to recruits as detailed in the lists
of free kits.

10. Metal collar badges will be fixed midway between top and
bottom of collar, and two inches from the centre of the badge to
the end of the collar. Collar badges will not be worn on khaki
drill frocks or service dress jackets.

A.C.D.
Clo. Regs.
1031
11. The position on garments of chevrons and badges for men
of normal dimensions is shown in Appendix XVII.

Table X.

PLAIN CLOTHES.

FOR SOLDIERS DISCHARGED FOR MISCONDUCT (£ee paragraph 121).

*1 cap   ..   .. ⎫
1 jacket   ..   .. ⎪
1 waistcoat   ..   .. ⎬ for each man.
1 pair of trousers   ..   .. ⎪
*1 neckerchief ..   .. ⎭

* Provided regimentally.

Table XI.

LIST OF TOOLS, &c., FOR SHOEMAKERS (referred to in paragraph 109).

Articles.	Large Chest.	Small Chest.
Aprons, basil	1	1
Awl-hafts, { closing or stabbing	6	3
pegging..	2	1
sewing	3	3
Awls, { closing	12	6
heel	12	6
pegging	12	6
sewing	24	12
stabbing	12	6
stitching	24	12
Breakers	1	1
Bristles .. .. ozs.	2	1
Chisels, hand cold, ¾ inch × 8 inch.. ..	..	1
Clams .. .. pairs	1	..
Cloth, emery .. .. sheets	4	6

Table XI—continued.

Articles.	Number.	
	Large Chest.	Small Chest.
Foot, iron, with leg	1	1
Files, seat	1	..
Flax, white ... lbs.	1	1
Hammers	1	1
Hooks, last	1	1
Horns, { paring	1	1
{ paste	1	1
Irons, { forepart, single, stout, ⅜-inch	1	1
{ glazing	1	1
{ lap	1	1
{ seat, wheel	1	1
Knives, { edge or scrapers	1	1
{ paring	2	2
{ peg	1	1
Lasts, men's, block ... pairs	4	4
Leathers, hand	..	1
Lifts ... pairs	12	..
Nails, tip ... lbs.	2	1
Nippers, cutting ... pairs	1	1
Pegs ... lbs.	1	..
Pincers ... pairs	1	1
Pliers, eyelet ... "	1	1
Punches, spring	1	1
Rasps, { 16-inch, peg	1	1
{ 9 " half file	1	1
Rivets, iron, { ½-inch ... ozs.	..	8
{ ⅝ "	..	8
{ ¾ "	..	8
Sand paper ... sheets	12	..
Screwdrivers	..	1
Sticks, { emery	..	1
{ long	1	1
{ size, outside single	1	..
Stirrups, made up	1	1
Tacks, lasting, { ⅞-inch ... doz.	2	½
{ 1 "	3	¼
{ 1¼ "	4	1
Tips, boot, heel ... pairs	24	12
Wax, shoemakers ... lbs.	1	½
Welt runners	1	..

Table XII.

ISSUES ON PAYMENT.

LEATHER.

A.O. 259 / 1911

		Average weight per hide, in lbs.
Bellies, struck		6 to 8
Calf skin, waxed		6 to 8
Kip butt, waxed		6 to 7
Sole, bend		15 to 16
Shoe butt, russet		12 per pair.
Shoulders	struck, English	7
	„ foreign	7 to 8
	welting	4 to 6
Lifts	pairs	
Soles, half	„	
Tip fillings	„	
Welts, boot	„	

GRINDERY.

57 / Gen. No. / 2111

Bills, steel.
Brads, cut, $\frac{1}{2}$, $\frac{5}{8}$, and $\frac{3}{4}$-inch.
Bristles.
Ends, waxed, 5-cord.
„ „ 10 „
Flax, white.
Heel balls.
Hemp, brown.
Lasts, men's, block.
Nails, { hob. / tip.
Pegs.
Plugs, toe tips.
Rivets, iron, $\frac{1}{2}$, $\frac{5}{8}$, and $\frac{3}{4}$-inch.
Tacks, lasting, $\frac{5}{8}$, 1, and $1\frac{1}{4}$-inch.
Tips, boot, heel, $2\frac{1}{4}$, $2\frac{3}{8}$, $2\frac{1}{2}$, $2\frac{5}{8}$, $2\frac{3}{4}$, $2\frac{7}{8}$, 3, and $3\frac{1}{4}$-inch.
Tips, toe $2\frac{7}{8}$, 3, $3\frac{1}{8}$-inch.
Wax, shoemakers.
Webbing, boot.

TOOLS FOR TAILORS' SHOP.

Boards, sleeve.
Bodkins, bone.
Chalk.
Edges, straight.
Irons, pressing, Nos. 7, 8 and 9.
Needles, sewing.
Scissors, pairs { tailors. / button-hole.
Shears, pairs, size 10.
Squares.
Tapes, measuring.
Thimbles.

TOOLS, &c., FOR SHOEMAKERS' SHOP.

Aprons, basil.

Awl-hafts, { closing or stabbing. / pegging. / sewing.

Awls, { closing. / heel. / pegging. / sewing. / stabbing. / stitching.

Bones, welt.

Breakers.

Chisels, hand cold, ¾ inch × 8 inch.

Clams, pairs.

Cloth, emery.

Compasses, pairs.

Eyelets, for boots.

Foot, iron, with leg.

Files, seat.

Hammers.

Hooks, last.

Horns, { paring. / paste.

Irons { forepart, single stout { ½″ / ⅜″ } / glazing. / lap.

Irons, { seat, wheel. / waist.

Knives, { edge, or scrapers. / paring. / peg.

Lasts, men's, block.

Leathers, hand.

Nippers, pairs.

Nipples, punch.

Pincers, pairs.

Pliers, eyelet.

Punches, spring.

Rasps, { 16 in., peg. / 9 „ ¼ file.

Rubbers, sandstone.

Sandpaper.

Screwdrivers.

Sticks, { emery. / long. / size, outside, single.

Stirrups, made up.

Tapes, measuring.

Trees, boot, with feet, sets.

Welt ploughs.

Welt runners.

Wheels, box.

Table XIII.
COLOURS, STANDARDS, GUIDONS, &c.

Household Cavalry	Four standards and cases and belts for each regiment every 10 years.
Dragoon Guards	One standard and belt for each regiment every 20 years.
Dragoons	One guidon and belt for each regiment every 20 years.
Foot Guards	Two colours and cases and belts for each battalion every 15 years.
Infantry (except Rifle regiments) and the West India and West African Regiments	Two colours and belts for each battalion every 20 years.
Cases for standards and guidons, Dragoon Guards and Dragoons, and for colours for Infantry	Every 15 years.
For guards of honour at Ballater and Dublin	King's colour and case and belt for each station, renewed when unserviceable.
Royal Military College Duke of York's Royal Military School Royal Hibernian Military School	Two colours and cases and belts, renewed when unserviceable.

Table **XIV.**

STATE CLOTHING.

HOUSEHOLD CAVALRY.

9 state coats and bags   ..   ..   ..
9 blue velvet caps and linen bags ..   ..
9 cloaks   ..   ..
9 pairs of leather pantaloons   ..   ..   quadrennially for each regiment.
9 sword belts ..   ..
1 pair of kettle-drum banners   ..   ..
8 pairs of trumpet banners with slings or cords   ..   ..

3 chests for state clothing ..   ..   ..   for each regiment—replaced when worn out, but not oftener than every fifteen years.
1 case for standards ..   ..

FOOT GUARDS.

1 state coat and bag..   ..   ..   ..
1 sash ..   ..
1 cloak   ..   ..
1 pair of short trousers   ..   ..   every six years for each household drummer to the Sovereign.
1 blue velvet cap and linen bag   ..   ..
1 belt ..   ..
1 pair of gaiters   ..   ..
1 pair of shoes*   ..   ..

1 box with lock and key   ..   ..   for each household drummer, replaced when worn out.

* Provided regimentally.

Table XV.

MISCELLANEOUS SUPPLIES.

(a) CLOTHING AND NECESSARIES FOR HOSPITALS.

Indented and accounted for by Officers in charge of Barracks, and issued to the troops on inventory.

Aprons, compounders .. .. ..
    „　cooks, dowlas .. .. ..
    „　mortuary .. .. ..
    „　operating .. .. ..
Brushes, blacking .. .. ..
    „　hair .. ..
    „　polishing .. .. ..
    „　shaving .. .. ..
Caps, cooks .. ..
Chevrons, 3-bar .. ..
    „　2　„ .. ..
    „　1　„ .. ..
Combs, hair .. ..
Crowns .. ..
Cloaks, germ proof .. .. ..
Drawers, cotton and flannel .. pairs
Forks.. .. ..
†Frocks, dowlas .. ..
Gowns, serge, lined and unlined ..
Handkerchiefs .. ..
Jackets, sleeping .. ..
Knives, table .. ..
Neckerchiefs .. ..
Overalls for nursing orderlies .. ..
*Shirts, cotton .. ..
*　„　flannel .. ..
Sleeves, compounders .. .. pairs
Slippers, carpet .. .. .. „
    „　leather .. .. .. „
    „　felt-soled .. .. each
Socks, brown .. .. .. pairs
Spoons .. ..
Strops, razor .. ..
Suits, working, for infectious and isolation cases, &c. .. .. ..
Trousers, pyjama, sleeping .. pairs
    „　serge, lined and unlined „
†　„　duck, for cooks .. „
Waistcoats, serge, lined and unlined ..

For lunatic patients, { Dresses, ticken .. ..
Hats, straw .. ..
Waistcoats, strait .. ..

Supplied in the proportions laid down in the Hospital Schedules, except in the case of the Royal Victoria Hospital, Netley, and the Royal Herbert Hospital, Woolwich, for which special scales are laid down.

A.O. 138
1913

A.C.D.
Reserves
3162

* 10 per cent. of cotton and 15 per cent. of flannel will be of the pattern for helpless patients. On mobilization for home defence the number of flannel shirts for helpless patients on peace charge of military hospitals at home will be increased to 25 per cent.
† The frocks and trousers for Native Cooks in Military Hospitals at Singapore will be provided locally.

CLOTHING AND NECESSARIES FOR HOSPITALS—*continued.*

For ditto at Netley only
{
Boots, ankle (with strap and buckle, to be affixed locally), pairs.
Braces, pairs.
Caps.
Covers, cap.
Frocks, serge.
Gloves, worsted, pairs.
Trousers, pairs, { moleskin.
serge.
tweed (for winter wear).
Waistcoats, cardigan.
Hats, white, linen (provided locally).
}

Special Articles.

Boots, ankle, pairs. | Veils, blue (for Egypt only).
Razors, plantagenet.

The special articles will only be supplied under exceptional circumstances to be explained when forwarding the indent.

The Deputy Director of Medical Services will take care that only such articles as are necessary are indented for.

Materials for the repair of hospital clothing, including needles, thimbles and sewings, are supplied as required.

For Station Veterinary Hospitals.

Aprons, operating ..
  „   veterinary ..
Strops, razor ..
Frocks, canvas, universal ..
Trousers „ .. pairs
}
As laid down in Barrack Schedules.

A.O. 49 — 1912

(Aprons, operating, will also be supplied for veterinary officers, as laid down in the Regulations for Army Veterinary Services.)

Indented for by Army Ordnance Department and to be accounted for as articles in use.

Hospital clothing and necessaries required for use on board ships conveying troops (except ships employed coastwise at home) will be supplied as laid down in the Equipment Regulations, Part I.

For men from abroad on leaving Hospital.

To be indented and accounted for by the Officer in Charge, Royal Victoria Hospital, Netley, or by the Officer Commanding the R.A.M.C. unit at Millbank or Woolwich. to which the men are attached, and to be issued under the conditions laid down in para. 195.

Waistcoats, cardigan.
Shirts, flannel.
Drawers, woollen, pairs.
  „   cotton, pairs.
Socks, worsted, pairs.

(b) ARTICLES SUPPLIED FOR USE OF SOLDIERS UNDER SENTENCE IN MILITARY PRISONS, OR IN DETENTION IN DETENTION BARRACKS, BRANCH DETENTION BARRACKS, OR IN BARRACK DETENTION ROOMS.

Indented and accounted for by Officers in charge of Barracks and issued on inventory.

Aprons, canvas   ..
Caps   ..   ..   ..   } for cooks.
Frocks, canvas   ..
Trousers, canvas, pairs

Aprons, cooks, canvas, for men employed cleaning barrack utensils, &c. (Mauritius).
Aprons, laundry.
Bags, clothes, for holding articles requiring to be washed.
Blacking. (Military Prisons only.)
Canvas suits (frock and trousers) for men who destroy their clothing.
Canvas trousers for men employed in cocoanut-husk beating (Ceylon).
Handkerchiefs.
Hones, razor.
Strops, razor.
Shoes, wood soled, for laundry work.
Shears, size 10, pairs.
Mud boots for men employed cleaning out ditches, drains, &c. (South Africa only).
Slippers, for wear in punishment cells.

Blue serge or service dress suits, ankle boots, braces, caps, drawers (cotton or woollen), shirts, socks, and towels will be allowed at the following military prisons and detention barracks, for wear by men whose clothing on arrival requires disinfection :—

		Sets.
A.O. 497 / 1912	Aldershot	8
	Bermuda	2
	Cairo	1
A.O. 275 / 1912	Chelsea	2
	Colchester	4
	Cork..	2
	Devonport	3
	Dublin	3
	Gibraltar	2
	Gosport	9
	Hong Kong..	2
	Jamaica	2
	Jersey	1
	Kandy (Ceylon)	3

ARTICLES SUPPLIED, &c.—*continued.*

						Sets.
Khartoum ..	..	..	..	..	..	1
Malta ..	..	..	..	..	..	4
Mauritius..	..	..	..	..	..	2
Pembroke Dock ..	..	..	..	..	..	2
Pretoria ..	..	..	..	..	..	3
Shorncliffe ..	..	..	..	..	..	2
Singapore ..	..	..	..	..	..	1
Stirling ..	..	..	..	..	..	4
Woolwich ..	..	..	..	..	..	2
York Castle	..	..	..	..	..	4

SOLDIERS UNDER SENTENCE TO BE DISCHARGED WITH IGNOMINY.

Additional clothing and necessaries, as under, will be held on inventory at military prisons where accommodation exists for soldiers sentenced to be discharged with ignominy for military offences.

For each man.

1 cap .. .. ⎫
1 jacket .. .. ⎬ Prison pattern.
1 waistcoat.. .. .. .. ⎪
1 pair of trousers .. .. .. ⎭
1 part-worn greatcoat.

Boots, ankle .. .. .. ⎫
Braces .. .. ⎪
Brushes ⎰ blacking .. .. ⎪
      ⎱ clothes .. .. ⎪
      ⎰ hair .. .. .. ⎪
      ⎱ polishing .. .. ⎪
      ⎱ tooth .. .. .. ⎬ To replace regimental
Canvas suits .. .. .. ⎪   articles worn out in
Caps, comforter .. .. .. ⎪   prison.
Combs, hair .. .. .. ⎪
Drawers (cotton and woollen) .. ⎪
Razors .. .. ⎪
Shirts, flannel .. .. .. ⎪
Socks .. .. ⎪
Spoons .. .. ⎪
Towels .. .. ⎭

1 jacket, bakers .. .. .. ⎫
1 waistcoat, bakers .. .. ⎬ For men employed
2 pairs trousers, bakers .. .. ⎭   in baking.

(c) WATCH COATS.

Indented and accounted for by Officers in charge of Barracks and issued on inventory.

Watch coats will be supplied for the undermentioned services:—

(a) For sentries.
(b) For soldiers of a fatigue party employed during target practice.
(c) For the garrison police at Chatham employed on duties which would otherwise be performed by sentries.
(d) For gate porters at the Royal Military Academy, Woolwich.
(e) For soldiers proceeding by boat to Upnor Castle in rough weather.
(f) For warders, guards, or watchmen of the Royal Engineer Establishment Staff.

Indented for by Army Ordnance Department and to be accounted for as articles in use.

For warders or night watchmen, to be given out nightly for use.

At home the issue will be made on the 1st November, and abroad during the winter months at such time as the general or other officer commanding shall direct.

Watch coats will be returned to store at home stations on the 1st April, and at stations abroad at the termination of the winter.

Watch coats will be required to last at least six years; but, if carefully repaired and looked after, will generally last much longer.

(d) WATERPROOF CLOTHING.

A.C.D.
Clo. Regs.
1050

I. Waterproof (indiarubber or oil-dressed) clothing will be supplied for such individuals and services (other than as provided for in Table III. of these regulations) as the General Officer Commanding the district or station may direct.

II. Care will be taken that its use is sanctioned only in exceptional cases. The issue will not be allowed for men who are not specially in need of the clothing, and for whom, having regard to the circumstances of their employment and the time they are liable to be exposed to rain while on duty, greatcoats should ordinarily be a suitable protection.

III. It should be noted that it has already been decided that waterproof clothing is not issuable to the classes detailed in Appendix II, unless specially authorized by the War Office.

IV. Waterproof clothing will not as a rule be supplied to civilian subordinates or ex-soldier employees unless they are supplied with uniform without a greatcoat and only then in exceptional circumstances.

WATERPROOF CLOTHING—*continued.*

V. An indiarubber coat only will ordinarily be required, but oil-dressed garments when suitable will be worn instead, *e.g.*,

Boats' crews   ..   ..   Frock and trousers, oil-dressed.
Barrack labourers   .. } Cape, oil-dressed.
Transport drivers   .. }

VI. Sou'-wester hats will also be supplied when necessary, and india-rubber leggings and pea jackets in certain special cases.

VII. The articles will be indented and accounted for by officers in charge of barracks, and issued to the troops on inventory after approval by the general or other officer commanding the district or station. In the case of look-out men in Q.F. batteries, the clothing approved will be indented and accounted for by the officers commanding the batteries.

VIII. Indiarubber coats, oil-dressed } 2 years at Jamaica and West
frocks and capes are ex- } Africa.
pected to last unless other- } 3 years at other stations.
wise specified }

Buttons will be renewed annually if necessary.

Pea jackets, indiarubber leggings and oil-dressed trousers are expected to last 2 years, and sou'-wester hats 3 years unless otherwise specified.

IX. Waterproof clothing required by the Army Ordnance Department, and for soldiers of Royal Artillery and Royal Engineers at camps of instruction will be indented for by that department.

WORKING CLOTHING.

Indented and accounted for by Officers in charge of Barracks, and issued to the troops on inventory.

(*e*) BOATS' CREWS.
Military Boats at Home and Abroad.

For each soldier forming part of the crew if certified to be necessary by the General Officer Commanding.

For Winter wear—
1 serge frock   ..   .. }
1 pair cloth or tweed trousers   ..   .. } annually.
1 hat, felt, japanned..   ..   ..   .. }

For Summer wear—
1 serge frock   ..   .. }
1 pair serge trousers   ..   ..   .. } biennially.
1 straw hat ..   .. }

One boat cloak for the use of officers will be issued once in six years for each boat.

A duck jumper in lieu of a serge frock, serge trousers in lieu of cloth trousers, and a sou'-wester hat, or a cloth cap, in lieu of the hat, felt, japanned, may be supplied at the discretion of the General Officer Commanding.

Mud boots .. .. } replaced when worn
Stockings, wadmill .. .. } out,

will be supplied at stations where their use is certified to be necessary by the General Officer Commanding.

(f) MISCELLANEOUS.

Boiler Inspectors will be supplied with a suit of overalls, to be provided locally. One suit of clothing will be supplied for each native employed in the bakeries at Malta.

Duck or canvas suits, sou'-wester hats, wadmill socks, and waders, will be supplied for students at the Royal Military Academy, the Royal Military College and Staff College, as may be necessary.

Two suits of serge clothing each will be supplied annually for the Serjeant-Major and Serjeant-Assistants at the School of Cookery, Aldershot, also 1 pair of serge trousers per man, and dowlas aprons as required for soldiers training as cooks.

A.O. 75
1911

A.O. 157
1912

150 suits of canvas clothing will be supplied for the use of officers and non-commissioned officers of classes, and of staff-serjeants at the School of Musketry, Hythe, whilst at work on machine guns, and 50 suits of canvas clothing for use of officers and non-commissioned officers attending machine-gun classes of instruction at the School of Musketry, Bloemfontein.

Canvas suits will be supplied for fatigue men engaged in operating aiming targets at the School of Musketry, Hythe.

Canvas clothing will be supplied for reservists of Royal Horse and Royal Field Artillery up for training as follows :

Twelve suits per Royal Horse Artillery Brigade.
Eighteen suits per Royal Field Artillery Brigade.

A pea jacket and two suits of dungaree clothing will be supplied biennially for each driver of Royal Artillery mechanical transport engines.

Canvas suits will be supplied for men attending horses suffering from contagious diseases.

A.O. 112
1911

Moleskin trousers and waistcoats, and wood-soled shoes, will be supplied for the non-commissioned officers and men employed as moulders in the Mechanical Transport Inspection Branch, Aldershot, and two sets of moleskin trousers and waistcoats and two pairs of wood-soled shoes to each Mechanical Transport Company, Army Service Corps, for the use of moulders.

Hospital gowns and slippers will be supplied for use of recruits awaiting medical inspection at large recruiting centres and depôts.

Sou'-wester hats and cloth caps will be supplied for ex-soldiers employed as markers and on range duties at the School of Musketry. The caps will be provided locally. A forage cap will also be supplied to the turncocks at Aldershot.

(*f*) Miscellaneous—*continued.*

At Gibraltar and Malta blue great coats will be held on inventory for the use of officers visiting the cold meat stores. A coat, warm, British, and a pair of service dress trousers will be supplied for each of the non-commissioned officers and labourers employed in the cold meat store. One blue jean frock and two pairs of canvas trousers will also be supplied for each of the labourers. | A.C.D. Malta 2343

Carpet slippers will be supplied for warders employed on night duty inside prisons, or detention barracks.

Warder cooks will be supplied with two canvas suits, an apron and a linen cap; the cap will be provided locally.

Knee or mud boots will be supplied for soldiers working in mud or water or on marshy ground, and overshoes or gum boots for Instructors drilling in open manèges. Wood-soled shoes will be supplied for use in stables at home stations; and to Cavalry, and Regimental Transport Drivers in South Africa. Four pairs will be issued to each Mechanical Transport Company Army Service Corps, for the use of drivers when washing down their vehicles. They will also be supplied to Cookhouses in South Africa, at the rate of 1 pair for each cook, and to the Royal Infirmary Laundry at Dublin for each man or woman employed. | A.C.D. R.S.F. 484.

Armlets will be supplied for military and hospital police.

Belts will be supplied for peons at Ceylon and Singapore.

50 pairs of goggles will be supplied for the use of sentries in North China. | A.O. 49 1912

Overcoats of sheeting, flax, made up in Aldershot, Dublin and Gosport Detention Barracks and Woking Military Prison for use of non-commissioned officers and Military Provost Staff Corps whilst superintending work in Detention Barracks and the Military Prison may be held as follows :— | A.O. 67 1913

Aldershot Detention Barrack		
Gosport Detention Barrack	8 each	
Woking Prison		
Cairo ..		
Colchester		
Dublin ..	Detention Barrack ..	6 each	Triennially.
Malta ..		
Pretoria..		
York ..		
Gibraltar		
Stirling ..	Detention Barrack ..	3 each	
Wynberg		

(*g*) **GYMNASIA (including Gymnasia at Detention Barracks and at Woolwich, Shorncliffe and Chelsea Branch Detention Barracks).** | A.O. 49 1912

| Shoes, gymnasia | { leather soles .. .. } as laid down in Barrack Schedules. | |
| | { rubber soles .. .. } | |

| Shoes, gymnasia, leather soled. | 50 pairs per brigade or depôt and 25 pairs per battery of Royal Horse and Royal Field Artillery. | For use during physical training at stations where there are no gymnasia. | A.O. 216 1912 |

65 pairs of gymnasia shoes will be allowed for the use of recruits drilling at the Cavalry School, Netheravon. | A.O. 266 1910

GYMNASIA—*continued.*

Instructors at all stations, including Detention Barracks.

2 pairs of blue serge trousers .. .. .. ⎫
1 pair of socks, worsted *.. .. .. .. ⎬ annually.
2 striped jerseys .. .. ⎭

Assistant Instructors, Temporary Assistant Instructors, and men under training for Instructors, including Branch Detention Barracks at Woolwich, Shorncliffe and Chelsea.

2 pairs of blue serge trousers .. .. .. ⎫ replaced when
1 pair of socks, worsted*.. .. .. .. ⎬ worn out.
2 striped jerseys .. .. ⎭

(*h*) **FIRE BRIGADES.**

(In addition to the uniform clothing of the corps to which the men belong.)

Aldershot Command, Bulford Camp, Colchester, and Curragh.

1 tunic .. .. sexennially.
2 pairs of trousers .. .. ⎫ annually.
1 overshirt, blue serge .. .. ⎭
1 pair of knee boots .. .. biennially.
1 frock, dungaree .. .. ⎫ annually.†
1 pair of trousers, ditto .. .. ⎭

Shorncliffe.

1 overshirt, blue serge .. .. annually.

General.

1 helmet per man, for all ranks of the fire brigade ⎫ every 10
at the above stations, and for the fire picquet ⎬ years.
at Netley .. .. ⎭

Indented for by the Army Ordnance Department, and accounted for as articles in use, except magazine clothing and canvas shoes for Royal Garrison Artillery, which will be indented for by the officer in charge of each armament district, and accounted for in his armament account (Army Form G 908A).

(*i*) **MAGAZINES, ‡ LABORATORIES, AND GUNPOWDER VESSELS.**

Magazines.

Boots, magazine, overall, pairs ⎫ As laid down in Part 2, Section XII (*a*),
Shoes, magazine, pairs .. ⎬ Equipment Regulations, and in Barrack Schedules.

Store Magazines and Laboratories, for each man.

A.O. 259 | Royal Artillery Magazines and Laboratories, see Table 19, Equipment
1911 | Regulations, Part 2, Section XII (*a*).

---

* Except Detention Barracks.
† In lieu of canvas frocks and trousers issuable under Table II.
‡ Magazine clothing is only supplied for use in buildings which are under magazine conditions, as defined by the magazine regulations.

MAGAZINES, &c.—*continued.*

In cold climates.	*In warm climates.*
1 jacket of lasting cloth.	1 jacket of lasting cloth.
1 pair of cloth trousers.	1 pair of trousers of lasting
1 glengarry cap.	cloth.
	1 pair of cloth trousers (Gibraltar only).
	1 glengarry cap.

One great-coat, part-worn (when certified by the General Officer Commanding to be necessary). The iron hook and eye on the collar, and the iron buttons at the back of collar and waist, will be removed locally before issue.

One cardigan waistcoat, and 1 pair of woollen drawers will be supplied for each man employed in laboratory operations and also to magazine men at Purfleet ; a canvas frock and pair of canvas trousers for each man employed at No. 1 Magazine, Plumstead ; knee boots for men at Tipnor, and pea jackets for men at Purfleet. Light hats may be provided locally for men employed in magazines on duties which expose the men to the heat of the sun. Flannel shirts may be supplied for use of men employed in rooms where picric acid is dealt with.

Floating Magazines, &c.

In Summer.

1 jacket of lasting cloth	..	..	..	..	}per man.
1 pair of cloth trousers	..	..	..	..	
1 glengarry cap	..	..	..	..	

In Winter.

1 jacket of lasting cloth	..	..	..	..	}per man.
1 pair of cloth trousers	..	..	..	..	
1 glengarry cap	..	..	..	..	
1 great-coat ..	..	..	..	..	

For gunpowder boat at Purfleet—

1 pea jacket ..	..	..	..	..	..	}per man.
1 pair waterproof leggings ..	..	..	..		

(*j*) DEPARTMENTAL BOATS.

Gun Wharves—Chatham, Devonport, Portsmouth, and Haulbowline—

For each man.

1 pea jacket ..	..	..	..	..	..	biennially.
1 jersey..	..	..	..	..	..	}triennially.
1 pair of cloth trousers	..	..	..	..	
1 cloth cap with ribbons	..	..	..	..	annually.

One jersey per man annually will be supplied for the crews of the Army Ordnance Department boats at Gibraltar and Malta.

(k) WAR DEPARTMENT VESSELS.
TO E ACCOUNTED FOR BY THE MASTERS OF VESSELS.

Home and Abroad.

57 Woolwich 4105	Clogs, wood sole, { As laid down in Approved Equipment, Consumable and other Stores, allowed for War Department General Service vessels at Home and Abroad.

Home Stations.

A.O. 75 1911	2 suits of canvas clothing (frock, canvas, laboratory, and trousers, canvas, universal), as a first issue, and 1 suit annually afterwards will be supplied for each seaman and boy. 2 suits of blue jean clothing as a first issue, and 1 suit annually and one suit biennially afterwards, in lieu of canvas clothing, will be supplied to each man of the engine-room staff. 2 jackets of lasting cloth, 2 pairs of cloth trousers and 2 pairs of magazine shoes, W.A. pattern, will be supplied to each steamship and barge ; to be worn by those of the deck staff engaged on their vessels in the stowage and trans-shipment of explosives. 1 jacket, 1 pair of trousers and 1 pair of shoes will be similarly issued to such tugs and launches as are fitted with holds for cargo or baggage. 1 pair of knee boots, Canada pattern, will be issued to each deck officer and seaman (but not to boys), and such boots will be repaired when necessary at the public expense.

(l) CIVILIAN SUBORDINATES.
Army Service Corps, Army Ordnance Department, and Manufacturing Departments.

A.O. 266 1910	Such special issues as may be decided upon from time to time. At central Ordnance workshops a supply of field dressings equal to 3 per cent. of the persons employed will be kept for use in emergency. The dressings will be expended and replaced every 12 months.
57 Southern 2385	Tooth brushes will be supplied to those employed in Painters' and Tinsmiths' shops in Army Ordnance Department Workshops and will be replaced when necessary.

(m) FIELD DRESSINGS (paragraph 170).

A.O. 275 1912	Field dressings for instructional purposes will be supplied on indent to units requiring them.

(n) BRUSHES, BRASS, for cleaning Rifles.

A.O. 67 1913	A "brush, brass" will be supplied as part of the equipment of each mobilization storehouse in which rifles are stored in regimental custody, for :—

(a) issue to army reservists on mobilization,

or,

(b) as part of authorized mobilization equipment held in unit charge during peace.

One brush will be supplied for any number up to 1,000 rifles, and an additional brush for each complete additional 1,000 rifles.

Time-expired great-coats will be supplied for military working parties; mud boots for men unlading vessels; knee boots for soldiers of Royal Artillery, Royal Engineers and Army Ordnance Corps at camps of instruction; straw hats will be supplied for working parties at Mauritius; waterproof coats and leggings for armament artificers; crossbelts for sentries on troopships.

Distinguishing cap bands for manœuvres will be provided locally by the Army Ordnance Department under the authority of the General Officer Commanding-in-Chief and the cost charged to the training grant.

NECESSARIES.

Table XVI.

FREE KITS.

MOUNTED SERVICES.

Articles.	Household Cavalry.	Cavalry of the Line.	Military Mounted Police.	B.H.A. and R.F.A.	Royal Engineers.*	Army Service Corps.†	Army Veterinary Corps.
Badges, collar, metal ... pair	...	1	...	1(a)	...	1	1
Badge for cap	2(d)	1	1	1	1	1	1
Bags { kit, universal	1	1	1	1	1	1	1
stable	1	1	1	1	1	1	1
Blacking ... tin	1	1	1	1	1	1	1
Boot laces ... pair	1	1	1	1	1	1	1
Braces ... „	1	1	1	1	1	1	1
Brushes { blacking	1	1	1	1	1	1	1
brass	1	1	1	1	1	1	1
clothes	1	1	1	1	1	1	1
hair	1	1	1	1	1	1	1
hard	...	...	...	1	1	...	...
lace	...	1	1	...	...	1	...
polishing	1	1	1	1	1	1	1
shaving	1	1	1	1	1	1	1
tooth	1	1	1	1	1	1	1
Button, brass	1	1	1	1(c)	1	1	1
Cap, comforter	...	1	...	1(c)	1	1	1
Case, plume	1	1	...	1(b)	...	...	...
Comb, hair	1	1	1	1	1	1	1
Disc, identity, with cord	1	1	1	1	1	1	1
Fork	1	1	1	1	1	1	1
Gloves, worsted ... pair	...	1	1	1	1	1	1
Holdall	1	1	1	1	1	1	1
Housewife	1	1	1	1	1	1	1
Jersey	1	...	...	...	...	...	...
Knife, clasp, with lanyard	1	1	1	1	1	1	1
„ table	1	1	1	1	1	1	1
Mineral jelly ... tin	1	1	1	1	1	1	1
Razor	1	1	1	1	1	1	1
Shirts, flannel‡	...	3	3	3	3	3	3
Shirts, cotton	3	...	...	...	...	...	...
Socks, worsted ... pairs	3	3	3	3	2	3	3
Sponge	1	1	1	1	1	1	1
Spoon	1	1	1	1	1	1	1
Spurs, swan-neck ... pair	1	1	1	1	1	1	1
Titles, metal, for shoulder straps sets	2	3	3	3	3	3	3
Towels, hand	2	2	2	2	2	2	2
Trousers, blue serge ... pair	1	...	...	...	...	...	...
Vests, flannel	2	...	...	...	...	...	...

A.C.D.
Cav.
1052

A.O. 307
1909

A.O. 83
1910

A.C.D.
Cav.
1053

* All soldiers of R.E. mounted units and sappers and pioneers of Signal Companies R.E., except "K" Company, will be supplied with kits as mounted men.
† All soldiers of the transport branch will be supplied with kits as mounted men.
‡ Men who join from the Special Reserve with 2 or 3 part-worn flannel shirts in their possession will receive, respectively, 1 or 2 new flannel shirts less with their free kit.   (a) Royal Field Artillery only.
(b) Royal Horse Artillery only.   (c) Except R.A. mounted band.
(d) Separate patterns are supplied for forage and service dress caps.

DISMOUNTED SERVICES.

Articles.	Royal Garrison Artillery.*	Royal Engineers.	Foot Guards.	Line Battalions, Garrison Staff and Army Pay Corps.	Rifle Regiments.	Highland (kilted) Regiments, and men of the Scots, Guards and Highland Light Infantry that wear the kilt.
Badges, collar ... pair	1(a)	...	...	1(a)	...	1
Badge { cap	1	1	1	1	1	1
{ purse	...	...	...	...	...	1(f)
Bag, kit, universal	1	1	1	1	1	1
Blacking ... tin	1	1	1	1	1	1
Boot (or shoe) laces ... pair	1	1	1	1	1	1
Braces ... „	1	1	1	1	1	1
Brushes { blacking	1	1	1	1	1	1
{ brass	1	1	1	1	...	1
{ clothes	1	1	1	1	1	1
{ hair	1	1	1	1	1	4
{ hard	1	1	...	...	...	...
{ lace	...	...	...	1(b)	...	...
{ polishing	1	1	1	1	1	1
{ shaving	1	1	1	1	1	1
{ tooth	1	1	1	1	1	1
Button, brass	1	1	1	1	1	1
Cap, comforter	1(e)	1(d)	1(d)	1	1	1
Comb, hair	1	1	1	1	1	1
Disc, identity, with cord	1	1	1	1	1	1
Fork	1	1	1	1	1	1
Gaiters, Highland ... pairs	...	...	...	...	...	2(c)
Garters and rosettes (g) ... pair	...	...	...	...	...	1
Gloves, worsted ... „	1	1	1	1	1	1
Holdall	1	1	1	1	1	1
Hose tops, tartan ... pairs	...	...	...	...	...	2
Housewife	1	1	1	1	1	1
Knife, clasp, with lanyard	1	1	...	...	...	...
„ table	1	1	1	1	1	1
Mineral jelly ... tin	1	1	1	1	1	1
Razor	1	1	1	1	1	1
Shirts, flannel†	3	3	3	3	3	3
Socks, worsted ... pairs	3	3	3	3	3	3
Sponge	1	1	1	1	1	1
Spoon	1	1	1	1	1	1
Titles, metal, for shoulder-straps, with grenades for Fusilier and bugles for Light Infantry regiments sets	3	3	1	3	3	3
Towels, hand	2	2	2	2	2	2

* Permanently mounted warrant officers, non-commissioned officers and men of heavy brigades and heavy batteries Royal Garrison Artillery, will be supplied with kits as for Royal Field Artillery.

† Men who join from the Special Reserve with 2 or 3 part-worn flannel shirts in their possession will receive, respectively, 1 or 2 new flannel shirts less with their free kit.

(a) Clerks entitled to blue clothing will receive two pairs in the Royal Artillery and Army Pay Corps. Not issuable to Oxfordshire and Buckinghamshire Light Infantry.

(b) Army Pay Corps only.

(c) One pair white and one pair drab for Highland (kilted) regiments and men of Highland L.I. wearing the kilt.

(d) Except band.

(e) Except R.A. band, Woolwich.

(f) Except Argyll and Sutherland Highlanders.

(g) A free issue will be made to Sergeant Piper, Queen Victoria School, on appointment, if not in possession.

A.O. 83
1910

Dismounted Services—*continued.*

Articles.	Army Service Corps.	Royal Army Medical Corps.	Royal Flying Corps.	Army Ordnance Corps.	Military Foot Police.	Schoolmasters.	Civilian Students, Duke of York's, Royal Hibernian Military Schools, and Queen Victoria School.
Badges, collar... pair	1*	1*	1	1*	...	...	...
Badge, cap	1	1	2(a)	1	1	1	1
Bag kit, universal	1	1	1	1	1	...	...
Blacking ... tin	1	1	1	1	1	...	...
Boot laces ... pair	1	1	1	1	1	...	...
Braces ... ,,	1	1	1	1	1	1	1
Brushes { blacking	1	1	1	1	1	1	1
brass	1	1	1	1	1	...	...
clothes	1	1	1	1	1	1	1
hair	1	1	1	1	1	1	1
hard	...	...	1	...	...	...	...
lace	1	...	...	...	...	...	...
polishing...	1	1	1	1	1	1	1
shaving	1	1	1	1	1	1	1
tooth	1	1	1	1	1	1	1
Button, brass ...	1	1	1	1	1	...	...
Buttons and rings ... sets	...	2	...	...	...	...	...
Cap, comforter	1	1	1	1	...	...	...
Comb, hair	1	1	1	1	1	1	1
Disc, identity, with cord	1	1	1	1	1	...	2
Drawers, cotton ... pairs	...	...	...	...	...	2	2
Fork	1	1	1	1	1	...	...
Gloves, worsted ... pair	1	1	1	1	1	1	1
Goggles... ,,	1‡	...	...	...	...	...	...
Holdall...	1	1	1	1	...	...	...
Hooks, waist	...	4	...	...	...	...	...
Housewife	1	1	1	1	1	1	1
Knife, clasp, with lanyard...	1	...	1	1	...	...	...
Knife, table	1	1	1	1	1	...	...
Mineral jelly ... tin	1	1	...	1	1	1	1
Razor	1	1	1	1	1	1	1
Serge frock	...	...	...	...	...	...	1
,, trousers ... pair	...	...	...	...	...	...	1
Shirts, flannel†	3	3	3	3	3	3	3
Socks, worsted ... pairs	3	3	3	3	3	3	3
Sponge	1	1	1	1	1	...	...
Spoon	1	1	1	1	1	...	...
Titles, metal, for shoulder-straps ... sets	3	3	1	3	3	...	...
Towels, hand	2	2	2	2	2	4	4
Waistcoat, cardigan...	...	...	...	...	...	...	1*

A.O. 83
1910
A.C.D
Aldershot
2685
A.C.D.
R.F.C.
45

* Clerks entitled to blue clothing will receive two pairs in the Army Service Corps, Army Ordnance Corps, and in the Royal Army Medical Corps.

† Men who join from the Special Reserve with 2 or 3 part-worn flannel shirts in their possession will receive, respectively, 1 or 2 new flannel shirts less with their free kit.

‡ Drivers of vehicles with internal combustion engines only.

(a) For field cap the badge will be fitted with shanks and pin, and for forage cap, with vertical shank.

LOCAL FORCES.

Articles.	Royal Malta Artillery.	Hong-Kong — Singapore Battalion, R.G.A.*	Sierra Leone Company, R.G.A.	Royal Engineers, Non-Europeans serving with Fortress Company, Sierra Leone.	West India Regiment.	West African Regiment.
Badges { cap	1	...	...	1	...	...
{ collar pair	1	1	...	...	...	...
Bag, kit, universal	1	1	...	...	1	...
Blacking tin	1	1	...	...	1	...
Bootlaces pair	1	1	...	...	1	...
Braces „	1	1	...	...	1	...
Brushes { blacking	1	1	...	...	1	...
{ brass	1	1	1	1	1	1
{ clothes	1	1	1	1	1	1
{ hair	1	...	...	...	1	...
{ hard	...	1	...	...	...	...
{ polishing	1	1	...	...	1	...
{ shaving	1	...	...	...	1	...
{ tooth	1	...	...	...	1	...
Button, brass	1	1	1	1	1	1
Buttons and rings sets	3	3	2	2	2	2
Cap, comforter	1	...	...	...	...	...
Comb, hair	1	...	...	...	1	...
Disc, identity, with cords	1	1	1	1	1	1
Fork	1	...	...	...	1	...
Holdall	1	...	...	...	1	...
Hooks, waist	4	4	...	...	4	...
Housewife	1	1	1	1	1	1
Knife, clasp, with lanyard	1	1	1	1	...	...
Knife, table	1	...	...	...	1	...
Mineral jelly tin	1	1	...	...	1	...
Razor	1	...	...	...	1	...
Shirts, flannel	3	3	...	...	3	...
Socks, worsted pairs	3	2	...	...	3	2‡
Sponge	1	1	1	1	1	...
Spoon	1	...	...	...	1	...
Titles (or badges), metal, for shoulder-straps sets	2	2	...	...	1	...
Towels, hand	2	2	2	2	2	2

A.O. 157
1912

* Cotton drawers will also be supplied, on repayment when indented for.
‡ Signalling and Telephone Section only.

A.O. 157
1912

APPENDICES.

APPENDIX I.

[Referred to in paragraph 17.]

1.—CLASSIFICATION FOR CLOTHING.

(a) Clothing of first-class quality.†

Armourer Quartermaster-Serjeant.
Armourer Staff-Corporal, Household Cavalry.
Artificer Quartermaster-Serjeant, Royal Artillery.
Band Corporal Household Cavalry.
‡Band Serjeant, except in Cavalry Regiments, Royal Artillery
and Royal Malta Artillery.
Barrack Wardens.
§Battery Quartermaster-Serjeant } Royal Horse Artillery.
§Battery Serjeant-Major ... }
*Chief Warder, Military Provost Staff Corps.
**Company Serjeant Major, Army Service Corps.
Corporal-Major ... ... } Household Cavalry.
Corporal-of-horse Trumpeter }
Company-Serjeant-Major, Instructor in Gymnastics.
Experimental Staff-Serjeant, Royal Artillery
Instructors, Manufacturing Departments.
Master Gunners, 3rd Class.
Port Serjeant, Gibraltar.
Quartermaster-Corporal-Major, Household Cavalry.
Quartermaster-Serjeant, except as stated in sub-head (b).
Schoolmasters.
Senior Drill-Serjeant, School of Military Engineering.
‡Serjeant-Bugler.
‡Serjeant-Drummer.
Battery and Company-Serjeant-Major-Instructor in Gunnery.
Colour-Serjeant-Instructor in Musketry.
Company - Serjeant - Major - Instructors — Orderly - room
Serjeants—Serjeant Instructors, and Serjeant Pioneer—
Schools of Musketry.
Serjeant-Piper.
Serjeant of the Band, Royal Artillery, Woolwich.
‡Serjeant-Trumpeter, Royal Artillery, and Royal Engineers.

A.C.D.
F.A.Dep.
2792

* The tartan frocks supplied to chief warders and warders are made of the same quality of material for all ranks.
† The frocks supplied to Cavalry Regiments are made of the same quality of material for all ranks.
‡ When requiring new clothing, while under instruction at the Royal Military School of Music, he will obtain the clothing of an ordinary serjeant, and the special clothing of the appointment will be indented for by the corps for issue to the non-commissioned officer doing the duty.
§ These non-commissioned officers have not so much gold trimming on their dress jackets as first class staff-serjeants, and receive worsted instead of gold lines for their busbies.
** If promoted to that rank prior to 1.11.98.

(C.R. 10544)   K

Squadron Corporal-Major Instructor in ⎤
   Fencing and Gymnastics ...   ... ⎟ Household Cavalry.
Squadron Corporal-Major Instructor in ⎟
   Musketry   ...   .⎦
Squadron Serjeant-Major Instructor in ⎤
   Fencing and Gymnastics ...   ... ⎟ Cavalry Regiments.
Squadron Serjeant-Major Instructor in ⎟
   Musketry   ...   .⎦
Staff Serjeants—Royal Military College.
Warrant Officer.
Warder Clerk, Military Provost Staff Corps.

(b) Clothing of Serjeant's quality.*

Bandsman, Highland, Scottish and Rifle Regiments.
Band Serjeant, Cavalry Regiments, Royal Artillery, and
   Royal Malta Artillery.
Bugler, Rifle Regiments.
Colour-Serjeant.
†Cook, Military Prison or Detention Barracks.
Engineer Clerk Staff-Serjeant.
Garrison Librarian.
Havildar   ... ⎫ Hong-Kong — Singapore Battalion, Royal
Havildar-Major ⎭   Garrison Artillery.
Kettledrummer, 3rd Hussars.
King's Gunner, Windsor Castle.
Musician, Royal Artillery.
‡Piper.
Quartermaster-Serjeant, recruiting district, not serving on an
   army engagement.
Quartermaster-Serjeant, squadron, troop, battery, or company,
   not included in sub-head (a) and having substantive (not
   acting) rank.
Royal Horse Guards, all ranks except those included in sub-
   head (a).
Serjeant (except lance-serjeant).
Serjeant Artificer.
Serjeant-Major, squadron, troop, battery, or company, not
   included in sub-head (a), and having substantive (not
   acting) rank.

---

* In the Life Guards, the ranks not included in list (a) receive special clothing.
Battalion drill-serjeants and orderly room-serjeants of Foot Guards will wear
forage caps of staff-serjeants' quality; and the tunics of the battalion drill-serjeant and
orderly room-serjeants will have extra lace.
† If receiving the pay of assistant warders, cooks will be entitled to have their
clothing made up of the same pattern as that for assistant warders.
‡ Soldiers authorized to be employed as pipers in the Royal Scots, Royal Scots
Fusiliers, the King's Own Scottish Borderers, or the Scottish Rifles, will not have
clothing of that rank, at the public expense, but the allowance for clothing of rank
and file will be drawn for them. Depôts of Highland regiments which have pipers on
the establishment of the regiment will be allowed clothing for two pipers. Acting pipers
of Highland regiments, to the number of 5 per battalion, and two extra pipers per
battalion in the Scots Guards, will be clothed as pipers.

Serjeant Trumpeter, Cavalry Regiments.
§Servant, Military Prison or Detention Barracks.
Staff-Serjeant Artificer.
Victoria Librarian.
Warders, Military Provost Staff Corps, except Chief Warders.

(c) Clothing of Rank and File quality.‖¶

All ranks not included in sub-heads (a) and (b).
Acting drummers of the brigade of Foot Guards will be
clothed as drummers.

APPENDIX II.

[Referred to in Table XV (d).]

List of details for which the use of waterproof clothing is
prohibited, except when specially authorized by the
War Office.

A.C.D.
Clo. Regns.
1050

Acting Barrack Serjeant.
Barrack Warden.
Butchers.
Camp { Serjeant-Major.
      { Quartermaster-Serjeant.
Clerks.
Draughtsman.
Expense Store Accountant.
Farrier N.C.O. Remount Co. A.S.C.
Fuel and Light Accountant.
Foreman of labourers and other employees A.O.D.
Garrison staff.
Instructor { Musketry.
           { Gunnery.
Issuers of rations, forage, coal, &c.

---

§ If receiving the pay of assistant warders, servants will be entitled to have their clothing made up of the same pattern as that for assistant warders.

‖ In the Royal Engineers, and in the Foot Guards, No. 2 cloth is supplied for tunics. In the Life Guards the ranks not included in list (a) receive special clothing.

¶ Bandsmen of cavalry regiments (except Household Cavalry) receive clothing of rank and file quality.

Band clothing will be allowed for boys, in addition to the regulated number of bandsmen, on the understanding that the difference in cost between rank and file and band clothing will be defrayed by the regiments or corps. In the bands of the Royal Artillery at Woolwich and Aldershot and of the Royal Engineers band clothing will be allowed at the public expense for boys and for the gunners and sappers authorized to be employed as bandsmen.

(C.R. 10544)   K 2

Master Gunners and N.C.Os. visiting forts, in charge of
batteries, gun firers, &c.
Musketry Range men.
Men on stable duty, Remount Depôt.
Magazine and Laboratory Foremen loading and unloading
vessels.
N.C.Os. Camp Staff.
N.C.Os. in charge of barrack labourers.
N.C.Os. and men on water fatigues and other out-door
employment.
N.C Os. and gunners R.G.A. employed at Range Naval Base,
South Africa.
N.C.O. i/c Wellington Front Class Room, Gibraltar.
N.C.Os. and ex-soldiers at Netheravon Cavalry School.
Native Magazine Keeper.
Orderly Serjeant.
Orderly Corporal.
Port Serjeant.
Pioneers.
P.F. Artificer.
Regimental Quartermaster Serjeant.
Regimental Waterman.
Serjeant Trumpeter.
Surveyor.
Shipping Clerk.
Shipping Foreman.
Storeman.
Storekeeper.
Storeholder.
Sluice Keepers.
Septic tank labourers, conservancy and sanitary men.
Sentries.
Verger, Garrison Church.
Warrant Officer i/c A.S.C. duties.
Wardmaster, Hospital.
Warrant Officer, R.A.M.C., making night calls.
Water Warden.
Watchers R.E.
Woodman Rifle Range.

APPENDIX III.

[Referred to in paragraphs 15 and 304.]

COMPANY INDENTS FOR CLOTHING AND NECESSARIES.

1. In units having quartermasters, indents corresponding in
period to the pay and mess-book (Army Forms H 1178 for mounted
services and H 1179 for dismounted services), for free issues of

personal clothing will be sent in duplicate by companies to the quartermaster. All men drawing clothing will be sent to the quartermaster's stores to be fitted.

2. The names of the recruits enlisted during the month* will be entered in the indent in the same order as in the pay and mess book. Only those articles actually issued during the month will be entered under each man's name, any articles withheld under para. 68, being included in the indent for the month in which the issue is made. The number of shirts included in the free kit of necessaries issued to a recruit enlisted from the special reserve will be entered at the foot of the column against each man's name. The Army Forms H 1157 received from special reserve units will be attached to the issue vouchers in such cases.

A.O. 48
1914

3. The quartermaster will return both copies to the company for the insertion of the names of any recruits who may enlist during the month. On the Tuesday immediately preceding the last pay day of the month* the quartermaster will enter the charge if any (*see* paragraph 369) for fitting, completing with chevrons and badges, and marking, in both indents, and after posting the issues in the clothing ledger, will insert the number of the ledger page and the issue voucher to the clothing account at the top of the forms and return them to the company. When the certificates and receipts have been signed, the officer commanding the company will forward one copy on the Wednesday immediately preceding the last pay day of the month to the regimental paymaster, and the other copy will be kept by the company and preserved in a guard book for future reference, and in this copy only the soldier will sign to the receipt of the articles at the foot of the form.

A.O. 285
1911

4. An indent (on Army Form H 1180 or H 1181) for personal clothing and necessaries on payment will be prepared by the company and sent at the commencement of each month* to the quartermaster, who will enter the prices of the articles indented for in accordance with the latest published Priced Vocabulary, and the amounts due by each man, and return it to the company for the insertion of the names of any other men who may require articles during the month. The names will be entered in the same order as in the pay and mess book, and the issues will be confined to one column for clothing and one column for necessaries for each man. On the Tuesday immediately preceding the last pay day of the month the quartermaster will complete the form, including the allowances, if any (*see* paragraph 369) for fitting, completing with chevrons and badges, and marking, and after posting the issues in the clothing ledger, and inserting the numbers of the ledger pages, will return it to the company for signature, &c. The soldier will sign to the receipt of the articles in the spaces at the foot of the columns. A copy of the form of indent (omitting the men's names and the details of issues) will be prepared by the company, showing the total number of each descrip-

A.O. 49
1912

* Signifies the period covered by the pay and mess book.

A.O. 284
1913

tion of articles sold, their value, and the total amount to be recovered from the company. The fitting, completing and marking charges will be added by the quartermaster, who will then return the form to the company for signature. Both copies will be forwarded on the Wednesday immediately preceding the last pay day of the month to the regimental paymaster. The first copy (containing the men's names and full details) will be certified by the paymaster and (when no longer required by him) will be returned to the unit, to be retained by the company for future reference. The second copy will be retained by the paymaster as a voucher to the pay list.

5. Articles required by regimental institutes for sale to soldiers will be indented for in bulk by the committee of management from the quartermaster on Army Form H 1180 or H 1181, as the case may be. At the end of each month the quartermaster will notify to the command paymaster the amount to be recovered from the committee of management, and credited to the public.

6. Before the completed indents for personal clothing and necessaries for issue free or on payment (Army Forms H 1178, 1179, 1180 and 1181) are returned to the company, the quartermaster will enter the total number of each article issued in kind to each company on one copy of the form of indent, and will obtain the signature of the officer commanding each company at the foot of the form in acknowledgment of the receipt of the articles. This form will be retained by the quartermaster. If it is necessary to issue any articles before the indent is closed at the end of the month, the quartermaster will obtain a temporary receipt for them upon Army Form G 1033. When the indent has been completed and the certificates signed, these temporary receipts will be given up and destroyed.

7. Indents for public clothing on Army Form H 1152 will be sent in duplicate to the quartermaster whenever necessary. The rates and amount for marking and for completing with chevrons and badges will be inserted by that officer, who will then forward them to the officer commanding the company for completion and signature. One copy will be returned to the quartermaster and retained by him, and the other copy will be attached to the company pay and mess book.

8. Indents from companies detached from headquarters will be forwarded as directed in paragraphs 1 to 7. The clothing and necessaries indented for will be despatched by the quartermaster as soon as possible after the articles have been marked. The officer commanding the company will make his own arrangements for fitting the personal clothing at the published rates, or, if the company is at a convenient distance from headquarters, the sergeant tailor may be sent with the clothing, and will bring back the articles which require alteration.

9. In units which have no quartermaster, the foregoing instructions will be carried out by the commanding officer of the unit, but the copy of the indent, prepared by the quartermaster, referred to in paragraph 6, will not be required.

APPENDIX IV.

[Referred to in Section XV.

INSTRUCTIONS FOR KEEPING THE CLOTHING LEDGER.

1. The general clothing ledger, Army Book 284 or 285, will be divided into seven sections :—

I. Personal clothing.
II. New public clothing.
III. Part-worn public clothing in store and in wear.
IV. Necessaries.
V. Materials and garniture.
VI. Mobilization clothing and necessaries.
VII. Record of charges for making up clothing.

Each section will be in two parts, receipts and issues.

2. Receipts under Sections I, II, IV, V, and VI will be posted from the delivery vouchers received from the Royal Army Clothing Department, the Army Ordnance Department, or other issuing depôt, and from bills for local purchases, &c.

3. Receipts under Section III will be posted from the company indents on Army Form H 1152* and Army Form H 1150, articles in possession of transfers from other units.

4. Issues under Sections I, II, and IV will be posted from the company indents on—

Army Form H 1178 or H 1179 ... Personal clothing and necessaries issued free.

 ,, ,, H 1180 or H 1181 ... Personal clothing and necessaries issued on payment.

 ,, ,, H 1152* ... ... Issues of public clothing.

 ,, ,, G 1033 ... ... New articles transferred to another unit or returned to A.O.D.

5. In units of more than one company, entries of issues shown in the company indents may be posted from consolidated vouchers containing summaries of the totals on Army Forms H 1178-81, instead of being posted from each individual voucher. The consolidated voucher should accompany the ledger when forwarded for audit.

6. Issues under Section III will be posted from—

Army Form H 1150 ... ... Articles in possession of men transferred to another unit.

 ,, ,, B 115 ... ... Clothing deficient on desertion.

---

* Articles issued to companies and struck off charge on the issue side of Section II will be brought on charge as in wear on the receipt side of Section III.

Army Form P 1954   ...   ...   Clothing deficient from other causes.

    „   „   G 1033   ...   ...   Part-worn public clothing in store transferred to another unit, and worn out public clothing sold to the contractor.

7. Issues under Section V will be posted from Army Form P 1925.

8. A record will be kept in Section VII of all charges made under paragraph 246 for making up garments issued in material.

A.O. 285
1911 9. All unmade garments received will be entered on the receipt side of Section VII as well as in Section I, and all charges preferred for making up garments will be entered under the heading "Articles Charged For." Charges for the conversion of garments need not appear in this section.

10. When garments in material are returned to the Royal Army Clothing Department, or to Ordnance Store, or are transferred to another unit, the transaction will be recorded in Section VII, under the heading "Articles Charged For."

11. A balance will be struck in Section VII when the ledger is forwarded for examination, and the remain will be carried to the next account in the usual way.

12. Immediately the ledger for one period is balanced and closed, a new ledger will be opened, into which the number of articles in store, as counted by the stocktaking board, will be carried forward.

13. The ledgers and other records will be posted daily, as the transactions occur.

14. Every entry will be supported by a voucher, or by a reference to a corresponding entry in another section of the ledger, and the 57
Gen. No
2322 number of the voucher will always be quoted. In cases where it is necessary to put up with the account blank vouchers to account for missing numbers, a brief explanation of the circumstances, signed by an officer, will be given on the blank vouchers. The addition of letters or sub-numbers to the numbers of vouchers is prohibited.

15. All articles received will be at once brought on charge in the clothing ledger, irrespectively of the year for which they may have been demanded, or in which they are intended to be used.

16. *All baling material and packages (except used tin cases, which may be destroyed) received with clothing and necessaries, will be brought on charge in the ledger.

17. Tools for marking will be accounted for in the equipment ledger.

18. Working and waterproof clothing in use at the School of Military Engineering and the School of Gunnery will be shown in a separate ledger, which will be forwarded for audit annually to the local auditor of the command.

---

* The canvas in the wrappers of bales will be computed at three yards per bale for home stations and six yards for abroad, except in the case of small bales of mobilization clothing which will be computed at one yard each for jackets, pantaloons and trousers, and two yards for greatcoats.

19. Clothing and necessaries issued to the Survey Companies, Royal Engineers, will be brought on charge in one ledger at the headquarters at Southampton.

20. Working clothing supplied for use in electric light duties will be accounted for as follows :—

(a) Articles supplied to units in the general clothing ledger (Army Book 284 or 285).

(b) Articles supplied to the School of Military Engineering in Army Book 247.

21. Badges, chevrons, footstraps, shoulder straps and titles, when supplied apart from the garments, will be brought on charge separately in the columns provided for the purpose. Buttons and rings received with canvas clothing need not be taken on charge. Greatcoats, capes, and full dress head-dresses for staff-serjeants will not be shown in separate columns from those used for other ranks.

22. Colour badges, crowns, footstraps, shoulder straps and similar articles, which are not shown separately in the company indents, will be entered in the ledger as issued for the corresponding number of garments for which they are necessary. The articles composing a free kit for the various services will be entered in the ledger for each free kit shown as issued in the company indents.

23. The entries striking off charge unserviceable articles sold to the contractor will be supported by the documents mentioned in Appendix XI.

24. A separate account will be kept of leather pantaloons and jack boots in the Household Cavalry, as per form, Appendix X. The account will show the date and cost of all repairs. This account will be subsidiary to the clothing ledger (which will show the articles in bulk only), and will be inspected by the board of survey inquiring into repairs or renewals.

25. Clothing for soldiers detached from their own units (except as provided for in paragraph 126) will be accounted for by the unit to which they are attached for pay.

26. The materials and garniture referred to in paragraphs 150 and 151 will be brought on charge in the clothing ledger.

27. Public clothing received with transfers will be at once entered in the ledger from the abstract on Army Form H 1150, or from a certificate voucher if no Army Form H 1150 is received.

28. The copy of the declaration of the court of enquiry referred to in paragraph 217 will accompany the account in which the deficient public clothing of a deserter is struck off charge.

29. Plain clothes provided by soldiers will not be brought on charge in the clothing ledger ; the allowance paid will be shown in the monthly indent (Army Forms H 1178 for mounted services, and H 1179 for dismounted services).

30. The entry in the ledger striking off charge empty packing cases or wrappers supplied to garrison needlework associations under paragraph 324 will be supported by the receipt of the honorary secretary of the association.

31. The authority of the general officer commanding, or of the medical officer, as the case may be, will be attached to the voucher striking off charge new issues (or supporting special credits) required to replace articles destroyed in consequence of exposure to infection (*see* paragraph 329).

32. A list of the articles taken on Imperial charge by units returning from India, in accordance with paragraph 353, will be attached as a voucher to the clothing ledger.

33. Before the ledger is closed, the balance of packages in each section will be transferred to Section III.

34. All surplus materials in possession of the serjeant tailor will be brought on charge as directed in paragraph 245.

35. The ledgers will (except for the regular establishment of the Special Reserve) be balanced, for comparison with the stock remaining in store, on the occasions mentioned in paragraph 305.

36. The ledger will be balanced by bringing the total issues in each section to the receipts side, and deducting them from the total receipts ; the "remain" will be the numbers for which the accountant is responsible. Immediately under this remain will be inserted the numbers in store as actually counted by the stock-taking board of survey and recorded in its report. The difference between the remain and the actual stock will be shown as "surplus" or "deficient" as the case may be.

37. The numbers in store as certified by the stocktaking board will be carried forward to the next year's account. As regards public clothing in wear, the numbers carried forward will be those shown in the statement referred to in paragraph 43 of the Appendix.

38. The clothing ledger (Army Book 284 or 285) will (except for the regular establishment of the Special Reserve) be closed on the 30th September in each year, or, in the case of the regular establishment of the Special Reserve, on the same date as that of the Special Reserve unit, and will be forwarded for audit as directed in paragraph 307. After being audited, it will be returned to the unit for retention, but the report of the stocktaking board and the vouchers will be retained by the local auditor (or by the Assistant Financial Secretary).

39. Any amendment of the opening balance of the new ledger rendered necessary by the audit of the old one will be carried out by means of certificate vouchers, and not by alteration of the original figures.

A.O. 83
1910
40. Officers receiving worn greatcoats for the use of recruits will account for them in Section III of Army Book 284 (or 285). The separate account of these articles formerly rendered on Army Form H 1163 will be discontinued.

41. All vouchers and bills for articles received or purchased, and all vouchers for articles struck off charge (except when the original has been sent to the paymaster), will be forwarded with the clothing ledger.

42. The reports of the stocktaking boards (or certificates in lieu) referred to in paragraph 300 will also accompany the clothing ledger when forwarded for audit.

43. A statement showing the public clothing in wear will be attached to the report of the stocktaking board, with a certificate that the numbers shown are (in the case of units of more than one company) a correct total of the balances in possession of each company as shown in Army Book 340, or that (in units of one company only) they have been verified by comparison with the numbers actually in wear. A further statement showing the remain of Section VII (see paragraph 11) will also be attached to the report of the stocktaking board.

44. In units having quartermasters, a ledger will be kept (Army Book 340) in which will be recorded the public clothing in possession of companies or detachments.

45. This book is the quartermaster's record of articles issued to and received from companies. One folio showing receipts on the left side and issues on the right side will probably be sufficient to record all transactions for twelve months for one company.

46. The receipt side will start with the total number of each article in possession of the company.

47. The postings on the receipt side will be made—

(*a*) From the company indent on Army Form H 1152.

(*b*) From an abstract of the transfer clothing statements received with transfers from other units (Army Form H 1150), or from a certificate receipt voucher if no Army Form H 1150 is received.

48. The postings on the issue side will be made—

(*a*) From the company delivery voucher for articles returned to store (Army Form H 1150).

(*b*) From an abstract of the transfer clothing statements sent with transfers to other units (Army Form H 1150).

(*c*) From Army Forms B 115 and P 1954 for losses, &c.

49. The ledger will be balanced on the same date and in the same manner as the general ledger. The remain in possession of each company should be carried to a recapitulation, and the total numbers of each article should be compared with the remain shown in Section III of the general ledger, with which they should correspond.

50. Army Form B 292 or 293, showing the public clothing in possession of squadrons, companies, or detachments, will be rendered monthly to the officer commanding the unit, who will compare the numbers shown in the returns with those in Army Book 340.

51. Officers will take care that the ledgers and vouchers are not ticked or altered with coloured pencil or coloured ink, that no correspondence is carried on upon them, and that no erasures are made. No entries in black lead pencil will be shown either in the ledgers or on the vouchers. Any necessary corrections will be made in black ink, and will be duly initialed, in the case of vouchers by the person who signs the vouchers, and in the case of ledgers by the responsible accounting officer, but the original entries should remain legible.

APPENDIX · V.—INSTRUCTIONS FOR MEASUREMENT AND FITTING.

[Referred to in paragraphs 247 and 249.]

1. The breast, waist, and breech measurements will be taken by measuring tapes under the tunic, frock or jacket, and over any underclothing. The exact measurements will be inserted in the measurement roll, as the proper extra allowance is made by the clothier. The size number of the garment required will be inserted opposite the man's name in the column prepared for that purpose in the company measurement roll.

2. The size roll, to accompany the indents for clothing will be prepared from the company measurement roll. Due allowance will be made for any surplus garments of corresponding sizes in the regimental store.

3. The soldier's height will always be given. The height will be taken (if possible) under a regulation standard, and the soldier will wear the regulation pattern boots.

4. Clothing in material is supplied for men of unusual dimensions who cannot be fitted from the ordinary sizes of made up garments; the measurements will be taken by a serjeant tailor where possible, and inserted with the name of the serjeant tailor on Army Form H 1119, any peculiarity in shape or build being carefully stated. Made up clothing will not be supplied for men of unusual dimensions, unless the unit has no serjeant tailor, or other special circumstances exist, to be explained when forwarding the indent.

5. Frocks and jackets of all descriptions will be fitted loosely over a cardigan waistcoat so as to admit of extra clothing being worn underneath in cold weather, and to allow for possible shrinkage of material. In fitting recruits and men returning from abroad, full allowance for future development should be made. Khaki drill clothing should be fitted very loosely on account of shrinkage in washing. The skirts of service dress jackets issued for wear with the kilt may be cut away in front regimentally.

6. In the case of first issues to recruits at depôts, the following garments will be fitted loosely (the cardigan waistcoat being worn under the tunic) :—

Dress jackets...	R.H.A.
Tunics and cloth or tweed trousers	Cavalry of the Line, R.F.A. and R.G.A.
Serge frocks	Cavalry of the Line.
Tunics	Infantry.

A.O. 112 / 1911

A second fitting will be carried out on the men joining a service unit or on completion of six months' service at the depôt. One-third of the rate will be allowed for the first fitting, and this portion only will be charged on Army Form H 1179 by the officer commanding the depôt. Two-thirds of the rate will be allowed for the second fitting, the charge for the latter being made on Army Form P 1918 by the commanding officer under whom the man is serving at the time.

The service dress clothing of recruits of R.H.A., R.F.A. and

R.G.A. will be fitted loosely at depôts, and the final fitting will be carried out on their joining a service unit. One-half of the fitting rate will be charged at the depôt, and the remaining half at the service unit.

7. All pantaloons when fitted, will be tight below the knee easy over the knee-cap, and loose round the thigh.

8. Each man requiring clothing will be paraded at the quarter-master's store, and in the presence of the officer commanding the company, the serjeant tailor will select the garments of sizes to correspond with the man's measurement, and fit them on the soldier.

9. The officer commanding the company will then parade the men, for the inspection of the commanding officer, who will see that the boots and clothing have been properly fitted; if any garments require altering he will cause such alterations as he may deem advisable to be recorded on an alteration sheet, which will be carefully preserved.

10. The captain will ascertain that the alterations noted in the " alteration sheet " have been completed, and will afterwards parade his men for the final approval of the commanding officer.

11. In the Royal Artillery the officer commanding a battery or company will not, unless required to do so, parade the men for the inspection of the officer commanding the Royal Artillery district or command until the alterations have been completed.

12. Cloaks and greatcoats will be carefully fitted; for trained soldiers, if the proper size for the man's height is supplied, the bottom of the garment from the ground, measured behind, will be about 9 inches for mounted and 12 inches for dismounted men. Recruits and growing lads will be fitted with cloaks of the next higher group of sizes, *i.e.*, men whose heights are 5 feet 5 inches or 5 feet 6 inches will receive garments sized for men 5 feet 7 inches and 5 feet 8 inches, to allow for subsequent growth in height and bulk.

13. Specifications showing the scales of fitting proportions for garments will be supplied on application to the chief ordnance officer, Royal Army Clothing Department.

14. The proper fitting of boots, on which the marching of an army depends, is a matter of the first importance. Company officers who superintend the fitting of boots will see that they are fully long enough, special care being taken that boys and growing lads are not allowed to wear boots of too small a size. As there is often a slight difference in boots of the same size number, great care is required in the fitting. The following instructions will be observed :—

2½ to 3 sizes will be allowed in length over the length shown on size stick, when sitting down, for the reasons (*a*), (*b*), and (*c*) below.

1½ to 2 sizes will be allowed in length over the measurements shown on a draft of the foot, taken standing, for the reasons (*b*) and (*c*).

(*a*) The foot expands and lengthens under pressure.

(*b*) Sufficient allowance must be made to allow of the proper motions of bones and muscles, expansion and contraction, otherwise the toes are thrust out of line or "stubbed," this being the most prolific cause of malform.

A.C.D.
Clo. Reg.
1090

A.C.D
Est.
7409

tion and bunions. In addition, if arteries and veins are compressed, swollen feet result, through faulty circulation.

(c) The contours or edges of the toe and seat of the bottom of the last are quite square, whereas the foot is rounded, and allowance must, therefore, be made.

15. Knee boots will be fitted so as to come to the top of the calf at the back of the leg, the top of the leg of the boot being about 3 inches below the point of the knee (centre of knee-cap). The size of the calf will regulate the size of the leg of the boot, care being taken to conform to the pattern, and to allow plenty of room at the instep and heel, to admit of their being easily drawn on or taken off when wet.

A.O. 83
—————
1910

16. Boots and highland shoes are supplied of five different fittings (Nos. 1, 2, 3, 4, and 5) for each size, in accordance with the scale of measurements. The sizes and fittings are marked on the insole and on the toe of the outsole. The correct size and fitting can be readily and accurately obtained by measurement and then by reference to the scale given on p. 159.

17. Canvas shoes will usually be required a size larger than boots.

18. The foot of every man will be measured on enlistment by a non-commissioned officer in the following manner :—Take the length (when man is sitting) with a size stick, and with a measuring tape the circumference of joints of toes (AB), the instep (CD), the heel and ankle (EF), and for knee boots the calf (GH), as shown in the diagram. These measurements, and the size of the boot required, will be passed with the recruit's documents to the service unit, where they will be recorded in a book specially kept for the purpose, and will be checked periodically. Where any difficulty is experienced in fitting from the ordinary stock sizes, a pencil outline of both feet, taken whilst standing on a piece of paper, together with the above measurements of each foot, will accompany the indent for the boots (*see* also paragraph 14 of the Appendix).

19. After the man is fitted, the toes of his boots should be raised by means of a last or piece of wood, and the whole of the upper well oiled with animal oil in order to make more room at this part. One pint of animal oil, for every hundred men, will be allowed for this purpose, in addition to that laid down in para. 7, Appendix VI, and will be obtained from the ordnance officer at the station as a free issue.

20. For taking the head measurement, a head-dress which fits the soldier should be measured, not the man's head, and the size number will be recorded.

21. A brass ring head measure will be supplied, on indent, to each unit at home and abroad.

22. Sealskin caps should be fitted half an inch larger than cork helmets.

A.C.D.
—————
Clo. Reg.
—————
1900

23. The sizes provided for all head-dresses are as follows :—

6, $6\frac{1}{8}$, $6\frac{1}{4}$, $6\frac{3}{8}$, $6\frac{1}{2}$, $6\frac{5}{8}$, $6\frac{3}{4}$, $6\frac{7}{8}$,   7, $7\frac{1}{8}$, $7\frac{1}{4}$, $7\frac{3}{8}$, $7\frac{1}{2}$, $7\frac{5}{8}$, $7\frac{3}{4}$,

$18\frac{7}{8}$, $19\frac{1}{4}$, $19\frac{5}{8}$,   20, $20\frac{1}{2}$, $20\frac{7}{8}$, $21\frac{1}{4}$, $21\frac{5}{8}$,   22, $22\frac{3}{8}$, $22\frac{3}{4}$, $23\frac{1}{4}$, $23\frac{5}{8}$,   24, $24\frac{3}{8}$.

The third and fourth rows of figures indicate the corresponding internal circumference of head-dress.

Scale of Sizes, Lengths and Fittings of Boots and Highland Shoes (*vide* para. 16).

A O. 83 / 1910

Foot lengths by size stick. Size.	Foot lengths by size stick. Inches.	Size of boot or shoe required.	Fitting.	Joint.	Instep.	Heel of last.	Knee Boots. Mounted Services. Calf.	Knee Boots. Mounted Services. Height of leg from the seat.
2 $2\frac{1}{2}$	9 $9\frac{1}{6}$	5	1 2 3 4 5	8 $8\frac{1}{4}$ $8\frac{1}{2}$ $8\frac{3}{4}$ 9	$8\frac{3}{4}$ $8\frac{15}{16}$ $9\frac{1}{8}$ $9\frac{5}{16}$ $9\frac{1}{2}$	13	$13\frac{3}{4}$ 14 $14\frac{1}{4}$ $14\frac{1}{2}$ $14\frac{3}{4}$	$16\frac{3}{4}$
3 $3\frac{1}{2}$	$9\frac{1}{3}$ $9\frac{1}{2}$	6	1 2 3 4 5	$8\frac{1}{4}$ $8\frac{1}{2}$ $8\frac{3}{4}$ 9 $9\frac{1}{4}$	9 $9\frac{3}{16}$ $9\frac{3}{8}$ $9\frac{9}{16}$ $9\frac{3}{4}$	$13\frac{1}{3}$	14 $14\frac{1}{4}$ $14\frac{1}{2}$ $14\frac{3}{4}$ 15	17
4 $4\frac{1}{2}$	$9\frac{2}{3}$ $9\frac{5}{6}$	7	1 2 3 4 5	$8\frac{1}{2}$ $8\frac{3}{4}$ 9 $9\frac{1}{4}$ $9\frac{1}{2}$	$9\frac{1}{4}$ $9\frac{7}{16}$ $9\frac{5}{8}$ $9\frac{13}{16}$ 10	$13\frac{2}{3}$	$14\frac{1}{4}$ $14\frac{1}{2}$ $14\frac{3}{4}$ 15 $15\frac{1}{4}$	$17\frac{1}{4}$
5 $5\frac{1}{2}$	10 $10\frac{1}{6}$	8	1 2 3 4 5	$8\frac{3}{4}$ 9 $9\frac{1}{4}$ $9\frac{1}{2}$ $9\frac{3}{4}$	$9\frac{1}{2}$ $9\frac{11}{16}$ $9\frac{7}{8}$ $10\frac{1}{16}$ $10\frac{1}{4}$	14	$14\frac{1}{2}$ $14\frac{3}{4}$ 15 $15\frac{1}{4}$ $15\frac{1}{2}$	$17\frac{1}{2}$
6 $6\frac{1}{2}$	$10\frac{1}{3}$ $10\frac{1}{2}$	9	1 2 3 4 5	9 $9\frac{1}{4}$ $9\frac{1}{2}$ $9\frac{3}{4}$ 10	$9\frac{3}{4}$ $9\frac{15}{16}$ $10\frac{1}{8}$ $10\frac{5}{16}$ $10\frac{1}{2}$	$14\frac{1}{3}$	$14\frac{3}{4}$ 15 $15\frac{1}{4}$ $15\frac{1}{2}$ $15\frac{3}{4}$	$17\frac{3}{4}$
7 $7\frac{1}{2}$	$10\frac{2}{3}$ $10\frac{5}{6}$	10	1 2 3 4 5	$9\frac{1}{4}$ $9\frac{1}{2}$ $9\frac{3}{4}$ 10 $10\frac{1}{4}$	10 $10\frac{3}{16}$ $10\frac{3}{8}$ $10\frac{9}{16}$ $10\frac{3}{4}$	$14\frac{2}{3}$	15 $15\frac{1}{4}$ $15\frac{1}{2}$ $15\frac{3}{4}$ 16	18
8 $8\frac{1}{2}$	11 $11\frac{1}{6}$	11	1 2 3 4 5	$9\frac{1}{2}$ $9\frac{3}{4}$ 10 $10\frac{1}{4}$ $10\frac{1}{2}$	$10\frac{1}{4}$ $10\frac{7}{16}$ $10\frac{5}{8}$ $10\frac{13}{16}$ 11	15	$15\frac{1}{4}$ $15\frac{1}{2}$ $15\frac{3}{4}$ 16 $16\frac{1}{4}$	$18\frac{1}{4}$
9 $9\frac{1}{2}$	$11\frac{1}{3}$ $11\frac{1}{2}$	12	1 2 3 4 5	$9\frac{3}{4}$ 10 $10\frac{1}{4}$ $10\frac{1}{2}$ $10\frac{3}{4}$	$10\frac{1}{2}$ $10\frac{11}{16}$ $10\frac{7}{8}$ $11\frac{1}{16}$ $11\frac{1}{4}$	$15\frac{1}{3}$	$15\frac{1}{2}$ $15\frac{3}{4}$ 16 $16\frac{1}{4}$ $16\frac{1}{2}$	$18\frac{1}{2}$

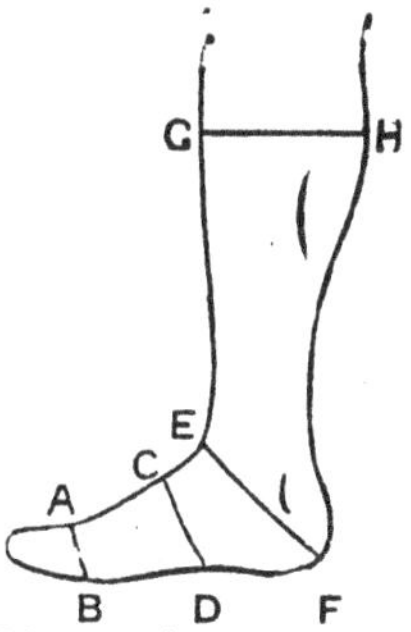

Diagram (*see* para. 18).

N.B.—The joint and instep measurements of the foot should be the same as those given above, but the heel of the foot should measure from $\frac{3}{4}$ to 1 inch less than the measurements shown for heel of last.

The heel measurement from one fitting to another is always an approximation: therefore the 3 fitting only is given with a gradation from one size to another of $\frac{1}{3}$ of an inch. As a fair average guide a $\frac{1}{3}$ of an inch allowance should be made in the heel measurement from one fitting to the next.

Wellington and knee boots.—Mounted men develop their insteps beyond the normal, and there should, therefore, be an extra $\frac{1}{4}$ inch allowance made for Wellington and knee boots in the girth of instep over and above that given in the scale. The boots themselves are made from lasts which meet this requirement, and which are altogether different from the lasts used in the making of ankle boots and highland shoes. This point must always be considered, as the foot is wholly enclosed in boots of the Wellington and knee boot type, whereas in the case of ankle boots and highland shoes, a slight variation in the instep is accommodated by these types of footwear being open-fronted or laced ones. A.C.D. / Clo. Regs.

When pencilled drafts are taken, two sizes in length will be sufficient to allow over length of draft, *e.g.*, a foot draft length of 10 inches (*i.e.*, size 5 will only require a size 7 boot, and so on.

APPENDIX VI.

[Referred to in Section XVII.]

CARE AND PRESERVATION OF CLOTHING, &c.

I. Care and preservation of clothing and necessaries, and of gold garniture.
II. Cleaning and removing stains from clothing.
III. Treatment of clothing infested with vermin.
IV. Washing flannel shirts, socks and woollen goods.

I.—Care and preservation of clothing and necessaries, and of gold garniture.

1. Surplus clothing and necessaries remaining in store will be carefully preserved from injury by moth, damp, or any other cause.

A O. 83 1910

2. Naphthaline will be placed among articles liable to be moth-eaten, kept loose in store or in other than the original packages. Russia leather parings, carbolized paper or turpentine sprinkled on brown paper, or on the garments, are also good for reducing the risk of moth. None of the ingredients named can, however, be relied upon as certain preventives, and the principal safeguard is for the articles kept loose in store or in other than the original packages to be frequently moved, brushed and exposed to the open air.

3. Naphthaline will be used for the preservation of clothing in departmental storehouses.

4. Gold lace, braid, cord or buttons, on garments or loose in store, will be carefully covered with gold tissue paper, and then wrapped in brown paper parcels, and placed in the clothing chest, or any air-tight chest available until they are required for issue. Care must be taken to use paper that is thoroughly dry, and to place the chest in a dry place. For the prevention of moth, the garments will be well brushed before being packed.

5. Gold trimmings and garniture that have become slightly tarnished will be cleaned locally with a mixture* of cream of tartar and dry bread rubbed up very fine, applied in a dry state, and brushed lightly with a clean, soft brass brush. The rule in paragraph 20 will also apply in this case. Brushes found to contain moths should be thoroughly cleaned and the boxes in which they are packed, sprinkled with turpentine.

6. Special care should be taken in the storage of oilskin clothing and indiarubber leggings. Each article should be invariably kept hung up in as cool and dry a place as possible and in a current of

---

* One teaspoonful of cream of tartar to one pint of bread-crumbs. The bread must be one or two days old, and must be well mixed with the cream of tartar.

air, where this can be arranged. They will be stored apart and will on no account be folded or piled one on the other. Indiarubber garments, will, as far as possible, be kept in store-room at an even temperature of 60 degrees F.

    7. Boots or shoes, surplus in store, will either be well dubbed, or have a coat of animal oil rubbed into the uppers at least once a year at home stations, and abroad as often as the general officer commanding, on the representation of the commanding officer, may certify to be necessary. Knee boots returned to store for further wear will be at once thoroughly cleaned and dubbed. One pint of animal oil, or one pound and a half of dubbing, will be allowed for every 100 pairs of boots or shoes (4 lbs. of dubbing will be allowed for every 100 pairs of sandals and 2 lbs. for 200 straps for sandals), and will be obtained from the ordnance officer at the station as a free issue. Dubbing for boots in wear will be supplied on payment by the Army Ordnance Department.

    8. The ordinary blacking of standard quality will be used to blacken boots supplied with the uppers unblacked as other ingredients harden and injure the leather.

    Welted boots should not under any circumstances be completely hobnailed as it would destroy the boots, but a few hobnails may be inserted in the parts most liable to wear.

    Ankle boots and highland shoes in wear will be kept soft with grease. They will be blacked only for full-dress parades and for walking out.

    9. A return will be furnished by officers commanding units to the chief ordnance officer in the district on the 31st March each year, and oftener if necessary, of any articles of clothing in store which are not likely to be wanted for issue within 12 months and cannot be transferred to other units at the stations, stating their sizes, when and under what circumstances they were indented for, and whether they are fit for issue as new. Instructions will then be given for their disposal.

    10. Surplus articles will not be returned to public stores without authority having been previously obtained. All clothing returned must, unless otherwise authorized, be of store sizes, not improperly altered, free from moth, and in a thoroughly serviceable condition and fit for re-issue.

A.O 75
1911

A.O. 112
1911

A.O. 49
1912

II.—*Cleaning and removing stains from clothing.*

Scarlet Clothing.

    11. Button or hook stains. Rub dry pipeclay over the stained part and brush with a clean hard brush, or as in (*a*), paragraph 12

    12. Oil and grease stains. (*a*) Rub the stain with a small piece of scarlet cloth soaked with methylated spirit or methylated ether ; or (*b*) powder dry pipeclay over the part, cover with clean blotting paper and press a hot iron upon the paper. Repeat until the stain is removed.

    (C.R. 10544)   L

13. Stains from perspiration or dirt. (a) Kersey and cloth frocks and tunics. A solution of salts of sorrel ($\frac{1}{4}$ oz. to 1 pint boiling water) should be applied all over the garment with a clean hard brush. Finish off by sponging well with cold water. (b) Scarlet serge frocks may be washed in lukewarm water in which some good yellow soap and a little oxalic acid ($\frac{1}{4}$ oz. per gallon) have been dissolved. Rinse off well in cold water.

14. Neither salts of sorrel nor oxalic acid should be applied to *parts of new scarlet garments.*

Blue Clothing.

15. Oil or grease stains may be removed with a mixture (in equal parts) of methylated spirit and turpentine, or with benzole.

16. For cleaning blue clothing, a weak solution of ammonia may be used, and well rubbed in with a hard brush after the garments have been well beaten and brushed. The solution must not be allowed to touch scarlet stripes or trimmings.

Drab Clothing.

A.C.D.
Clo. Regs.
1074

17. A solution of soap in hot water will be applied lightly with a brush, or a pad of drab material, and the garments then well-rinsed in clean tepid water to remove the soap, neither soda nor ammonia will be employed, and the soap used should be of best yellow quality. The cleaning with the soap solution should be carried out on a table covered with double thickness of drab material; this should be frequently washed. The clothing, when dry or nearly so, will, when considered necessary, be carefully pressed.

Service Dress Caps.

A.C.D.
Hants S.R.
42

18. Caps will be cleaned with methylated spirit carefully and lightly applied with a brush.

Moleskin Strappings of Pantaloons.

19. The moleskin strappings of pantaloons should not be cleaned with soda or ammonia. Benzole or turpentine should be used for this purpose.

General Instructions.

20. Before being subjected to any of the foregoing processes, the garments should be well beaten and brushed, and should be carefully stretched whilst under treatment to prevent shrinking.

21. Care must be taken not to use ether or benzole in the presence of any light or fire. The vapour of ether should not be inhaled.

22. If the weather permit, the cleaned garments will be dried in the open air, if not they will be hung up in a dry place, but not near fires or stoves.

23. No expense for the provision of the ingredients nor for workmanship will be allowed, except for new garments found to be stained on receipt, when the cost will be charged against the public.

III.—*Treatment of clothing infested with vermin.* ·

24. Clothing infested with vermin will be treated as follows:—

(a) The infested clothing will be hung up in a small room in such a manner that the fumes of burning sulphur will have access to all portions of the garments.

(b) About half a pound of flour of sulphur will then be put into an earthenware saucer and ignited.

(c) All doors, windows and other openings in the room will be closed before commencing the fumigation of the garments.

(d) After from three to four hours the doors and windows will be opened and free ventilation established.

(e) The clothing will subsequently be well aired and shaken.

25. Materials for the purpose will be obtained from the officer in charge of barracks.

IV.—*Washing flannel shirts, worsted socks and woollen goods.*

26. The water in which the articles are washed should be lukewarm only; they should on no account be put into boiling or even very hot water, as it tends to shrink the material. The articles must be well rinsed in clean tepid water before drying. Yellow soap only should be used, and the use of washing powder is prohibited. A little ammonia (one tablespoonful to two gallons of water) may be added to remove grease and perspiration.

27. After the water has been completely wrung out of them, the articles will be well pulled out by hand before drying.

APPENDIX VII. — DESIGNATION WORN ON THE SHOULDER STRAPS, AND COLOUR OF THE SHOULDER CORDS WORN ON THE TUNICS, JACKETS, AND FROCKS OF THE VARIOUS SERVICES.

CAVALRY.

Corps.	Tunics.		Serge Frocks, Service Dress Jackets, Khaki Drill Frocks, and Drab Greatcoats.	Remarks.
	Numerals and Initials on Shoulder Straps.	Colour of Shoulder Cords.	Numerals and Initials on Shoulder Straps.	
Household Cavalry—				Plain shoulder strap on jacket, undress.
1st Life Guards	...	...	1 L.G.	
2nd Life Guards	...	...	2 L.G.	
Royal Horse Guards ...	...	...	R.H.G.	
Dragoon Guards and Dragoons—				
1st Dn. Gds.	1 D.G.	...	1 D.G.	
2nd Dn. Gds.	2 D.G.	...	2 D.G.	
3rd Dn. Gds.	3 D.G.	...	3 D.G.	
4th Dn. Gds.	4 D G.	...	4 D.G.	
5th Dn. Gds.	5 D.G.	...	5 D.G.	
6th Dn. Gds.	Not worn	Yellow	6 D.G.	
7th Dn. Gds.	7 D.G.	...	7 D.G.	
1st Dragoons	1 R.D.	...	1 R.D.	
2nd Dragoons	2 D.	...	2 D.	
6th Dragoons	6 D.	...	6 D.	
Hussars—				
3rd Hussars	...	...	3 H.	
4th Hussars	...	...	4 H.	
7th Hussars	...	...	7 H.	
8th Hussars	...	...	8 H.	
10th Hussars	...	...	10 H.	
11th Hussars	...	...	11 H.	
13th Hussars	...	...	13 H.	
14th Hussars	...	...	14 H.	
15th Hussars	...	...	15 H.	
18th Hussars	...	...	18 H.	
19th Hussars	...	...	19 H.	
20th Hussars	...	...	20 H.	
Lancers—				
5th Lancers	...		5 L.	
9th Lancers	...		9 L.	
12th Lancers	...	Yellow	12 L.	
16th Lancers	...		16 L.	
17th Lancers	...		17 L.	
21st Lancers ...	embroidered strap.	...	21 L.	

ROYAL ARTILLERY AND ROYAL ENGINEERS.

Corps.	Tunics. Colour of Shoulder Cords.	Serge Frocks. Initials on Shoulder Straps. Colour of Shoulder Cords.	Service Dress Jackets, Khaki Drill Frocks, and Drab Great-coats. Initials on Shoulder Straps.	Remarks.
Royal Artillery—				
Horse batteries ...	...	...	Initials R.H.A. ...	Yellow shoulder cords on dress jackets.
Field batteries ...	Yellow	Yellow shoulder cords ...	Initials R.F.A. ...	
Garrison companies ...	Yellow	Yellow shoulder cords ...	Initials R.G.A. ...	
Clerks' Section ...	Yellow	Yellow shoulder cords ...	Initials R.A. ...	Initials R.A. on blue tartan frock.
Schools of Gunnery ...	Yellow	...	Initials S. of G.	
Local forces—				
Royal Malta Artillery ...	...	Maltese cross ...	Initials * ...	* Maltese cross on khaki drill frocks, initials R.M.A. on drab great-coats.
Hong Kong — Singapore Battalion, R.G.A. ...	...	Yellow shoulder cords ...	Initials H.K.S.-R.G.A. ...	
Sierra Leone Company, R.G.A. ...	...	Initials S.L.R.A. ...	Initials S.L.R.A ...	
Royal Engineers ...	Yellow	Yellow shoulder cords ...	Initials: R.E. ...	

FOOT GUARDS, INFANTRY, &c.

Regiment.	Tunic and Full Dress Frocks. — Designation (or Device) on Shoulder Strap.	Jackets, white. — Colour of Shoulder Cords.	Service Dress Jackets, Khaki Drill Frocks, and Drab Great-coats. — Title, &c. on Shoulder Strap.	Remarks.
Foot Guards—				
Grenadier Guards ...	Grenade	White	Initials G.G. and Grenade	No title on blue-grey great-coats.
Coldstream Guards ...	Rose		,, C.G. and Rose ...	
Scots Guards ...	Star		,, S.G. and Thistle ...	
Irish Guards ...	Star		,, I.G. and Star ...	
Infantry of the Line—				
Argyll and Sutherland Highlanders	A. & S. H.	White	A. & S. H.	
Bedfordshire Regt. ...	Bedford	...	Bedford.	
Berkshire Regt., Royal	Royal Berks	...	Royal Berks.	
Border Regt. ...	Border	White	Border.	
Cameron Highlanders	Cameron	...	Cameron.	
Cheshire Regt. ...	Cheshire	...	Cheshire.	
Connaught Rangers ...	Conn. Rangers	...	Conn. Rangers.	
Devonshire Regt. ...	Devon ...	...	Devon.	
Dorsetshire Regt. ...	Dorset ...	...	Dorset.	
Dublin Fusiliers, Royal	R.D.F. and Grenade	...	R.D.F. and Grenade.	
Duke of Cornwall's Light Infantry	Cornwall and Bugle	...	Cornwall and Bugle.	
Durham Light Infantry	Durham and Bugle	...	Durham and Bugle.	
Essex Regt. ...	Essex ...	...	Essex.	
Gloucestershire Regt.	Gloster ...	White	Gloster.	
Gordon Highlanders	Gordon ...	...	Gordon.	
Hampshire Regt. ...	Hants ...	...	Hants.	

Highland Light Infantry	...	H.L.I. and Bugle.
Inniskilling Fusiliers, Royal	...	R. Inniskilling and Grenade.
Irish Fusiliers, Royal	White	R.I.F. and Grenade.
Irish Regiment, Royal	...	Royal Irish.
Irish Rifles, Royal	...	R.I.R.
Kent Regt., East	...	Buffs.
Kent Regt., Royal West	...	R.W. Kent.
King's Own Scottish Borderers	...	K.O.S.B.
King's Royal Rifle Corps	...	K.R.R.
Lancashire Fusiliers	...	L.F. and Grenade.
Lancashire Regt., East	...	E. Lancashire.
Lancashire Regt., Loyal North	...	N. Lancashire.
Lancashire Regt., South	...	S. Lancashire.
Lancaster Regt., Royal	...	King's Own.
Leicestershire Regt.	...	Leicester.
Leinster Regt.	...	Leinster, R.C.
Lincolnshire Regt.	...	Lincoln.
Liverpool Regt.	...	King's.
Manchester Regt.	...	Manchester.
Middlesex Regt.	...	Middlesex.
Munster Fusiliers, Royal	...	R.M.F. and Grenade
Norfolk Regt.	...	Norfolk.
Northamptonshire Regt.	...	Northampton.
Northumberland Fusiliers	...	N.F. and Grenade.
Nottinghamshire and Derbyshire Regt.	...	Notts and Derby.
Oxfordshire and Buckinghamshire Light Infantry	...	Oxf. & Bucks with Bugle.
Rifle Brigade	...	R.B.
Royal Fusiliers	White	R.F. and Grenade.
Royal Highlanders	...	R.H.
Scots, Royal	...	Royal Scots.
Scots Fusiliers, Royal	...	R.S.F. and Grenade.
Scottish Rifles	...	S.R.

FOOT GUARDS, INFANTRY, &c.—*continued.*

Regiment.	Tunic and Full Dress Frocks. Designation (or Device) on Shoulder Strap.	Jackets, white. Colour of Shoulder Cords.	Service Dress Jackets, Khaki Drill Frocks, and Drab Great-coats. Title, &c., on Shoulder Strap.	Remarks.
Infantry of the Line—*continued.*				
Seaforth Highlanders ...	Seaforth	White	Seaforth.	
Shropshire Light Infantry ...	Shropshire and Bugle	...	Shropshire and Bugle.	
Somersetshire Light Infantry	Somerset and Bugle	...	Somerset and Bugle.	
Staffordshire Regt., North ...	N. Stafford	...	N. Stafford.	
Staffordshire Regt., South ...	S. Stafford	...	S. Stafford.	
Suffolk Regt.	Suffolk	...	Suffolk.	
Surrey Regt., East ...	E. Surrey	...	E. Surrey.	
Surrey Regt., Royal West ...	Queen's	...	Queen's.	
Sussex Regt., Royal ...	Royal Sussex	...	Royal Sussex.	
Wales Borderers, South ...	S.W.B. ...	...	S.W.B.	
Warwickshire Regt., Royal...	R. Warwickshire	...	R. Warwickshire.	
Welsh Fusiliers, Royal ...	R.W.F. and Grenade	...	R.W.F. and Grenade.	
Welsh Regt.	Welsh ...	...	Welsh.	
West Riding Regt. ...	Duke of Wellington's	...	Duke of Wellington's.	
Wiltshire Regt. ...	Wilts ...	...	Wilts.	
Worcestershire Regt. ...	Worcestershire	...	Worcestershire.	
York and Lancaster Regt. ...	Y. & L. ...	...	Y. & L.	
Yorkshire Light Infantry ...	Yorkshire and Bugle...	...	Yorkshire and Bugle.	
Yorkshire Regt. ...	York ...	...	York.	
Yorkshire Regiment, East ...	E. York ...	...	E. York.	
Yorkshire Regt., West ...	W. York	...	W. York.	

			Remarks
Army Service Corps	White shoulder cords	A.S.C.	
Royal Army Medical Corps	Cherry red shoulder cords	R.A.M.C.	
Royal Flying Corps	R.F.C.	Royal Flying Corps.‡	‡ Worn on the arm. $\frac{87}{687}$
Army Ordnance Corps	A.O.C.	A.O.C.	
Army Pay Corps	A.P.C.	A.P.C.	
Army Veterinary Corps	A.V.C.	A.V.C.	
Military Mounted Police	Yellow shoulder cords	M.M.P.†	† Also on blue tartan frocks.
Military Foot Police	" "	M.F.P.‡	
Military Provost Staff Corps	" "	Royal Cypher.	
School of Musketry	S. of M.	S. of M.	
School of Gymnastics	Royal Cypher	Royal Cypher.	
Garrison Staff	"	"	
Royal Military College	R.M.C. "	R.M.C.	
Royal Military Academy	R.M.A.	R.M.A.	
Schoolmasters	Shoulder knots or cords	Shoulder knots or cords.	Shoulder knots for Warrant Officers, cords for Schoolmasters, not Warrant Officers, are worn on frock coat, frock cloth, or serge and frock khaki drill. A.C.D.
Barrack Wardens	B.W.*	...	*On collar only. Clo.
Local forces—			
West India Regiment	...	West India Regiment.	Shoulder cord on Reg. blouses (natives). 1076.
West African Regiment	...	W.A.R. (Europeans only)	

APPENDIX VIII.

MODE OF MARKING.

[Referred to in Section XII.]

(a) Public Clothing.

Articles.	Marks to be put on each article.	Position of Marks.	Stamps to be used.	Materials to be used.
Boots, { jack		Inside top of leg	¼-inch stamps	
{ knee		On the inside "	½-inch stamps	Marking ink.
Busby		„ outside	„	
Bag, cotton for do.		„ head lining	„	
Cap, bearskin		„ outside	„	
Bag for do.		„ leather top, inside	„	
Cap, Lancers		„ inside	„	
Oilskin cover for do.	Regt. or Corps, No., and date of issue	Inside lining of body	„	
Cap, sealskin		On the outside	„	
Bag for do.		„ inside	„	
Chaco		„ outside	„	
Cover for ditto		Inside, on the skirt at the back	„	Paint.
Cloak*		„ on middle of back	„	
Belt for do.		Inside kilmarnock	„	
Cape for do.		On the inside	„	
Feather bonnet		Along the front	„	
Oilskin bonnet cover			„	
Oilskin hackle cover			„	
Cocked hat, master gunner's		On the head lining	„	
Greatcoat*		Inside, on middle of back	„	
Cape for do.		„ „	„	

Helmet, {metal, cloth}   Bag for helmet   Leggings   Purse and belt   Spurs, {jack, for jack boots}

Regt. or Corps., No., and date of issue

On the rim at the back	½-inch stamps	
" inside	⅛-inch stamps	
" outside		Paint.
Inside on the facings	½-inch stamps	
On pocket and strap	"	
Inside the bow	⅛-inch stamps†	

Winter Clothing.

Cap, fur   Coat, warm, British   Drawers   Mitts, leather, lined with lambskin   Vest

Regt. or Corps, No., and date of issue

On the inside	½-inch stamps	
Inside on middle of back	"	
On inside of band	"	
" front of the mitt on the wrist	"	
" skirt	"	Paint.

Clothing for Military Mechanist, Coxswains, &c.

Boots, knee   Hat, sou'-wester   Frock, oilskin   Jacket, pea   Trousers, oilskin

Corps, Number, and date of issue

Inside, top of leg	½-inch stamps	
" of back face	⅛-inch stamps	
" top of back lining	"	
" top of seat "	"	Paint.

* Cloaks, greatcoats, and capes may be marked with a stencil plate with letters of the same size as those on the stamp, provided that no expense is caused to the public for stencil plates or brushes.

† In units which have no ½ inch stamps, $\frac{7}{16}$-inch stamps may be used.

MODE OF MARKING—*continued.*

(b) Personal Clothing.

Articles.	Marks to be put on each article.	Position of Marks.	Stamps to be used.	Materials to be used.
Boots { ankle	Regt. or Corps, No., and date of issue	Inside, top of quarters...	¼-inch stamps	Marking ink.
Boots { Wellington		Outside, top of leg, behind	„	Marking ink.
Breeches		Inside the waistband	½-inch stamps	Paint.
Cap, forage		„ „ the crown	„	Marking ink.
Cover for do.		On the waistband	„	Paint.
Drawers		Inside the crown	„	Marking ink.
Fez		On one end	„	Marking ink.
Turban cloth		Inside on right front facing	„	Paint.
Frock		„ „ „	„	Marking ink.
Frock coat		Inside the collar	„	Paint.
Frock, khaki drill		On the inside	„	Marking ink.
Gaiters		„ web	„	Marking ink.
Girdle		„ inside	„	
Gloves		„ outside	„	Paint.
Helmet, drill		„ inside	„	
Bag for helmet		Inside on right front facing	„	
Cover for helmet		on plaits at back	„	
Jacket		„ the waistband	„	Marking ink.
Kilt		„ at top	„	Paint.
Pantaloons			„	
Plaid			„	
Scarf	Not marked ...	Not marked		

A.O. 307 / 1909

A.O. 49 / 1912

Article	Mark	Location	Size of stamp	Medium
Puttees	Regt. or Corps., No., and date of issue	On back in centre	½-inch stamps	Paint.
Pagri	(Regt. or Corps., No., and date of issue)	On one end	,,	Marking ink.
Sash	Not marked	Not marked	...	...
Shoes {leather	Regt. or Corps, No., and date of issue	Inside top of quarters	1-inch stamps	...
Shoes {canvas		,, sole at instep	1-inch stamps	Paint.
Stockings		Upper part of the leg	½-inch stamps	Marking ink.
Trews	Regt. or Corps, No., and date of issue,	Inside the waistband	,,	
Trousers		,,	,,	Paint.
Tunic		,,	,,	
Waistcoat {with sleeves / without sleeves}		Inside on right front facing	,,	

(c) Condemned public and personal clothing delivered to contractors or sold to dealers.

Article	Mark	Location	Size of stamp	Medium
All articles of cloth or similar material	Inverted broad arrows	On the inside of the article, as near the Government mark as possible	2-inch stamps (each broad-arrow 1-in. long)	Paint.
All articles of leather or other similar material	Inverted broad arrows		1-inch stamps	...

(d) Necessaries.

Article	Mark	Location	Size of stamp	Medium
Bags {clothes / kit / stable}	Regiment or Corps and Number	On the outside	½-inch stamps	{Marking ink. / Paint. / Marking ink.}
Blacking, tin of	Not marked	...	...	...

MODE OF MARKING—*continued*

(*d*) Necessaries—*continued*.

Articles.	Marks to be put on each article.	Position of Marks.	Stamps to be used.	Materials to be used
Braces	Regiment or Corps and Number	On the webbing...	½-inch stamps ...	Marking ink.
Brushes — blacking ...	Regiment or Corps and Number	On the edge	¼-inch stamps ...	...
Brushes — brass ...	Regiment or Corps and Number	" "	" ...	...
Brushes — cloth ...	Regiment or Corps and Number	" "	" ...	...
Brushes — hair	Regiment or Corps and Number	" "	" ...	...
Brushes — hard ...	Regiment or Corps and Number	" "	" ...	...
Brushes — lace ...	Regiment or Corps and Number	Along the handle	¼-inch branding irons	...
Brushes — tooth ...	Regiment or Corps and Number	" "	¼-inch branding irons	...
Brushes — polishing ...	Regiment or Corps and Number	On the edge	¼-inch stamps ...	...
Brushes — shaving ...	Regiment or Corps and Number	Round the side	Sharp pointed knife	Marking ink.
Button, brass	Regiment or Corps and Number	Along the side	¼-inch stamps ...	...
Cap comforter	Regiment or Corps and Number	On the end	½-inch stamps ...	Paint. A.C.D. / 39 / 426
Case, plume	Regiment or Corps and Number	Along the front	" ...	"
Comb	Regiment or Corps and Number	" side	¼-inch branding irons	...
Disc, identity	Number—name—regiment—religious denomination	... ...	⅛-inch stamps ...	...
Drawers, cotton ...	Regiment or Corps and Number	On the waistband	½-inch stamps ...	Marking ink.
Dressings, field ...	Not marked.			

Article		Where marked	Size	Medium
Fez		Inside the crown	$\frac{3}{8}$-inch stamps	Paint.
Fork		Along the handle	$\frac{3}{8}$-inch "	...
Frock		See clothing	...	...
Gaiters		On the inside	$\frac{1}{2}$-inch stamps	Paint.
Garters	Regiment or Corps and Number	As decided by the Commanding Officer	...	...
Gauntlets		On inside of sleeve part	$\frac{1}{2}$-inch stamps	Paint.
Gloves		On the inside	"	"
Holdall		" centre band	...	Marking ink.
Hose tops		As decided by the Commanding Officer	...	...
Housewife		On the inside	$\frac{1}{2}$-inch stamps	Paint.
Jersey		On the welt at bottom	$\frac{1}{4}$-inch branding irons	"
Knife {clasp		Along the handle	$\frac{1}{4}$-inch stamps	...
table		" "	$\frac{1}{4}$-inch branding irons	...
Razor		" "	$\frac{1}{2}$-inch stamps	Marking ink.
Shirt, flannel	Not marked	On tape below front opening	$\frac{1}{2}$-inch stamps	Marking ink.
Socks		On upper part of leg	"	Paint.
Sponge, pipeclay		Not marked	...	...
Spoon	Regiment or Corps and Number.	Along the handle	$\frac{1}{4}$-inch stamps	...
Spurs, swan-neck		Inside the bow	$\frac{1}{16}$-inch stamps	...
Stockings		On the upper part of leg	$\frac{1}{4}$-inch stamps	Paint.
Towel		On one corner	"	Marking ink.

TOOLS AND STAMPS FOR USE IN

[Referred to in

Articles.	Regiment of Cavalry and Cavalry Depôts.	Royal	
		Horse and Field Bat-teries, Depôts, and Riding Establishment.	
Anvils, 5-lb. 10-oz.	1	1	1
Brushes, sable, writing, duck, large	2	2	2
Hammers, riveting, 8-oz.	1	1	3
Irons, branding { $\frac{1}{4}$-inch { figures (0 to 8) .. .. sets	1	1	4
letters, 1-letter, regimental initial „	1	1	5
$\frac{3}{16}$-inch letters, 1-letter, terminal .. „	..	..	6
Stamps .. { copper, inlaid, $\frac{1}{2}$-inch, figures (0 to 8).. „	..	1	7
steel { $\frac{1}{4}$-inch { figures (0 to 8) .. „	1	1	8
letters, 1-letter, regimental initial .. .. sets	1	1	9
$\frac{3}{16}$-inch letters, 1-letter, terminal „	..	..	10
brass or wood 2-inch	1	1	11
steel $\frac{1}{4}$-inch	1	1	12
Typeholders	..	2	13
„ blocks	..	2	14
Typeholders, { $\frac{1}{4}$-inch letters, regimental, initial .. sets	..	1	15
type .. { $\frac{1}{4}$ „ „ „ terminal „	..	..	16

Commanding officers in making indents will be careful to indent for the proportions of large and small letters strictly in accordance with the regimental abbreviations. All initial letters should be of the larger size; the terminal, or others, of the smaller. Thus, the Highland Light Infantry would require the initials "H.L.I.," all of the larger size, while the Leicestershire Regiment would require the combination of large and small letters in the abbreviation "Leic." A set comprises one letter of each kind required.

IX.

MARKING CLOTHING; AND NECESSARIES.

paragraph 262.]

	Artillery.	Royal Engineers.							
	Garrison Companies, Depôts, and District Staffs.	Each Mounted Unit, except Field Telegraph Companies.	Each Dismounted Unit, and each Telegraph Company.	Battalion of Foot Guards or Infantry.	Mounted Company of Army Service Corps.	Dismounted Company of Army Service Corps and Company of Army Ordnance Corps.	Company or Detachment Royal Army Medical Corps, Military Provost Staff Corps, and Army Veterinary Corps.	Regimental District.	Each Corps of local troops abroad.
1	1	1	1	1	1	1	1	1	1
2	2	2	2	2	2	2	2	2	2
3	1	1	1	1	1	1	1	1	1
4	1	1	1	1	1	1	1	1	1
5	1	1	1	1	1	1	1	1	1
6	..	..	..	1	..	..	..	1	..
7	3	1	3	3	..	3	3	3	3
8	1	1	1	1	1	1	1	1	1
9	1	1	1	1	1	1	1	1	1
10	..	..	..	1	..	..	..	1	..
11	1	1	1	1	1	1	1	1	1
12	1	1	1	1	1	1	1	1	1
13	2	2	2	2	2	2	2	2	2
14	2	2	2	2	2	2	2	2	2
15	2	1	2	2	..	2	2	2	2
16	..	..	..	2	..	..	..	2	..

The sable writing brushes are for use in finishing off marks where necessary. The anvil and hammer are for use with the steel stamps.

When any of the above articles are supplied, under the Equipment Regulations, for marking equipment, they will be utilized for marking clothing and necessaries, and the numbers allowed under this Appendix reduced accordingly.

None of the tools or stamps will be accessible to unauthorized persons.

APPENDIX X.

[Referred to in paragraph 97.]

HOUSEHOLD CAVALRY.

Account of jack boots (or leather pantaloons).

Consecutive Number.	Date of Issue.	Regimental Numbers.	Trooper's Name.	Date repaired and amount expended.						Remarks.
1	19.6.88	200	Jones, John	10.89 2s. 6d.	10.90 5s.	...	...	...	...	
		230	Smith, Thomas	...	...	10.92 10s. 4.93 1s.	10.94 5s.	10.96 12s. 6d.	...	{ Condemned 1.10.98 replaced by No.
		300	Robinson, Henry	...	...	...	...	...	...	
2	19.10.89	150	Atkins, T.	10.90 1s.	10.92 2s. 6d. 3.93 1s.	10.93 5s.	10.95 10s.	...	...	
		180	Brown, W.	...	...	...	...	...	...	

APPENDIX XI.

INSTRUCTIONS FOR THE DISPOSAL OF WORN-OUT PUBLIC CLOTHING.

1. Worn-out public clothing, except at Sierra Leone, will be given over to the contractor under the following arrangements :—
(*a*) The articles will, if possible, be removed at the same time as the worn-out personal clothing.
(*b*) A list of the clothing, duly completed with the rates and amounts, will be prepared in triplicate on Army Form H 1172 ; one copy will be sent to the contractors and two to the command paymaster, who, after the money has been paid, will return one copy to the unit to support the write-off in the clothing account. The date on which the paymaster notifies to the unit that credit has been given for the value of the articles will be quoted on the voucher for marking the articles with the condemned stamp.
(*c*) On receipt from the command paymaster of Army Form H.1172 showing that payment has been made, the commanding officer will then arrange with the contractor for the removal of the articles. An officer of the unit (not the quartermaster) will be detailed to witness the delivery of the condemned clothing to the contractor.

2. Articles for which there is no contract will, at home stations, be disposed of as may be ordered by the chief ordnance officer, Royal Army Clothing Department ; at stations abroad, except Sierra Leone, the chief ordnance officer will make arrangements for their sale to the best advantage. The regulations to be observed in all cases of sales are laid down in paragraphs 6 to 20 of Appendix XVI. | *A.O. 112.*
 1911

3. At Sierra Leone all articles will be disposed of as directed in paragraph 89.

4. Bearskin caps, with fittings, will be returned to the Royal Army Clothing Department. Metal furniture, if unserviceable, of all other full dress head-dresses which are disposed of under the contract for worn-out clothing, and metal helmets and spurs will be returned annually to a clothing depôt, if convenient, otherwise to an ordnance depôt to be broken up for sale as old metal. | *A.O. 266.*
 1910.

5. Any worn-out public clothing except bearskin caps required for repairs will be retained and struck off charge on the certificate of the commanding officer when the garments have been expended in repairs, reference being given to the report of the Board of Survey by which the articles are condemned. | *A.O. 259.*
 1911.
Small pieces of old bearskin suitable for petty repairs of bear-skin caps will be supplied on indent, if available.

6. The entries in the clothing account will be supported by a copy of Army Form H 1172, and also by the receipt of the con-tractor, when the stores are sold, and by a certified explanatory

statement, when they are otherwise disposed of. A copy of the report of the board which condemned the stores will also be attached.

<u>A.O. 138</u>
1913

7. The contractors for the purchase of worn-out clothing are as follows:—

Great Britain and Ireland—
    (1) Coats, great, without capes
    (2) Coats, great, drab ....

Messrs. Coleman, Jonas & Son,
8, Springdale Road,
Green Lanes,
London, N.

    (1) Capes, all descriptions ....
    (2) Cloaks without capes ....

Messrs. Mallett, Porter & Dowd,
Ltd.,
465, Caledonian Road,
London, N.

All other clothing and miscellaneous articles detailed in Part III.-X. of Priced Vocabulary of Clothing and Necessaries

Mr. H. Marchinski,
114, Commercial Street,
London, E.

Gibraltar, Malta, Cyprus, Egypt, Ceylon, Bermuda and South Africa—
All clothing and miscellaneous articles detailed in Part III.- X. of Priced Vocabulary of Clothing and Necessaries

Messrs. Coleman, Jonas & Son,
8, Springdale Road,
Green Lanes,
London, N.

<u>A.C.D.</u>
<u>China</u>
132

North China—
Coats, great, drab

Messrs. Samuel Moses & Sons,
Ltd.,
65, Mansell Street,
London, E.

<u>A.O. 275</u>
1912

8. The worn-out public and personal clothing will, as a rule, be removed by the contractor at intervals not exceeding 3 months.

9. In the event of a unit being about to leave the station or other special circumstances, the contractor may be called upon to remove the articles at any time.

10. The worn-out rates for personal and public clothing will be published periodically, with the Priced Vocabulary of Clothing and Necessaries in Army Orders.

APPENDIX XII.

[Referred to in paragraph 103.]

STANDARDS AND COLOURS.

Standards and Guidons of Cavalry.

1. The standards of regiments of Dragoon Guards are to be of crimson silk damask embroidered and fringed with gold. The guidons of regiments of dragoons are to be of crimson silk damask. The tassels and cords are to be of crimson silk and gold mixed. The lance of the standard or guidon, including the Royal Crest which surmounts the lance, is to be eight feet six inches long.

2. The standard is to be two feet five and a half inches wide without the fringe, and two feet two inches on the lance : the corners to be square. The guidon is to be three feet five inches to the ends of the points of the swallow-tails, exclusive of the silk on the pole and of the fringe, and two feet three inches on the lance. The upper and lower corners to be rounded off at twelve inches from the end. The point of the slit to be two feet seven inches from the lance and equidistant from the upper and lower edges. The width of the slit at the points of the swallow-tail to be thirteen and a half inches.

3. The standard or guidon of each regiment is to be of a crimson colour, and will bear (unless otherwise authorized) the Royal or other title in letters of gold on a red ground in a circle, and the rank of the regiment in gold Roman characters on a crimson ground, in the centre,—the whole within a wreath of roses, thistles and shamrocks on the same stalk, ensigned with the imperial crown. The white horse, on a green mount on a crimson ground, will be in the first and fourth compartments, within a scroll : and the rose, thistle and shamrock conjoined, on a ground of the colour of the facings of the regiment, within a scroll, will be in the second and third corners. In the case of a regiment having a particular badge, such badge will be embroidered in the centre, and the rank of the regiment will be put in the second and third corners, within a wreath of roses, thistles and shamrocks.

4. The standard or guidon is also to bear the devices, distinctions and mottoes, as given in the Army List, which have been conferred by Royal authority ; the motto is to be under the wreath in the centre.

Colours of Infantry.

5. The Royal or first colour, hereinafter called the King's colour, of the regiments of Foot Guards is crimson. They severally bear the distinctions, as given in the Army List, conferred by Royal authority upon the respective battalions as well as those authorized for the second colours (company badges excepted).

6. The regimental or second colour, hereinafter called the regimental colour, of each battalion of the regiments of Foot Guards is the Great Union, and bears the badges and distinctions, as given in the Army List, granted to the regiment in commemoration of war services, and also one of the ancient badges conferred by Royal authority on each of the companies composing the respective battalions; the badges being borne in turn as the colours are renewed

7. The colours of infantry are to be of silk; the dimensions are to be three feet nine inches flying, and three feet deep on the pike, exclusive of the fringe, which is about two inches in depth :— the length of the pike, including the Royal Crest, is to be eight feet seven and a half inches; the cords and tassels are to be crimson and gold mixed.

8. The King's colour of every regiment (except as provided in paragraph 5) is to be the Great Union, the imperial colour of the United Kingdom of Great Britain and Ireland, in which the Cross of St. George is conjoined with the Crosses of St. Andrew and St. Patrick, on a blue field, as modified by Her late Majesty Queen Victoria, in 1900. The first colour is to bear in the centre the territorial designation on a crimson circle with the Royal, or other title, within the whole, surmounted by the imperial crown.

9. The regimental colour is to be of the colour of the facing of the regiment, except in those regiments which are faced with scarlet or white, in which the second colour is to be the Red Cross of St. George in a white field, with the territorial designation and the Royal or other title displayed as on the Royal, or First, colour within the Union-wreath of roses, thistles and shamrocks, and ensigned with the imperial crown.

10. The regimental colour is to bear the ancient badges, devices, distinctions and mottoes, as given in the Army List, which have been conferred by Royal authority. The number of each battalion is to be placed in the dexter canton; but in the case of regiments which are entitled to carry honorary distinctions on all the four corners of the colours, the number of the battalion is to be placed below the honorary distinction in the dexter canton. When regiments of infantry are not entitled to a Royal or ancient badge, and have not a combination of territorial and Royal or other special designations, the number of the battalion will be placed on the colours within the circle bearing the name of the regiment instead of in the dexter canton. In those regiments which bear any ancient badge, the badge is to be on a red ground in the centre. The territorial designation is, if practicable, to be inscribed on a circle, within the Union-wreath of roses, thistles and shamrocks, and the Royal or other title in an escroll underneath, the whole ensigned with the imperial crown.

11. In those regiments where the number of actions exceeds nine, laurel branches are to be introduced, and the scrolls bearing the names of the actions entwined thereon.

APPENDIX XIII.

(Referred to in para. 11.)

A.O. 35
——
1914

STORAGE AND TURNOVER OF CLOTHING AND NECES-SARIES HELD FOR RESERVISTS AND FOR MEN TO BE SPECIALLY ENLISTED ON MOBILIZATION.

1. Clothing and necessaries to the scale laid down in Table I., Clothing Regulations, Part III., will be stored for regular reservists at their place of rejoining, and will be in charge of officers commanding depôts, or, in certain cases, of other units.

Officers commanding who have mobilisation clothing on charge are responsible that it is correct in every respect and fit for issue.

REGULAR RESERVISTS.

SIZES AND QUANTITIES STORED.

2. The measurements of soldiers on transfer to the Army Reserve are shown in Army Form B 2056, and officers commanding will be responsible that garments, &c., of suitable sizes, and boots of correct magnitudes are provided for all reservists. Clothing and boots of abnormal sizes will not, however, be stored. (*See* also paragraphs 3 and 4.) On mobilization, if it is found that men cannot be fitted from stock sizes, idents and size-rolls will immediately be forwarded to the Royal Army Clothing Department for any garments required, and special size boots and highland shoes, when necessary, will be provided regimentally, at the rate published in the Priced Vocabulary of Clothing and Necessaries.

3. Infantry reservists will be re-measured on coming up for training, as provided for in Army Form D 430, and the measurements recorded on the detachable slip will be retained by the officer commanding the depôt, who will make any adjustments necessary in the articles stored.

4. For reservists of Cavalry, Royal Artillery, Army Service Corps and Royal Army Medical Corps, whose measurements are not periodically verified, and for Royal Engineers reservists rejoining at Aldershot and Chatham, a proportion of each group of sizes of the jackets, trousers and pantaloons stored will be of the larger dimensions of that group, instead of those recorded on Army Form B 2056, as the measurements of the men.

5. Subject to paragraph 8, clothing and kits will only be stored for the number of reservists on the books, and indents will

be made quarterly for any articles, required, owing to changes that have occurred during the quarter. In the event, however, of any abnormal increase in the number of reservists, intermediate indents may be put forward.

6. On the outside of each pigeon-hole a label (Army Form H 1117 or G 1091) in a tin frame will be attached, showing the name and regimental number of the man, and the articles and sizes stored for him.

7. A nominal roll of the reservists, showing their measurements, the sizes of the articles stored for them, and the number of the pigeon-hole allotted to each man, will be kept in Army Book 250.

METHOD OF STORAGE.

8. Greatcoats, jackets, trousers and pantaloons will be kept in bales in separate racks for each kind of garment, and in the case of depôts holding large stocks (units at Aldershot excepted) each bale will contain 10 garments of one size and description with the exception that sizes for men of 5 feet 11 inches and upwards, will, if convenient, be packed together in bales of ten.

9. The description, size and number of articles, also the date of packing, will be marked on the end of the bales, which will, as far as possible, be placed in the racks so that the marks are visible.

10. The remaining articles of the reservist's kit will be packed as follows in the pigeon-hole allotted to each man.

(a) In front of the accoutrements except mess tin.

Kit bag pressed flat placed crossways and containing the articles of clothing and necessaries (except those referred to in paragraph 8) and the service dress cap, boots, kilt (Royal Highlanders only), spurs and cutlery.

The service dress cap will be wrapped in brown paper and placed on top of the kit bag.

(b) In front of the pigeon-hole.

One pair of boots with laces on each side of the pigeon-hole well to the front so as to be clear of the kit-bag. The boots of each pair to be placed one inside the other without severing the string fastening them together ; the uppers not to be folded in.

(c) Between the two pairs of boots.

Clasp and table knife, fork, razor in case, spoon, and spurs, wrapped in waterproof paper ; mess tin.

11. Half a sheet of " paper, brown, double imperial cap, 168 lbs." and one yard of " thread, sealing " will be allowed for wrapping up each cap ; and a quarter of a yard of waterproof paper and half a

yard of "twine, baling, plain" for each set of cutlery. The brown paper and "thread, sealing" will be supplied on indent from the War Office and the waterproof paper and twine from the clothing depôt supplying the district. Waterproof paper must be used for the cutlery but any suitable paper and string received with stores, &c., may, when available, be substituted for the other materials.

12. The instructions in paragraphs 10 and 11 are a general guide. Provided that the system adopted is uniform for any one unit or depôt and that all the articles named are kept in the pigeon-holes, the details of the arrangement may be slightly varied at the discretion of commanding officers concerned. For special reservists and specially enlisted men see paragraph 32.

13. Kilts for reservists of highland regiments, except the Royal Highlanders, which will be made into a parcel and placed in the pigeon-hole, will be kept stored in the cases in which they are issued, and racks will not be required for them.

14. Chevrons, badges and titles, as under, will be stored in the kit-bag, and will be sewn or fixed on garments or caps under regimental arrangements immediately mobilization is ordered :—

Chevrons, 1 bar... ...	6 per man for 4 per cent. of cavalry and infantry reservists on the books. 6 per man for 6 per cent. of reservists of other services except Foot Guards.
Chevrons, 2 bar... ...	6 per man for 3 per cent. of reservists except Foot Guards, who will store 6 per man for 7 per cent., viz., 4 per cent. for lance-corporals and 3 per cent. for corporals.
Chevrons, 3 bar... ...	6 per man for $1\frac{1}{2}$ per cent. of reservists on the books.
Guns (R.A. only) ...	2 per man for $1\frac{1}{2}$ per cent. of reservists.
Grenades (R.E. only) ...	4 per man for $1\frac{1}{2}$ per cent. of reservists.
Crosses, Geneva... ...	6 for each R.A.M.C. reservist.
Cap badges	1 per man.
Titles, metals, sets ...	2 per man.

Badges and titles stored for reservists of cavalry regiments stationed abroad will be of the patterns of the affiliated home units.

Four of the six chevrons per man will be for jackets, and two for greatcoats.

15. As soon as a soldier is transferred to the Reserve, the articles detailed in paragraphs 10 and 14 will be assembled as follows :—

    (a.) From regimental stocks.
    (b.) By means of indent on the clothing depôt.

It is essential that the articles be (a) of recent manufacture and perfectly sound ; (b) of latest manufacture. A suspense account in manuscript will be kept of the numbers taken from regimental stocks, and at the end of the quarter the totals will be transferred in the clothing ledger from peace to mobilization charge.

16. The sizes of baled garments in mobilization stores not appropriated for other men will be checked to see whether they are suitable for newly transferred Army reservists. Garments due for turnover under paragraph 19 (a) are not suitable.

17. The articles stored in the pigeon holes will be taken out once a quarter, when the boots will be rubbed over to prevent mildew, the knives, forks, razors and spurs wiped with an oiled rag, the contents of the kit bag shaken out, and all the articles examined for signs of deterioration. If they are in good order they will be re-folded, &c., and put away again, naphthaline being renewed if necessary. The boots will be dubbed and the spur straps greased once a year. Any of the articles found at the quarterly examination to be motheaten, or otherwise damaged or deteriorated will be exchanged.

18. An annual allowance of 10 lb. of naphthaline, and 2 pints of animal oil (or 3 lbs. of dubbing) for every 100 reservists will be granted for the preservation of clothing, necessaries and boots. Supplies will be obtained from the Army Ordnance Department.

TURNOVER.

19. Turnover will be made as follows :—

(a) *Baled garments.*—When the bales are 5 years old, or, subject to paragraphs 22 and 25, whenever they are found to contain sizes no longer required.

(b.) *Kilts.*—May be retained 1 year longer than baled garments, and will be exchanged with supplies from the Royal Army Clothing Department under special arrangements.

(c.) *Other articles.*—

(i.) For men who have to serve over 6 years in the Reserve.	At the end of the fifth year in the Reserve and again on the termination of engagement.
(ii.) For other men	On the termination of engagement.

20. Pigeon-hole articles will be taken out of the pigeon-holes at the end of the periods named in paragraph 19 (c) and, except at Aldershot, where special arrangements are in force, will be trans-

ferred to regimental stocks by certificate voucher. A record will be kept in one of the spare columns in Section I. of Army Book 250 showing the dates on which pigeon-hole kits are withdrawn.

21. Except at Aldershot, units holding mobilization clothing and necessaries will at the end of each quarter prepare a list of articles remaining in store that have been withdrawn from pigeon-holes under paragraph 20. After deducting the quantities they can utilize within a reasonable period, they will communicate with other units at or near the station, with a view to the balance being transferred. Units must be prepared to accept on transfer such of the articles as they anticipate they will require within the following six months. After all possible transfers have been effected the balance remaining in store will be reported to the Clothing Depôt supplying the district.

22. The sizes of stocks of garments in bales should be reviewed quarterly, with a view to adjusting them to the actual sizes of the men on the books, but turnover for the sake of a few garments in each bale should be avoided.

23. During the course of each year the Chief Ordnance Officer of the clothing depôt will (except at Aldershot) call on each unit in his area of supply that holds mobilization clothing to furnish a return of bales in mobilization store that have been packed five years. The return will show the number of each bale, size and description of contents, and the numbers and sizes of the garments that can be utilized for ordinary issue by units at or near the station (*see* paragraph 21). The numbers and sizes required in replacement will at the same time be indented for on the prescribed forms.

New bales will then be issued for mobilization store, and instructions given for the disposal of the bales due for turnover.

24. The active co-operation of units in promptly using up articles transferred to them under paragraphs 21 and 23 in preference to others in regimental store of more recent date of manufacture is essential.

25. Complete bales only will be utilized for turnover of such articles as are stored in bales, and no articles of mobilization clothing or necessaries will be utilized for ordinary issue until similar articles are on the spot to replace them.

INSPECTION.

26. The clothing and necessaries will be inspected approximately every six months alternately by the Assistant Director of Ordnance Stores and by the Chief Ordnance Officer. In commands where both appointments do not exist, another ordnance officer may be detailed to carry out one of the half-yearly inspections.

The results of the inspections will be reported on Army Form G 1097 to the headquarters of the command, but will not be transmitted to the War Office, unless the General Officer Commanding desires to do so.

Accounts and Stocktaking Boards.

27. Reservists' clothing and necessaries will be held on mobilization charge in a separate part of the clothing account furnished under paragraph 307, unless there is not sufficient room in the ordinary account, when a separate one will be rendered on Army Book 285.

28. The annual stocktaking board will verify the stock of mobilization clothing with the ledger balances, the proceedings on Army Form H 1164 being forwarded as directed in paragraph 300.

29. Boards of Survey will also be held on change of commanding officers or quartermasters, or on the transfer of mobilization clothing from one unit to another, subject to the conditions of paragraphs 294 and 295.

30. A record by sizes will be kept in Army Book 250 of the numbers of garments stored in bales, and of the numbers actually required for the total strength of Army reservists.

Marking.

31. The clothing and necessaries will not be marked until mobilization is ordered, when they will be dealt with as laid down in the Mobilization Regulations. Identity discs will, however, be stamped in accordance with paragraph 137.

Special Reservists, Royal Engineers (Cyclists Section).
Special Reservists (Category (c)), Army Service Corps.
Specially Enlisted Men, Army Service Corps.

32. Clothing and necessaries for these men will be stored in bulk in the original packages, which will be dealt with as follows :—

(a.) Cases of boots will be opened every 12 months, and the boots rubbed over to prevent mildew, and dubbed, *see* paragraph 17.

(b.) Knives, forks, razors and spurs will be wiped with an oiled rag once a year, or oftener if necessary Spur straps will be greased once a year.

(c.) Service dress caps will be examined and brushed every 12 months, and napthaline renewed if necessary.

(d.) Articles found to be defective at the periodical examination will be exchanged.

(e.) Turnover of all the articles will be made every 5 years, and will, as far as possible, be effected as directed in paragraph 21.

33. Chevrons and badges will be stored for Special reservists for the percentages laid down in paragraph 14, except that four sets per man only will be held—two for jacket and two for great coat.

RECORD OF STOCKS OF BALED GARMENTS.

Jacket, service dress.

	Size 6. Nos. required, 82. Nos. on charge, 80.			Size 8. Nos. required, 28. Nos. on charge, 30.			Size 10. Nos. required. Nos. on charge.			Size 12 Nos. required. Nos. on charge.	
In bale No.	Date of bale.	No. of rack.	In bale No.	Date of bale.	No. of rack.	In bale No.	Date of bale.	No. of rack.	In bale No.	Date of bale.	No. of rack.
4583	$\frac{4}{12}$	17	426	$\frac{7}{12}$	20						
4584	$\frac{4}{12}$	17	895	$\frac{9}{12}$	20						
4587	$\frac{4}{12}$	17									
4586	$\frac{4}{12}$	18									

APPENDIX XIV.
(Referred to in para. 12.)

INSTRUCTIONS FOR THE TRANSFER OF CLOTHING AND NECESSARIES BETWEEN UNITS AT HOME ON CHANGE OF STATION.

1. On a unit changing stations, all new articles of the following description, common to all services, will, if possible, be transferred from the outgoing to the incoming unit :—

Bags, kit.
  ,,   stable.
Blacking, tins.
Braces.
Brushes, blacking.
   ,,   clothes.
   ,,   hair.
   ,,   hard.
   ,,   lace.
   ,,   polishing.
   ,,   shaving.
   ,,   tooth.
Caps, comforter.
Combs, hair.
Drawers, cotton or woollen.

Forks.
Frocks, canvas.
Greatcoats, drab.
Holdalls.
Housewives.
Knives, table.
Mineral jelly, tins.
Razors.
Shoes, canvas.
Socks, worsted.
Spoons.
Spurs, swan-neck.
Towels.
Trousers, canvas.
Waistcoats, cardigan.

2. The officer commanding the outgoing unit will inform the officer commanding the incoming unit as long in advance as possible of the descriptions, quantities and sizes which will probably be left, and will prepare the necessary vouchers for the transfer.

3. Articles, other than those detailed in paragraph 1, in excess of the quantity necessary for the unit up to the date of departure or surplus to the weight authorized by the Allowance Regulations will, under the instructions of the general officer commanding, be transferred to other units at the station or to the incoming unit if of the pattern for that unit.

4. Garments trimmed with gold lace or made to abnormal sizes will not be included with the articles to be transferred unless with the consent of the officer commanding the incoming unit.

5. When the outgoing unit leaves before the arrival of the incoming unit, an officer or a responsible non-commissioned officer will be left behind to hand over the articles to be transferred.

6. In the event of a unit leaving a station and not being relieved by another, or where the interval between the departure of the outgoing unit and the arrival of the incoming unit is likely to be inconveniently long, the officer commanding will apply to the general officer commanding for instructions as to the disposal of articles surplus to the weight authorized by the Allowance Regulations, who will direct their transfer to other units or their return to the Ordnance Clothing Depôt according to circumstances.

7. All articles transferred must be new and without regimental marking.

8. When a unit is notified that it is to proceed to another station, all indents for articles to be sent to the station the unit is leaving will be limited to the minimum quantities necessary while at that station.

APPENDIX XV.

INSTRUCTIONS FOR THE MAINTENANCE OF RESERVES OF CLOTHING AND NECESSARIES AT ORDNANCE CLOTHING DEPÔTS, OR ON ARMY ORDNANCE CHARGE AT COLONIAL STATIONS.

1. Authorized reserves of clothing and neessaries will be maintained intact and will not be drawn upon without previous War Office authority.

2. The turnover will be effected as laid down in the Regulations for Army Ordnance Services.

3. To enable the turnover of reserves at Colonial stations in charge of the Army Ordnance Department, to be effected, officers commanding units will forward their indents and size rolls to the

chief ordnance officer at the station, who will cause to be inserted thereon in red ink the numbers and sizes of articles which can be supplied from store, including, when necessary, articles in the reserves that require to be turned over. Any of the articles that are to be taken from the reserves will be at once set aside, but, if they are to be replaced, will not be issued until articles to replace them have been received. (*See* also Section XIII.)

The articles not noted by the chief ordnance officer at the station for issue locally will be supplied from the Royal Army Clothing Department direct to the unit. Those shown in red ink will be sent and charged to the chief ordnance officer at the station, unless it is stated on the indent that the whole or any portion of them will not require replacement.

4. General officers commanding-in-chief at Colonial stations will render annually on the 31st March, to the War Office, a certificate that the reserves of clothing and necessaries are maintained complete and in good order. In instances where the reserves are incomplete, details of the deficiencies will be given, stating reasons and quoting the War Office authority for depleting the reserves, and the number and date of any demands which may have been put forward to complete them.

A.C.D.
Clo. Regs.
1073

5. At home a certificate will be rendered annually by general officers commanding-in-chief concerned, except the general officer commanding London district, stating that reserves of clothing and necessaries ordered to be maintained at ordnance clothing depôts in their commands are complete and in good order, or setting forth in what respects the reserves were not complete on the 31st March and the reasons therefor. The certificate will be rendered as early in April as possible to the chief ordnance officer, Royal Army Clothing Department, Pimlico, who will furnish a consolidated certificate to the War Office.

APPENDIX XVI.

(Referred to in Appendix XI.)

SALES.

General Regulations.

1. The only circumstances in which it is permissible to dispose of army stores or supplies, without previous reference to the War Office are specifically laid down in Army Regulations. Warlike stores or serviceable uniform clothing will not in any case be disposed of without previous War Office sanction.

2. In certain special circumstances, such as the conclusion of hostilities, or the reduction or removal of the garrison from a station, when considerable quantities of stores or supplies are to be disposed of, the general officer commanding-in-chief will

report in general terms the stocks of supplies and store existing, and make his recommendations to the Army Council as to the quantities to be held and quantities to be sold, stating on what grounds his recommendations are based, what the future consumption will be, how it is proposed to provide for such future consumption, and when fresh purchases will become necessary.

3. In arranging for the quantities to be sold, careful consideration must be given to the future requirements of the troops. The sale and repurchase of the same goods, or purchase of similar goods shortly after the sale, should only be resorted to in the most exceptional circumstances, and with the express sanction of the general or other officer commanding-in-chief, who will in all such cases forward an immediate report to the War Office.

4. Only supplies and stores in excess of the authorized reserves and general requirements for issue to troops will be regarded as surplus. The surplus will be made up of the older or inferior goods. Perishable articles will be considered first.

5. If the surplus quantities are not required for the troops elsewhere, and are not ordered to be sent home, instructions will be given by the War Office for their local disposal, which will be carried out under the following regulations.

6. The stores or supplies will be sold as a rule by open competitive tender or by auction as may be most expedient, at the places where they lie, if possible, or at the nearest commercial centre, if their probable sale price will justify expenditure in removal.

7. All goods are to be sold duty free, and attention will be called to this in notifying the sale. Before sale, steps will be taken to ascertain the amount of Customs or other duties payable, so as to prevent the acceptance of prices which do not admit of a reasonable margin after payment of any duties or other charges arising out of the proposed sale.

8. When the quantities are considerable, and an immediate sale is likely to result unsatisfactorily, the sales should, if possible, be spread over a period with a view to securing the best price.

9. The utmost vigilance will be exercised by all officers concerned in the question of sales with a view to securing the greatest advantage to the Government in dealing with the goods, a reserve price being fixed in all cases of auction sales and in other cases when necessary.

10. Public advertisement to a reasonable extent should be made of the goods for disposal by the officer responsible for the sale.

11. In every case of sale, before parting with the goods sold, the officer concerned will obtain the certificate of the command paymaster that they have been paid for. This certificate will support the write off of the stores or supplies in the accounts.

12. The cash debit voucher will in every case show the nature of sale, whether by auction, tender, or private treaty, and will be supported by a certificate from the responsible officer that the method of disposal was the most advantageous in the circumstances, and that the best prices obtainable were realised. If and

whenever goods are sold below normal prices, their condition or other circumstances accounting for such prices will be explained on the debit vouchers.

13. No officer or other person in the services of the Crown or in the departments of the army will be permitted to purchase army stores or supplies, except as provided for in Army Regulations.

Sales by tender.

14. Forms of tender should be issued to likely contractors. These should provide for—

    (a) Facility to firms tendering to inspect goods for sale.

    (b) Sale by lots, if the quantities offered for sale at one tendering are large.

    (c) Payment before removal—the officer to whom payment is to be made and the mode of payment to be stated. Security for fulfilment of contract.

    (d) Removal within time fixed. Any articles not so removed to be forfeited and resold, and security forfeited. Loss, if any, to be recovered from first buyer.

    (e) Goods to be taken with all faults and errors of description, and without question on part of buyer.

    (f) Goods to remain at buyer's risk until removal, and no expense to be borne by Government, except such as may be incurred in loading up when it is considered desirable that this should be carried out by the military.

    (g) Goods to be sold duty free.

15. The tenders will be dealt with as far as possible in accordance with the paragraphs relating to contracts in the Regulations for Supply, Transport, and Barrack Services.

The material particulars of each contract will be given to the accountant who will arrange for payment of proceeds of sales.

Sales by auction.

16. Only firms of the highest standing should be employed as auctioneers. An officer should attend the sale, and certify lots sold, and report in writing how the sale was conducted, such report to be attached to the cash debit voucher.

When stores or supplies are few and of small value, they may be disposed of by a subordinate in the presence of an officer who will certify the debit voucher. The subordinate will not be entitled to any remuneration.

The conditions of sales by auction will follow generally those laid down for sales by tender in paragraph 14, a reserve price being fixed in each case on the basis of paragraph 7.

(C.R. 10544)   N

17. When an auctioneer is employed, the officer in charge of the stores or supplies will (in conjunction with the auctioneer, if necessary) prepare an inventory or catalogue of the stores or supplies to be sold. The conditions of sale will be plainly stated thereon.

18. The auctioneer will recover the amounts due from purchasers and pay them over, less his agreed commission, to the command paymaster, who will credit the amount in his accounts.

Sales to public bodies.

19. Sales to Government, municipal, and local authorities, may be made by special negotiation if circumstances justify this course, and the prices agreed on are advantageous to the Imperial Government.

Sales by private treaty.

20. Sales by private treaty will not be made without the express sanction of the general officer commanding-in-chief, and a special report of the circumstances attending each transaction will be attached to the accounts.

If in any case it is considered necessary in the public interest, on grounds of very special urgency, to depart from this rule, an immediate application for the covering sanction of the general officer commanding-in-chief will be made.

APPENDIX XVII.

[Referred to in paragraph 11, Table IX.]

POSITION OF CHEVRONS AND BADGES ON GARMENTS FOR MEN OF NORMAL DIMENSIONS.

A.C D.
Clo. Regs.
1081

1. The point of the 1-bar chevron will be 9 inches, the 2-bar 9½ inches, and the 3-bar 10½ inches from the top of the sleeve of tunics, frocks, and jackets, all services except Household Cavalry, and tunics and red tartan frocks, Foot Guards.

2. On tunics, Foot Guards, the serjeant-major's badge will be 10 inches, the quartermaster-serjeant's chevron 12 inches, the 3-bar chevron 11 inches, and the 2-bar 10½ inches from the lower edge of badge or point of chevron to the top of the sleeve. The bottom

point of the serjeant-drummer's chevron and of the good conduct or skill-at-arms badge will be about half-an-inch above the hand slash, except that in the Grenadier Guards the bottom points of the bandsman's good conduct badge will be one inch above the top of the cuff.

3. On red tartan frocks, Foot Guards, the badges and chevrons will be worn in the same position as on the tunic, except that those worn below the elbow will follow the rule for garments with pointed cuffs.

4. The centre of the good conduct badge, the 4-bar chevron, and the warrant officer's or skill-at-arms badge worn on tunics, frocks or jackets with pointed or braided cuffs will be about half-an-inch above the point of the cuff or braiding.

5. On service dress and other jackets and frocks with plain cuffs, the lower edge or points of the warrant officer's or skill-at-arms badge will be 6½ inches, the point of the 4-bar chevron 9 inches, of the 1-bar good conduct badge 7½ inches, the 2-bar 8 inches, the 3-bar 8½ inches, and the 4-, 5- and 6-bar 9 inches from the bottom of the sleeve.

6. On tunics and frocks, Scottish regiments, and tunics, serjeant-piper and piper, Scots Guards, the bottom points of the 4-bar chevron, or good conduct badge, will be half an inch higher than the highest point of cuff or braiding. The lower edge or points of the warrant officer's or skill-at-arms badge will be 6½ inches from the bottom of the cuff.

7. The lower edge or point of the trade badge, Geneva cross or badge of appointment when worn by privates on tunic, frock or jacket will be 9 inches from the top of the sleeve.

8. Trade badges worn by non-commissioned officers (except quartermaster-serjeants) should be affixed with the lower edge 3/4ths of an inch above the point of the V of the chevron, and the Artillery gun, or gun and crown when worn, about the same distance above the trade badge. The grenade in the Royal Engineers will be worn immediately above the trade badge.

9. Trade badges and crossed trumpets are worn on the 4-bar chevron in the Royal Artillery and Royal Engineers, but above the chevron in other units.

10. The following badges are also worn on the chevron, viz.: colour badge, Foot Guards, and the serjeant bugler's badge, Royal Engineers.

11. When a skill-at-arms badge and a good conduct badge are worn the former will be placed above the latter.

12. The braid worn by second class orderlies of the Royal Army Medical Corps will be placed one inch above the knot of the tracing on the right sleeve of tunic or frock. The second bar worn by first class orderlies will be half an inch above the first. On the service dress jacket the first bar will be 6½ inches from the bottom of the sleeve.

13. On drab greatcoats the point of the 1-bar chevron will be 9 inches, the 2-bar 9½ inches, and the 3-bar 10½ inches from the top of the sleeve, and of the 4-bar 11 inches from the bottom of the

cuff. The lower edge of the warrant officer's Geneva cross will be 6½ inches from the bottom of the cuff, and the lower edge of the private's Geneva cross 9 inches from the top of the sleeve. Crowns will be worn immediately above the Geneva cross and the Geneva cross immediately above the chevrons.

14. When warrant officers wear more than one badge the foregoing measurements will apply to the lowest.

15. On the Foot Guards greatcoat the point of the 2- and 3-bar chevron, and the bottom points of the 4-bar chevron will be 1 inch above the top edge of the cuff, and the lower edge of the warrant officer's badge will be 6½ inches from the bottom of the cuff.

INDEX.